# CRAZY OR NOT HERE I COME

## Healing through the eyes of a Wounded Healer

WALTER W SWINHOE (M.Div)

ISBN: 978-1-7357050-0-2

# PREFACE

The healing journey is not the storyline of this book. The storyline is being written by you, through your interaction with the words and stories you will read.

You will become the author of your own story while breaking through your unconscious chains that bind you. The images of your soul will flash upon these pages, giving you the ability to experience your inner child. The child within you will no longer be covered by the mask you wear. The mask is what the world and you see that reflects a hollow image of your authentic self. The goal of this is to break the chains of oppressive relationships, mood, habits and experiences.

Healing is what all of us crave but few of us know. The ability to heal is needed and yearned for by us all. I put off writing this book for over ten years. I heard the Holy Spirit within my Soul calling forth daily for me to begin writing. I was asked to write this book by my clients, friends, and peers during this time. I remember leaving seminary when my theology professor, Dr. C. Penrose St. Amnant said, "when you write your book, keep the theology personal and practical." When I finished my residency from Dallas Pastoral Counseling and Education Center Dr. Kenneth Pepper said, "trust yourself when you write your book". I am honored God would use me to write a book on healing and finding your authentic self.

Seven years ago, having been guided by God's Word, I was moved by the Holy Spirit to write a book for soul healing using regression. I was a License Marriage and Family Therapist and supervised other licensed therapists. I trained other healers to heal for more than twenty years. This was part of my identity as a counselor; the other part was being a Pastoral Counselor. Along my journey to the Soul, I gave up my license as a Marriage and Family Therapist to stop the tempest of my Soul. My story will be highlighted throughout the book so you may know your guide and to model the process of healing. I am a Wounded Healer who now trains others to heal.

God wanted me to write on the spiritual process of healing using regression. Regression allows you to dwell in your temple while listening to your inner child. Attending to your inner child and old wounds will allow you to be able to reclaim your God given spontaneity, creativity, and child-like innocence. I knew healing was a journey to the Soul and regression would pave the way.

Each chapter is self-contained while remaining essentially connected to the whole. You will use forms of regression to unearth your authentic self while nurturing the child within you. Practitioner-based exercises developed from decades of client work will guide you on your hero's journey. Each revealing step you take on this journey will be in the light of God's Word and plan for your soul.

**If you are:**

- stuck in depression, frozen in anxiety, or haunted by past abuse issues this book will be curative.
- stuck in an internal indulgence like self-doubt, self-loathing, self-pity or self-despair you will be given ways to break the shame that binds you.
- stuck in external-indulgences like alcohol, drugs, work, gambling, shopping, gluttony, or pornography, this healing journey will empower you to find freedom.

You will build healthy coping skills, boundaries, and self-control while connecting with the image of God in you. You will be able to:

- write a new storyline for your early learned scripts while changing the neurological structure of your brain.
- deal with outdated defense mechanisms to deal with reality.
- recover your authentic self and the child within you.

This book offers a dynamic path to healing by going to the root cause of your present symptoms. It is guided by psychology, neurology, and theology. As the author and a Wounded Healer personally, constructing this material helped me integrate my knowledge of God with knowledge of the psyche. The result has been a cure for the soul that has worked for hundreds of clients over the last thirty-five years.

# DEDICATION

A special thanks to each of my clients for teaching me, through their suffering and authentic, the path for the Hero's Journey.

# CONTENTS

# CHAPTER ONE

## IMAGO DEI

"And God said, let there be light: and there was light. And God saw the light, that it was good: and God divided the light from the darkness."

(Genesis 1:3 AVS)

**Key Points**

- God is your most important ally on your path to healing.
- Many people, especially those with past trauma, struggle to connect with God.
- Effective healing must begin with cleaning up distorted ideas we have about God and transform negative conditioning from our past.

**Reflections**

- We are created in God's image and given life with His breath.
- Have you brought your darkness to God?
- Are you masking your pain or reconceptualizing your past beliefs?
- Do you have two people to support you on this journey?

# Welcome

God's first experience of the world was void and dark. God brought light into the world's void and darkness. As any scientist will tell you, darkness does not actually exist; it is only the absence of light. You live in a world that has missed God's mark, and as a result, darkness exists. Figuratively, "darkness" can be seen as the absence of God. You are living in the light yet shield it from yourself and God. Emotional Darkness can be scary without the knowledge of God. Yes, there are degrees of darkness we all carry. Yet the question is: How do I bring radiant light or God into the darkness I carry within me?

Would your darkness of past emotional bruises, neglect, unwanted touch, or sexual abuse change with the knowledge of God? Probably not. The knowledge of light is one thing, while bringing light to your darkness is another. You can know you are created in the image of God and still carry the darkness. Yet, the imago Dei (image of God) you were created in seeks its creator: "And God created man in his own image, in the image of God created him; male and female created he them." Genesis 1:27

The connection with God was broken in the Garden of Eden. This does not diminish your soul's yearning for its creator. Your psyche carries the relic of God which it was created for. You will strive for meaning to fill this void. Many of my clients attempt to fill the void with Google, Facebook and Twitter, while others medicate their darkness with internal or external indulgences.

You may want to experience this true connection with your creator, God. Humankind lost God's Spirit due to Adam and Eve's disobedience. Even though you live East of Eden, the relic of God and Eden still exist within you; however, they can only flourish in a relationship and communion with God. This fellowship with God brings the light of hope and healing. The absence of God or carried darkness corrodes your installation of hope, happiness, and trust. I have seen the cost of darkness in the form of mental illness and "addictions."

As a pastoral counselor, I have seen many clients of faith seeking to experience fellowship with God. Many came to counseling in hopes of experiencing the Holy Spirit through therapy. They come aware of some unnamable barrier between themselves and God and are full of confusion. Some would ask, "Is there something wrong with me?" They were doing all the "right things" for the "right reasons," yet they were missing an intimate connection with God. In many cases, there were no signs of mental disorder or addictions due to the mask covering their darkness. Through my years of work, it has become abundantly apparent that we are all seeking a Higher Consciousness: a spiritual connection between ourselves and God.

## About Trauma: Critical Spirituality

It is possible to be in a relationship with God and still have a void in your Soul. This void may be from your old emotional "logic," or childhood wounding, which is clouding your connection with God in the present moment. Think about it: today, many Christians look sad, like they have lost a friend, or they are very unhappy. They have the greatest gift anyone could ever have but are not able to enjoy it.

You may suffer from the same spiritual void even when acting Christ-like in your life. Your relationship with God is not the issue. This issue is your past trauma, and how this learning has colored your spiritual relationship with God. You will need to reconceptualize your memories if you want to see God clearly. I would not have experienced a loving God today, if I did not take my image of God out of the seat he used to share with my alcoholic father.

Matthew 11:30 (NASB) tells us God desires that we lay our heavy burdens upon Him. God desires to provide us with rest. His burden is light. How can you lay your burdens upon God if you are unwilling to hold them yourself? God is not going to take away your early wounding because you would lose your inner child this way - your creativity, spontaneity, and innocence. The more sacred traits of your inner child were created by God. 2 Corinthians 5:17 tells us "Wherefore if any person is in Christ, he is a new creature: The old things are passed away; behold, they become new."

If you are not aware of your history of abuse, then allow yourself to be mindful and proactive in being with yourself and God. Practicing being present with yourself will lead you to be present with God. The New

Commandment can be practiced once you are truly present with yourself and God. In Matthew 22:37-39 from the NIV says; "Jesus replied: 'Love the Lord your God with all your heart and with all your soul and with all your mind.' This is the first and greatest commandment. And the second is like it: 'Love your neighbor as yourself.'" The ten commandments were not new to them and they knew of the need to love God. What was so new was that Jesus was encouraging them to love themselves, which was revolutionary for the Jewish community.

One of the main premises of this book is for people to love themselves before they can love others. Notice that loving God is primary, then your neighbor, and lastly, yourself. Most of the time the last is more powerful than the first, in God's Word. The last of the three, in this passage, is to love yourself. The Greek word for love is *Agape*, which means "God's unconditional love." In this passage, *agape* references loving God, your neighbor, and yourself. The fact that you have heard that loving yourself is a sin is what makes loving yourself difficult. The love of the flesh and indulgences of the flesh are sins. To love yourself as God loves you is to love your heart, mind, and Soul, which is not of the world. Loving yourself as God loves you is healthy and encouraged. The heart of these commandments is *agape* love: the essence of God.

You may not be able to experience the essence of God, which is love. Instead, you may experience God as a judgmental and condemning God. The fear of condemnation is learned from your early emotional learning. Your child-like emotional brain may have experienced judgment and condemnation by your church leaders, teachers, or parents. It is sad that you and so many other "believers" who accepted Jesus as their personal Savior were not able to accept His true essence, which was love. In my clinical experience, the clients who were unable to live under God's unconditional love struggled with experiencing God's true forgiveness or grace. You cannot give to yourself or others that which you do not have yourself. Having this New Commandment will be difficult to fulfill without experiencing God's steadfast and unconditional love for yourself.

Do you remember times in church when you were two, four, seven, or nine years old? Do you remember the "fire and brimstone" sermons? You may have heard, "Get right with God or you are going to Hell" or "You know you're a sinner. Don't give Satan a foothold because you will burn in hell" or "You can burn in hell if you're not right with God." Even if you did not go to church, as a child you could have heard scary messages that colored your view of God. Your early learning carries more weight than your knowledge today.

Your emotional brain and its logic could have demonized God and made Him the tyrant. If you heard messages like the ones mentioned above, you need to reconceptualize your past learning. Think back and feel the emotions of that time and then put it into perspective with your knowledge of a loving God. It is not hard; this is called regression. Let us say your childhood experience of church was "God is mean" or "He doesn't care about me."

Your child-like emotion could have been scared and hurt. If you took time today you could know the reasons for your early belief. You may have a memory of a Pastor or Sunday School teacher reprimanding you. Now you can look at the memory with your rational mind and put your emotional logic and its emotions of scare and hurt into perspective which changes the logic and emotions. By changing your thought processes, you can uproot an early mental weed and plant a flower.

Many memories may surface as you read about or hear examples of other childhood memories. You will need to take time to listen to what you heard, feel the feelings you had then and bring your truth to your past learning. You were a child, and children fabricate things about themselves to understand. Having these feelings can create distorted beliefs about God. Remember that children seven and under make everything about themselves; they would hear words like, "There are some here today who are going to Hell," or "If you are a sinner, you know who you are. Repent because God is coming back but is he is coming for you?" How would a child take this teaching? If a child saw this God, would he/she run up and sit in his lap? or say, "I love you daddy?"

I hope you will remember what you heard as a child. If you remember "scary messages," write them down in the book, on paper, or in your journal. Do not allow them to be suppressed and buried again. Just being aware of what you heard growing up is not curative. Writing it down while confronting it with truth is like pulling a weed. When you write down how you felt, you will become aware of the emotional "logic" you had as a child. You can change this "logic" with your present truth.

What about those of you that did not hear fire and brimstone sermons? You heard sermons on heaven and hell, good and evil, and sinner and saints. Do you think a child's mind can differentiate these two different views? A child will have difficulty differentiating these because it takes rational thinking of the frontal lobe to do so, which was still developing. The child heard death and may have gotten lost in fear that colored everything else. Listen to what you heard about God growing up and about how you felt. Then record what you experienced or saw.

I remember going to church with my papa when I was about 10 years old; I was so happy that I was with him. He was a loving man, for me, growing up. I remember sitting beside him during the sermon and everything was fine. The next thing I knew people were "speaking in tongues" "filled with the Holy Ghost" and being "Slain in the Spirit." I did not know what those words meant but I knew they scared me. What scared me more was watching people speak a foreign language and pass out in the aisles. I left his church that day scared to death. I had bad dreams for weeks. These spiritual experiences scared me as a child because my rational mind was still developing.

I am not saying anything is wrong with speaking in tongues or being filled with the Spirit. I just know I was traumatized that day. I began wetting the bed again and would not stay with my Papa anymore. In college, I recognized my fear of God, which stemmed from my childhood experience with my papa. I dealt with the weeds which sprung forth from my earlier spiritual trauma by taking time to hear my scare and my emotional logic at that time. When I was in my twenties I began to journal and process these experiences. By journaling I heard my emotional logic: "people are speaking crazy and being knocked out by God." This logic created fear. My fear went away when I confronted the logic with truth, "The Holy Spirit is speaking through them and they are being healed and not knocked out."

Only after I put these intense feelings of fear into perspective emotionally and confronted my "logic" at the time with my present knowledge, did these memories become meaningful. They helped me understand the strength of my papa's faith, the power of the Holy Spirit, and its transforming nature.

I believe once you have experienced the true love of God, you can then experience His power, comfort, forgiveness, and grace. If you are not able to experience God's power, comfort, forgiveness, and grace you will need to re-write your script. You need to re-wire your beliefs of God by confronting your old messages and beliefs. If you are not confronting your old beliefs, then you may feel God is judging and condemning you; you are listening to your old tapes or script.

My God has little likeness to my alcoholic biological, earthly father, the old church women, or the pastors who preached fire and brimstone sermons. It is sad that these people were my first experiences of God. Now they give me fruit of a lifetime. Take some time to reflect on the following questions to discover how old memories can affect your beliefs today.

## Exercise: Your Imago Dei

*This is not a regression exercise. There are no special instructions included. Answer simply and directly in your journal.*

1. Who were your first God images?
2. What were your emotional experiences growing up concerning God?
3. What was your emotional "logic" or thoughts of God at the time?
4. How would you use your current knowledge and experiences to plant a flower?

Here are a few questions that may help identify some spiritual weeds of your Soul. Allow yourself to be honest as you answer the following questions:

1) When you sinned, what feelings did you experience after your prayer asking for forgiveness? Peace joy, guilt, shame, love, fear or ________?

(Circle one or list a different feeling)

2) What would you experience from your earthly parent once you confessed or said you were sorry? Peace, joy, guilt, shame, love, fear or _______?

3) When you remember your poor choices, wrongs, or sins that you have already confessed what the first feeling you experienced? Peace, joy, guilt, shame, love, fear or ______?

4) Do you hold grudges, or do you offer forgiveness to those who wrong you? ___________.

5) The next time you are around a person who wronged you, what feeling will you experience? Peace, joy, guilt, shame, love, fear, anger or __________?
*(What you experience with others will more accurately describe your experience of God's forgiveness, grace, and love for you. If you experience shame this may not be true. Look at your first two answers. Remember shame is a feeling that you are flawed, which is not okay.)*

6) When you are praying for God's answers or forgiveness in your life, is it conditional on how good you have been as His child? Yes. No.

7) If you were in front of God, at this very moment, what feelings would you experience? joy, guilt, shame, love, peace, fear or________?

Are you experiencing grace and love from God, or judgment and condemnation from Him? If your answers are not peace and joy, then do you feel that your Heavenly Father is judging and condemning you? Are you putting past authority figures beliefs and actions on God? This is called projecting.

If your answer to question #6 is yes, then you need to revert to your memories and ask yourself "Who? What? When?" formulated your memories. If you are not giving forgiveness to others, then you are not totally experiencing God's forgiveness. You will get a better picture of your God and belief system as you continue the work in this book.

## Breaking The Chains: Your Imago Dei

The meaning that comes from the Spirit of God's intercession for us is three-fold. First, the Spirit of God is interceding before God with groaning. The Greek word for groaning is present tense, meaning present activity. The Spirit's groaning is for your present pain and suffering now. If you are experiencing emotional, mental, or physical pain from sexual abuse or trauma, the Spirit is interceding on our behalf.

As a Christian, this same Spirit of God resides in you and hurts for you while interceding for you before God. The Holy Spirit is not interceding with words because His agony is too great for words. The Holy Spirit is the guide you want to have on your journey to find your authentic self because the Holy Spirit is neither minimizing your struggles nor decreased by your defense mechanisms.

You may be like many of my clients who minimize their experiences and feelings because "others have it worse," or "it wasn't that bad," or "it's okay." Such self-defeating thoughts belittle your pain and suffering and will lead to justifying your hurts, fears, and behaviors. Your use of defense mechanisms will stop you from being authentic, protecting yourself with boundaries, and hearing (following the guidance of) the Spirit of God. Refusing to take yourself seriously takes an emotional and spiritual toll. You are living while not being "fully" awake.

Second, the Spirit will give you wisdom to understand and counsel you with strength and knowledge (Isaiah 11:2). As you gain wisdom to understand a topic both objectively and subjectively, it will lead you to safety. Knowledge and understanding are great, but wisdom tells you how to use knowledge and understanding in a meaningful way. This "counsel" grants you the understanding that you are not alone in your struggle; when you are weak you will have strength.

Third, the Spirit that raised Christ from the dead is also in you. The Spirit provides life, empowering righteousness and power over sin and death. You will have all these blessings or gifts, but they are useless if you have not opened them. You will need to open yourself up to your God and know you are not alone unless you want to be. God will honor your choices. If you implore the Spirit to be a part of your good and bad experiences, you will experience the Fruit of the Spirit.

Christ endured pain and suffering without using defense mechanisms or turning to addictions. If you can comprehend that your suffering will pass, then affliction may become more bearable. Hope comes from the realization that suffering can bring glory to you and to God. Remaining in the present moment and willingly experiencing your pain or suffering energizes you to be fully alive in Christ.

You can now be present, awake, and alive in the moment. God has given you the ability to listen to your innermost feelings without fear. The Holy Spirit will guide, restore, and empower your life. As you listen to and honor yourself and confront your old emotional logic and defense mechanisms, you will be more open to life's meaning.

Are you willing to hear and take seriously your inner-most thoughts, feelings, and experiences? Are you willing to experience your Holy of Holies and the wealth that lies within your past truth? Are you willing to allow yourself to create a support system or call upon a friend? Are you going to allow the Spirit of God to be your guide?

Reconceptualize your past negative beliefs of yourself and others and life will create meaning in the present. If so, you will experience healing on this journey to your soul. But if you do not face those past thoughts and feelings, you will likely, and unconsciously, act out the past in the present. You may recreate your past in your future and not be aware of it. The sad thing is, like Paul, what you do not want to do is the thing you will do.

Meaning making in any form leads to transcendence of your emotional, mental, and spiritual situation. You are using your conscious mind to move toward your goals. This is a conscious act of your will. You live East of Eden, but you still have the relic of God in you. The creator of heaven and earth has empowered mankind with the ability to transcend and rise above any situation. The Relic of God in all mankind calls out to create meaning with ultimate meaning, coming from finding a transcendent God.

Remember, you can create meaning, regardless of the circumstances. Meaning does not just happen; people pursue and chase it with heart, mind, and soul. Meaning and the pursuit of meaning creates a transcendence with each step, each dream, and each thought. Meaning that comes from one thought can lead a victim to acknowledge that they cannot be victimized again; meaning can help addicts acknowledge daily sobriety while experiencing God is "aha" moments. Making meaning is not a passive experience, but an act of the Will that is empowered by the freedom of the human spirit.

Meaning is neither dependent on your circumstances, nor can it be taken away through suffering.

The apostle Paul is a great example of making meaning despite his circumstance and suffering, which can be seen in his letter to Philippians. Paul was looking through the eyes of his faith and that gave him meaning. The church at Philippi supported Paul while he was in prison and during his ministry. In Philippians 4:11-13, Paul writes, "I can do all things through Him who strengthens me" (NASB). Paul was aware of how to be content in all things. Paul was present and he counted all things as gain since he was in Christ. Paul's meaning came from being in Christ which gave him strength.

Paul was not in denial. He did not minimize, rationalize, or dissociate himself from his sufferings or joys. Paul had meaning through his belief in God. He was awake and experienced life by living in Christ Jesus. He was present in the moment with himself, others, and God. Paul was aware of this "thorn in the flesh" (2Corn. 12:7) and still experienced the power of God or love the church of Philippi. Paul was conscious of his circumstance and his emotions. He brought that awareness of himself to the whole church. He was not scared of ridicule, rejection, or other's judgment. Paul was vulnerable even when he was suffering from depression and wishing to die or "depart" (Phil. 1:23).

I have had clients who will not tell their closest friends of their sexual or emotional abuse. Clients will not tell their bible study class or the church about their struggle. Other clients struggle with infidelity, substance abuse, or pornography and refuse to ask for support. Paul could bring himself and his sinful nature into relationship with God. When he struggled with sin Paul said, "For the good that I wish, I do not do: but I practice the very evil that I do not wish." (Roman 7:19) While such behaviors may make Paul appear hypocritical, struggle is normal when residing in a world complicated by sin. Right now, more than ever, it is important to allow others to encourage you and to bolster your belief in God to sustain you on this journey.

Paul lived East of Eden, and unlike Adam and Eve, he did not hide behind a fig leaf, a tree or hide his sin by defensive mechanism. Paul was conscious of his pain and suffering while in prison. He suffered from "a thorn in the flesh" in service to his God. No one knows what Paul's "thorn" was, but I believe we all have such a weakness. The lesson here is confronting our weaknesses while staying in fellowship with others and God. Fellowship gives support and accountability and will decrease your need to medicate or use a defense mechanism. The unconscious use of defense mechanisms causes deception. Fellowship with God will add meaning while empowering the Holy Spirit to shield you against self-deception.

The Spirit of God will provide comfort, healing, knowledge, and life. The Holy Spirit will sustain and guide you as you examine yourself on this journey to the soul. Here are some biblical references to the truths of the Spirit of God that dwells in you.

The Spirit gives:

(1) "In the same way the Spirit also helps our weakness; for we do not know how to pray as we should, but the Spirit Himself intercedes for us with groaning too deep for words" (Romans 8:26, NASB).

(2) "The Spirit of the LORD will rest on Him,
The spirit of wisdom and understanding,
The spirit of counsel and strength,
The spirit of knowledge and the fear of the LORD" (Isaiah 11:2 NASB).

(3) "If Christ is in you, though the body is dead because of sin, yet the spirit is alive because of righteousness. But if the Spirit of Him who raised Jesus from the dead dwells in you, He who raised Christ Jesus from the dead will also give life to your mortal bodies through His Spirit who dwells in you" (Romans 8:10, 11 NASB).

# Managing the Process:

# Defense Strategies & Spirituality

Rebellion, or the drive toward disobedience, is often considered man's original sin. However, perhaps a close second is the drive to hide ourselves, from each other, and from God. Adam and Eve first hid their naked bodies with "fig leaves" in Genesis 3:7 and then in Genesis 3:8, they hid their physical bodies from God "among the trees of the Garden." Lastly, they hid their consciousness with the use of defense mechanisms in Genesis 3:12. The sin of hiding, originating out of deceit and selfishness, created a defensive wall between humans, their authentic feelings and thoughts, and God. It was from these choices that the unconscious mind, which continues to store our blind spots and hide our wounding, was born. We use the word "Fall" to signify our descent from full awareness of ourselves and God.

From the choice to hide flowed other significant defense strategies that continue to operate within the human experience. After Adam ate the fruit from the tree of Knowledge of Good and Evil, he denied, rationalized, blamed, and justified his actions before God. Adam lost a little of himself and more of his awareness each time he used these lies. The primary defense strategies that present in psychological analysis are as follows. Some, or all, of these may be active in your own life today. If so, like Adam, they will be causing you confusion, pain, and separation within yourself, God, and others.

1. **Rationalization:** Rationalizing is attempting to present a reasonable excuse to make behavior logical; a way to justify one's actions.
2. **Intellectualization**: Intellectualizing is using our intellect to escape emotions by focusing on the intellectual aspects.
3. **Minimization**: Minimizing is decreasing the intensity of an emotion, thought or experience.
4. **Denial**: Denial is a refusal to accept reality.
5. **Compartmentalization**: Compartmentalization is putting your emotions and thoughts out of awareness and into a mental compartment; usually not thought about.
6. **Projection**: Projection is an unconscious way of placing undesirable thoughts, feelings, or impulses onto another person.

7. **Displacement:** Displacement is an unconscious way to release emotions by placing the feeling onto another person.
8. **Suppression**: Suppression is a conscious act of pushing thoughts, feelings, and experience out of awareness.
9. **Repression**: Repression is an unconscious way of pulling suppressed emotions from awareness
10. **"Acting Out:"** Acting out is showing extreme behavior to express thoughts and feelings that could not otherwise be expressed; usually by inappropriate behavior.
11. **Numbing**: Emotional numbing is a way to detach from emotions by increasing memory and decreasing emotions.
12. **Blaming**: Blaming is a form of attack on another person to make unwanted feelings, thoughts, and behaviors about someone else.

Defense mechanisms are the ways we lie to ourselves, and thus, remain locked in the prison of unconsciousness.[1] Defense mechanisms feed the unconscious. They do not protect our soul, and they keep us from being conscious of God and His healing, and thus, making progress inward toward our deeper wounds. It is amazing how these lies separate us from ourselves, leaving wounds on top of the wounds we carry from earlier times in our lives.

[1] I believe the only God given or healthy defense mechanism is dissociation, which does not carry the element of deceit, yet protects your mind and soul by "not remembering" abuse, trauma or significant loss until you are mentally and emotionally able to handle the unconscious or forgotten experience. Dissociation is an emotional and cognitive amnesia that allows you to continue to function in life, despite your trauma. The dissociated experience will likely surface when you can consciously deal with your wound. Yet, dissociated experiences need to be brought to awareness before they become septic.

# Exercise:

## Locating Your Defense Mechanisms

*This is not a regression exercise. There are no special instructions included. Answer simply and directly in your journal.*

In this section, we will focus on examining your present awareness for the presence the defense strategies in your life. We are looking for where you are currently trapped in unconsciousness. The scars left by your current defense mechanisms will influence your thoughts, feelings, and behavior. They likely connect with forgotten emotional wounds that are out of your adult awareness. We will have to follow your present signs and symptoms to discover the historic hurts that haunt your psyche.

If you are like most people, you avoid the painful aspects of your inner experience through defense strategies. These can manifest in self-medicating (emotional numbing, indulging with food, alcohol, drugs, gambling, or other assorted external excesses) or battling oneself with internal distortions such as self-pity, self-despair, or self-doubt (to name a few). Because you are human, you may have sharpened these defense mechanisms to a razor's edge. You may deny, rationalize, or intellectualize to avoid emotional pain. If your wounds are more severe, you may use stronger defense mechanisms such as suppression, repression and/or dissociation.

The more aware you are of your present moment or adult self, the greater your chance at healing. You will need to look at your present signs or symptoms and find the reason they are in your life. Answer the following questions as honestly as you can in your journal. Like before, do not pause or overthink these answers. Write down the responses that feel most authentic and instinctive.

## Exercise: Religious Wounds.

*This is not a regression exercise. There are no special instructions included. Answer simply and directly in your journal.*

If a friend, family or church member asked about the "secret" that you haven't shared with anyone, such as: being raped, touched inappropriately, or another other matter you don't remember or want to talk about:

1 - What would you say?
2 - Would you share your authentic experience?
3- Would you share your real feelings concerning the asked about experience?

If they told you they would speak to others to get you help:

4- What would you do while waiting for them to break the secret?
5- What defense mechanisms did you employ?
6- What defense strategies did you do wait for your secret to be revealed to others?
7- Did these questions trigger you to revisit your experience of the previous secret?

## Breaking the Chains:

## Patterns of Defense

The way a wound heals is not with time, as many of my clients think, but through steps. A wound heals from the inside out; it is necessary to open the wound to release the infection. This process may extend weeks or months. Cleaning the wound depends on the depth and the amount of toxins present at the time of the wound, and the length of time it festered. The best path to take to healing is *making yourself a priority* without the use of defense mechanisms. Give yourself time, energy, and attention.

Making yourself a priority may challenge you. Looking honestly at those who have hurt you, listening openly to your thoughts and feelings, and revisiting your pain is hard work. It is far easier to create defenses against this pain. Unfortunately, as discussed, this only creates more wounds that need healing - both in your life and in the lives of others.

## Managing the Process:

## Fellowship & Support

It is easier to face yourself if you have someone to share in your experience. It would be helpful to have a friend, a group, or bible study group doing this work with you. Yet, the fear of what others will think often hinders fellowship on this personal level, which is sad. I hope you will have a friend who will honor, stand beside, and support you as you find your authentic Self. You will probably be like most of my clients who do the work by themselves. Always remember the Holy Spirit is present with you and will support you. Matthew tells his readers that God knows what you are going to ask before you even ask Him (Matthew 6:8, NASB), and this is the kind of guidance you need on this journey.

## Conclusion Exercise:

Journal your thoughts, feelings and experiences concerning any "secret" you may consciously carry yet do not want to acknowledge.

## Remember:

The Holy Spirit resides in you and hurts for you while interceding for you before God. The Holy Spirit is the guide you want to have on your journey to find your authentic self because the Holy Spirit is neither minimizing your struggles, nor decreased by your experience.

"Darkness is cloaked in defense mechanisms and hides the way we miss the mark. Jesus brought Light into the world, so that everyone who believes in Him will not remain in darkness." (John 12:46 NASB)

# CHAPTER TWO

## WALTER'S STORY[2]

"Therefore, I urge you, brothers, and sisters, in view of God's mercy, to offer your bodies as a living sacrifice, holy and pleasing to God—this is your true and proper worship. 2 Do not conform to the pattern of this world but be transformed by the renewing of your mind. Then you will be able to test and approve what God's will is—his good, pleasing and perfect will." Romans 12:1-2

### Meet Walter: Early Childhood

Like many of you, I had an earthly parent who fell far short of God's best. And, like many of you, most folks who met my earthly parent loved him. Dad was willing to do anything for anybody. He could make you laugh, and folks felt special under his attention. He was always immaculately dressed in pressed shirts and pants. His boots shined - not a speck of dirt anywhere.

My dad would have genuinely enjoyed your company and you may have seen him have a drink or two, but you would have never seen him lose control. The truth is that he would sit in his chair under his favorite tree and drink a case or more of beer a day. Despite this intoxication, his hand waved at every car. Many honked back. A mean drunk was not the man the public knew. This man was aware of his appearance. He took pride in it and fought

[2] This is the "Lost Chapter." While I was reviewing this manuscript, an awareness came over me. The increasingly edited original document had become devoid of its original heart: my own. And thus, the manuscript lacked personal rawness and vulnerability. This is honesty that I ask you, the reader, to trust in. Share yourself here. This was the case in all but one chapter - the first one. And so, I have come to call this "The Lost Chapter," or "Nearly Lost," the passage that God would not let be deleted. This chapter that looks directly at my own experience with this, the work that healed my life. The work that can heal your life, too.

to preserve it at all costs.

Behind the scenes, the father I knew yelled, screamed, and beat me daily. In addition to his struggle with addiction, my dad was a hard man - an authoritarian. "It's my way or the highway," he repeatedly said. While Christianity was not a part of my dad's life, he did know the verse, "If you spare the rod, you spoil the child." If a dish were not clean or dried well in the cabinet, he would snatch one of us out of bed to "wash every dish in the house." Dad would pull his white handkerchief out of his pocket and run it over and through the cracks of the furniture. If he found dust on the handkerchief, he would beat us. Then we would have to, "clean the filthy shit again."

As a child, I hated when he came home. My mom would tell me to go to my room when he pulled into the driveway. I would do so, but soon enough he would ask about me. Amongst my siblings, my Dad believed I was the "hard case." So hard, in fact, he made a special belt to spank me with. Each time he swung it, the black belt would hit my skin several times. His abuse was more extreme, due to my empathetic gift. I could feel his rage as I was being whipped, but as a child I could not understand my empathetic gift nor my gift of discernment. My discernment knew his intent was to hurt me with a deep desire to kill me. I worked to suppress these God given gifts to protect myself.

Like many others, the pain I endured from my father's words far surpassed the pain I endured at his hands upon my psyche. He would cuss me like a sailor in spaces safely away from the public and those words cut to the bone. He called me many names like "idiot" or "stupid fucker." He poked fun at my glasses. He would send me away because he "couldn't understand the shit that was coming out of (my) mouth."

My dad often said I was "not a Swinhoe." Never truly knowing what that meant, I took it to mean I was not actually his son: a belief that haunted me as a child. Perhaps I "wasn't a Swinhoe" because I had a severe stutter. For years, my last name came out "Winhoe," which infuriated him. He believed that I was doing this on purpose and beat me for it.

For years, I struggled with disfluency. Often, the words I had in my head were not the words that came out of my mouth, which was confusing for me. For example, if someone asked if I wanted a glass of milk and I did, my head would say, "yes" but my mouth said, "No." The real struggle was that I didn't realize I had said no -- I heard, "yes" in my head. I would get so frustrated in these situations. I was certain I had said yes and did not get what I thought I was offered! Communication with anyone was a problem, but this problem drove my dad, especially nuts. My father expected perfection, and I was not even in the same area code.

I truly feared my father as a child. I never knew what would happen in his presence. I believed I could be thrown out of my family at any time and left to grow up with the other rejects on the Island of Misfit Toys.

## School Years.

If I said these were the only personal struggles I had growing up, I would be lying. I was a big kid for my age - usually 6 to 8 inches taller than my peers. I also suffered from "lazy eye" or amblyopia. My right eye might be looking at you while the left one would appear to "wander." Others told me I looked "retarded," which bothered my dad more than my speech problem. He would throw all sorts of objects at me trying to make me "stop looking that way;" he rarely missed. Dad hit me in the head with full or half-empty beers, salt and pepper shakers, and ashtrays. Anything close enough for him to grab was fair game.

Life got harder when I started school because my learning disabilities, speech problems, and poor self-esteem; the belief that, "I couldn't pour piss out of a boot with the directions on the sow." I honestly believed I was stupid and as a result earned D's and F's, which did not go over well at home. The school culture was different in those days. I was often set aside and taunted by my teachers.

Despite the problems with my eye and unusual height, my most serious struggles in elementary school were with communication. I hated having to answer questions in class because no one understood me. To correct my communication problems, I went to speech class, which I hated because kids laughed and mocked me. I could not defend myself in these situations because my frustration made my speech worse.

Without a doubt, speech was my hardest class in school. I did not know that I was not pronouncing certain letters my teachers asked me to say. It was hard to fix something I did not know was a problem; I would have sworn I was saying those sounds. I thought everyone else was crazy.

Finally, in the fourth grade, a speech teacher taped me speaking and played it back to me. I thought it was a trick. He recorded me several times. I listened to each one of those blank tapes before he recorded me to confirm that nothing was on them. Once I believed they were blank, I would speak into them. I finally heard myself mispronouncing those sounds and believed it was me saying them.

This was one of many moments that changed my life. Once I accepted that I had a problem, I could fix it. It was just exceedingly difficult to see or understand the problem. My speech improved within a year. Fifth grade was a huge breakthrough for my self-confidence. I learned to speak properly and had a teacher willing to prove to me I was not stupid. That truth validated that I was okay and that my dad was wrong.

Unfortunately, while my interactions with teachers and classmates improved, my home life became much, much worse. Despite his best efforts, I no longer felt defective in front of my father. As a result, I defied him more and received more beatings with the black belt. Not surprisingly, this belt went missing before long.

With his favorite tool of abuse missing, I expected things to change, and they did. Although Dad found other handy things to abuse me with, finally being able to speak clearly, I had a new freedom. For the first time, I knew I was okay. As I began telling dad what I thought and could speak the words clearly, he got angrier and more abusive; however, there was a light of hope in this dark time: I discovered sports, the saving power of friends, good humor, and a had a walk with God.

I received a lot of praise playing football and baseball. I was good at these sports and found I often did not have to work hard. Athletics helped me channel my energy and provided a reason to be away from home. There were still chores, but I was often gone when my dad was at home.

Learning to laugh and play with friends made life fun. But, when my dad saw me smiling, he would ask, "What's up smiley?" There was rarely a "right" answer with my dad. I would earn more chores, be sent to my room, or get a whipping. An odd sense of humor began to develop when my dad was whipping me. I would chuckle and laugh at him, which drove him nuts and prolonged the whippings.

There were usually bruises on my body. Blood blisters from the belt would be on my legs and back. Finally, I was strong enough physically to laugh until my dad was totally exhausted. He would literally have to kill me to stop my laughter. My mom would beg me to stop and just go to bed. "Just be quiet, Wally." However, I could speak clearly and that was worth the beating.

The beatings stopped in the seventh grade, possibly because I was close to six feet tall. Then again, perhaps, Dad had started focusing his energy on my two younger brothers. I was playing every school sport and, by this time, making B's and C's, which seemed to pacify him. He was still a hard man, but now his words became his weapons toward me; whippings were just a threat.

Dad would not make us work on Sundays if we went to church. Thus, sports, a defiant sense of humor, and church became a refuge during this time. I went to church as often as I could and accepted Jesus as my savior when I was about eight or nine years old. Like many children, I did this mostly out of fear of "going to hell" at the time.

## Discovering God.

Despite being "saved" young, my first true experience with God occurred years later at a Baptist church camp in South Texas. Nature has always healed my soul and the camp was established in a beautiful setting on the banks of the Frio River. Even now, I can go back there instantly in my mind. The rock formations, the piney cedar air, and the flowing crystal waters brought a natural reverence, peace, and joy to my heart.

Throughout my time at camp, I experienced what can only be described as divine grace channeling throughout me regularly on the banks of the Frio. This happened again sitting in the back of the tabernacle with friends during a preaching. Suddenly, I was flooded with a profound sense of bliss and fellowship with God. In a way, it was an out of body experience.

Like many children growing up with trauma, "out of body" experiences were not new for me. I was familiar with these sensations from many moments in my past where I was scared and hiding or being beaten by my father. This experience was different than those past ones, however. I was not looking down on myself or watching what was happening. I watched the Evangelist tear up the Bible, equating it with how we treat Christ and God's Word in our lives. Watching him created powerful images that brought me face-to-face with God. I felt a sadness unlike any I had felt in the past. This sorrow spoke to me, not in words but in "knowing." I deeply felt God's love for His Son, Jesus. Seeing through my Heavenly Father's heart changed me that night. Suddenly, I had a grasp of how profoundly God loves us.

After many years, I still have no words for this experience of love. It is like trying to tell someone how an orange tastes. Words fall short of peeling the rind off and smelling the aroma, biting into the fruit, and feeling your taste buds explode with the experience of the fruit's flavor. While I had heard many pastors preach about God's love, grace, and forgiveness over the years, these experiences only left me with some small remnant of the truth. Looking through God's eyes and experiencing His true love for His Son, and for all of us, was transforming. I have never been the same.

The clinical term for this experience is disassociation. Based on each type of my experiences with disassociation (in both positive and negative situations) I believe it is a God given gift. In one case it exists to protect the mind, body, and soul. In the other, it serves to give one release from the physical body and entry into that of the divine.

I left camp that year looking and acting the same but deeply changed. Eagerly, I shared all that had happened with my dad, hoping he would have a small taste of God's heart, but he did not understand my words. My dad was not a Christian at that time. My mom's father, the Godliest man I ever knew, prayed for him each night. When I stayed with my Papa, I would hear him "speaking in tongues" in the kitchen. I once walked in on him praying; I thought he was hurt, because of the crying and what sounded like pleading before God. Papa was on his knees with his face prone on the floor. He would raise his hands to the ceiling while raising his voice in this unknown tongue. He would do this for hours.

## Teenage Turmoil.

After some time, life continued like it always had for both of us. I wish I could say my actions and behavior changed after my experience with God. My heart was changed, my mind renewed, but I continued to make poor choices. I was still "Wally." I played sports hard and lived life hard. My heart had changed, yet my actions stayed the same: working during the summers, making money so I could "play" at the creek with friends. Drugs and alcohol were always available, and I indulged in them freely and willingly. Life was good! Our parents were distracted, and we often partied all day and night. All I had to do was make good grades and plays sports and my freedom was secure.

It is hard to keep secrets in a small town. Over time, I got into more and more trouble at school and with the police. My work on the field and in school was good, but my life outside was getting more attention. Rumors of my drinking, drug use, fights, and stays in jail began to spread. I was glad the rumors were only shadows of the truth, but my life was reeling out of control.

During my junior year, I was kicked out of my parent's house. One night, my dad was belittling my mom at the kitchen table and I told him to stop. This was like pouring gasoline on fire. I remember walking to his chair and telling him to shut up or stand up. He did not shut up, so I poured my glass of milk over his head and demanded that he stand up. At that moment, everything in my mind, body, and soul wanted him to challenge me. He remained seated. In hindsight this was a blessing. I left that house that night and never lived there again. I returned the next day to find my clothes on the back porch. Dad had knocked out the walls of my bedroom to enlarge the dining room.

Over the next two years I lived with friends or on my own. While I continued to attend church, I lived a life totally opposite of Christian values or teachings. I had a passion for God and a calling to ministry, but I did not pursue these spiritual urgings in my life. In retrospect I can see that I had not yet graduated from the University of Hard Knocks. I started skipping school and meeting friends in the evening to drink beer and go dancing.

One evening after a fun night at the clubs I heard a friend had been in a fight and needed help. Running outside, I found my friend beaten and unconscious. He had been drinking, and his mother had told me long ago that he had an allergy to alcohol. He risked death with even slight consumption. Quickly, we put him in the back of a truck and rushed to the hospital in Huntsville. I was driving. Speeding like a bat out of hell, I did not see the red light until it was too late. Unable to veer off the road because of raised walkways, I could not stop the truck in time.

The next 30 seconds changed my life. It all happened so quickly but took forever to end. I hit two vehicles that were shot out of the way by the force of the collision before hitting the next two that quickly hit oncoming cars in their own paths. Next, I struck cars passing through a four way stop which then hit other cars. Finally, I hit a van. In total, eight vehicles and two police cars were involved in the wreck. Within minutes, I was being booked into the Huntsville jail on charges of Reckless Endangerment and Driving While Intoxicated.

The jail was on the same block as the accident. Sitting in the holding cell, I heard dozens of ambulances and fire trucks at the scene. Somewhere down the hall, I overheard "the others" in the truck were hurt and at the hospital. When I asked the police officer for information, he told me "shut the fuck up." That night was so long. The police treated me much like my father, and I responded in kind. Before the night was over, I was beaten by the police and put in the cell block with seven other prisoners from Huntsville State Prison. I felt so sick and alone, and in my hour of complete desperation called out to God.

Immediately, I felt comforted. My God was with me. I spoke to my Abba all through the day and night. There was a peace that could only come from my Heavenly Father. There was no judgment or shame. There was more love than at any other time I could recall. God and I spoke about my future. I knew God was in control. There was hope because my God had always been bigger than my circumstances.

I found myself talking about my relationship with God to a couple of inmates when another inmate came by and said, "Man, you are in Huntsville jail, boy. Where is your God?" What a strange question. In my darkest time, I experienced the greatest love from God.

I planned on staying in jail for a couple of weeks, but my mom bailed me out Sunday or Monday morning. The police told me repeatedly that I would have to appear in court and that I might not get released. After meeting the judge the next morning, the only good news was that my friend had not died, so involuntary manslaughter was not one of the many charges. I was released that afternoon.

I stayed one night at home and left the next day. Somehow, I knew I was living out my father's old behavior and wanted to get as far away from it as I could. It was also odd that my dad and I had bonded somewhat over this negative event. He, too, had experienced abuse from the Huntsville jail. He knew about the small rubber clubs they used and how it hurt to the bone. Dad's empathy was a surprise. This was nice, but he continued to discount my experience with God. He said, "Any man would call on God when his ass was on fire."

My dad encouraged me to get a lawyer. He knew, as well as I did, that I had huge legal problems on the horizon. I prayed about these legal matters and again had a strange peace. When I thought about receiving a jail sentence, I heard God say, "That is not in my plans." I rested in this reassurance often over the following months and continued to hear this answer from God whenever this worry entered my mind. This was a spiritual healing time in my life. I rededicated my life to God.

## Turning to the Light.

The small Baptist church I found during that time was an oasis for me. Through sermons from the pastor, Brother Hardy, I experienced God's love and grace. Brother Hardy had the heart of God. I had heard many pastors preach better sermons, and they might say the same things, but Brother Hardy knew the same love and heart of God I had experienced. Brother Hardy had a revival on sin vs God's unconditional love. God used this revival to show me that His love was much bigger than my sin. I decided to listen to God's lead which many would call " walking on faith."

God put it on my heart to stop by my parents' house and invite my dad to the revival. I admit, I did not want to do this at all, but I did as God asked. My dad was clear that he did not intend to go to any revival. Honestly, I did not want him there either. The next three nights of the revival meetings were enjoyable. I did not look for my dad because I neither expected him to come, nor did I want him to show up.

While sitting in a pew near the front of the church, I felt the Holy Spirit speak to me. I heard, "Forgive your dad," and "Tell him you love him." Telling my dad I loved and forgave him was going to be difficult. When I pondered saying " I forgive you." I began to flashback to times he beat me. I did not think I could forgive him. I felt God's sorrow for how my father treated me as the Holy Spirit encouraged me to forgive my dad. I began bargaining with God. I said, "I will tell my dad that I love him and forgive him if he comes to church." Then I said, “this church."

I literally heard God say, "Go." I looked around because I believed that others could hear it. I was not finished bargaining. I told God, “I'll go only if he is in this church tonight." I knew that was my final offer to God and I was not going to do it any other way. The pastor wrapped up his sermon and he asked the congregation to stand as he gave the invitation. As I stood up, I felt God's sorrow for me and His love for my dad. Then I heard audibly, "Go my child." I was filled with an eerie feeling, a sense that my father was in the back of the church. I did not want to turn around, hoping I was wrong.

The church was signing the invitation, and I tried to turn to see but could not make myself. I wanted the service to end when Brother Hardy gave another call. While another stanza of the invitation played, I made up my mind to turn around at the end of this song. As the song ended, I turned to my right and left and did not see my dad. I felt such relief. I felt almost giddy. Again, I told God, I would tell my dad I forgave him if he was there that night.

I heard the Holy Spirit speak and I turned and looked right behind me. A couple of rows from the back sat my dad. Without any hesitation, I said, "Shit" aloud as if I was the only one in the church. I remember a little old lady just shaking her head, as if she were telling me "No," while others just looked at me, I turned around and faced forward. I believe one of my friends hit me in the arm. I stood facing the pastor in disbelief. My body started shaking from the ground up. If you know nothing else about me, know this: if I tell you I will do something you can take it to the bank.

As a victim of severe emotional and physical abuse, I did not know if I could tell my abuser those few words. God gave me a nudge when the pastor said, " There are some of you who need to say something to someone here today. "Will you do it now?" I said, "Shit" again. As my body began to shake and my heart filled with anxiety, I tried to move towards my dad. I moved enough because the man on my right moved back to allow me to step around him. I put my hands on the pew to move down the row because my legs felt like they could not bear my weight. They began to shake and feel weak. I stood there trying to move when the pastor said, "You have more time."

I do not remember making it to the aisle, but there I stood facing the back as everyone else was facing the front singing the verse again. I began walking to the back of the church and suddenly thought about walking out. A feeling of relief flooded my body. I began walking to the back and looking at the back doors, thinking about leaving. Stopping three or four pews from the back where my dad was standing, I moved past a couple who was standing in the pew as I moved toward my dad. I flashed back to some of the truly brutal and cruel things he had done to me as a child.

My mind flashed to the time he hung my sheets out in front of the house to show I had wet the bed. I remember him saying, " if you do it again you will take them to school." I recalled him pushing a sock in my mouth which pushed my tongue back in my throat. I could feel the flesh ripping under my tongue. The next memory was being in a crib and him putting something in my mouth to stop my crying. Being one person from my dad, I remembered feeling of the belt cutting my skin. Everything in me wanted to turn around and leave. The guy standing next to my dad stepped back to let me pass.

At a proverbial crossroads, I stood there, as my dad turned toward me. I reached out and hugged him and said, " Dad I love you and forgive you." I do not remember if he replied. Of course, I would like to think he said, " I love you, too." I turned to leave, to get out of the church. I was in tears as I left the church. I was just trying to make it back to my car without sobbing. All I wanted was to get in my car and cry. I cried tears of relief, thanking God for my dad being there and for God's patience with me. I do not remember seeing my dad leave the church that night. I believe this was the first and last time I ever saw my dad in church.

Even then, I knew somehow that forgiving my dad was more for me than for him. While I did not understand the whys, I knew it was for me. God was cleaning my mind and heart while my actions were recreating my father's teaching. I was living in my alcoholic father's footprints while wanting to walk in my Heavenly Father's. I spent more and more time in the only earthly place I could find peace - the creek. I loved the white sand, running water and fresh air, yet the creek also brought more temptation to drink and party. I had friends breaking into houses and stores, selling drugs and others that wanted to party. I was in a tough spot. My heart was for God, yet my life had remnants of everything contrary to Him.

No longer a rebel, I no longer had a cause. As it turns out, I did not receive direction until I lost my ability to walk. God works that way sometimes. Once when fasting, one of my best friends asked me to come to his party. After I refused a couple of times, he said, " You don't have to drink." I decided to go for a few minutes. There were several offers to use alcohol or drugs before I even got to his front door. I told them I rededicated my life to Christ and had just come to enjoy their company.

It was nice to be around friends and laugh again. I found more of my friends in the kitchen funneling beer. After much encouragement, I funneled a few beers. Somehow, there was an altercation with the boyfriend of one of the partygoers. He was much older than I and threatened me. At that time in my life, I did not deal well with threats. In the midst of the fight, I felt a severe pain in my foot. I could not stand on my left foot and had to ask a friend to drive me home. By the time I got home the floorboard of his car was covered in blood. The tendons were cut near my ankle. There was no movement in my foot or toes.

My friend took me to the emergency room. The doctor informed me I might not be able to walk again; I needed a specialist. A foot specialist was in the hospital. He was not on call but happened to be in the hospital documenting. He agreed to do surgery and they wheeled me directly back to the operating room - because I had been drinking they did not anesthetize me for surgery.

I was lying in bed that night feeling thankful when God told me to go to Texas Tech University and play football. I thought God certainly had a sense of humor - a doctor had just told me I might not walk again. The trial was still looming. The irony of how I had made fun of all my college-bound friends was humorous. Outside of my physical and legal problems, I wondered, "How will I get into Texas Tech? And how will I pay for it?"

The next morning, I told Mom about my foot and that I need to apply to Texas Tech. I asked her not to tell anyone, including my dad. Since I was severely hurt, I moved in with my sister. I continued living life as I always had with the addition of daily talks with God. I was transforming from the inside out and beginning to walk by faith. God was speaking to me in a personal way; however, I still had one more hurdle to cross.

One of my friends asked me to go fishing, which seemed safe at the time. We were out in the middle of the lake when a storm began to blow in. With the fish biting like crazy, we did not want to go back to shore. While we were fishing, whitecaps began to overtake our boat, so we thought it was time to return to safety. We started the outboard engine and headed back. The boat struggled to get over the whitecaps and suddenly, it was too late.

In a split second, the boat that was on top of the water was pointing towards the bottom of the lake. When I came to the surface, I could barely see my friend due to the wind, rain, and whitecaps. I followed him as best I could to the distant shoreline. My left leg, still in a cast, was pulling me down with each wave that washed over me. I was growing weaker trying to fight the rain, waves, and wind. I was swimming on top of the water, yet these elements were on top of me, especially with the anchor on my leg. The wind and rain were relentless as my strength and hope grew weary. I asked God to help my friend make it to the shoreline. My prayer was not humble; I just did not believe I would survive.

Being an athlete, I was able to push myself past ordinary limits as I continued to swim and push back all the pain and exhaustion. When I rested from swimming, I found myself 4 to 6 inches below the surface of the water. I was losing hope, until I felt a physical manifestation of a hand under my chest. God's hand was holding me on the surface which allowed me to breathe. As I used my arms and legs to swim; I had such peace and assurance that I was not alone. I cannot tell you how far or long I swam in that storm. I can remember mentally and physically the feeling of His hand holding me up. Though still spiritually immature, I knew something supernatural was happening to me. The next thing I knew we were swimming onto shore.

The following week, I had an appointment with my leg specialist. He cut off the cast and became visibly upset: the wound was necrotic. He cut the deteriorating stitches and dead skin away as he cleaned the wound. He scraped and cleaned until he reached the bone. Over and over he asked the nurse to pour antiseptic and he would begin again. It was incredibly painful. Once he was finished cleaning the wound he said, " I'm going to leave it open and trust that it will heal." The doctor informed me that the wound was necrotic and might not heal and I might not be able to walk again. I did not dare tell him I was going to play football in under two months.

The following week, still reeling with pain, my mother and I had an appointment with my lawyer. When we saw his office, I knew that we would not have the money to pay him. He was sitting at a huge desk in the biggest office I had ever seen. He knew most of the story and only asked me a couple of questions. Then he looked at me and said, "Your mom can't afford me." Mercifully, he agreed to take the case and told me to show up at the courthouse for trial.

The day of the trial I got to the courthouse 30 minutes before the hearing. That hearing was the first time I had ever been aware of having anxiety and was close to having a full-blown panic attack. My thoughts raced as my palms sweated and my heart felt as if it were going to beat out of my chest. I felt totally out of control; however, once my lawyer arrived my anxiety disappeared.

He showed up 5 minutes before the trial with specific instructions: I was only to say, "No contest." I must have said it seven or eight times. The hearing seemed brief. I was given probation for several counts and charged with a DWI. Before my lawyer left the courthouse, he informed me that my bill would be paid in full if I graduated from Texas Tech. I never saw him again.

That same week, my mom handed me my acceptance letter from Texas Tech. I did not tell anyone. I still did not know if I was going to be able to walk or if my wound would heal in time. There was extraordinarily little time to get in shape to play division one football. I followed the doctor's instructions to the letter. The necrotic wound was healing well but I could not move my foot. A couple of weeks later, I could move my toes, which gave me hope. I was aware of the doctor's statement that the stitches had been compromised by the infection on the muscles and tendons, yet the timelines for my recovery and reporting for practice at Texas Tech overlapped. I knew I must start working out, and this could create a problem. I decided I needed to walk or run in two weeks.

Over the next two weeks, I was being spiritually intentional by walking in God's footprints and not my early learning.  I was being intentional by praying and fasting. I had faith I would be able to work out again. The negative messages, " You're not good enough," " You're not smart enough to go to college", " I won't pay a red cent to send you to college," would plague me through the day. I confronted them with God's Word or with prayer. As my faith and fasting prevailed, the negative notations would play less in my mind.

Quickly, the time came to run. I sat up in bed and asked God for the strength and healing to run. I was hoping for a miracle as I took the wrap off my foot. No miracle. The wound was red, yellow, and white. It was still open as I cleaned the debris away. I put on a new dressing and  felt good about the wound, but I did not know if the stitches on the muscles or tendons would hold together. I had severe pain as I began running. I ran 3 miles in one direction and was on my way back when my foot gave out and I could not run. It felt exactly like the night I was injured. I stood up, and without thinking yelled, "Get behind me Satan!" I said this so loud that a lady raking her yard ran into the house. My faith in God allowed me to begin running again, as I had when I started that day.

## College Years.

When the time came to go to Tech, I had thirty-four dollars in my pocket. I had never been to the Texas Tech campus. I did not have a room, but I knew I was accepted and enrolled in school. My ride dropped me off at the football stadium sometime after midnight. I sat there alone in the dark and thanked God for so many blessings. I was overwhelmed with joyful tears.

After paying for gas to get to campus, I now had less than two dollars, no room to sleep in, and nothing to eat, which brought concerns. While I should have been worried, I knew faith was going to open doors I could not open myself.

I "walked on" to the Texas Tech football team that Monday. A resident assistant allowed me to stay with him that week. He was a Christian and was impressed I had simply shown up. He walked me through the steps to get a room between practices that week. I had not eaten for three days and was playing football for about six hours a day. I was becoming weak. When I felt hungry, I asked God to sustain me and give me strength. He did, but I did not know if I could last a week.

Walking back to the dorms from morning practice, I decided to look at the rest of the university. It was around noon when a guy walked up and began asking me about the campus. I told him all I knew about the campus, which was not much. He invited me to go eat lunch with him, saying he wanted company. We went to a sandwich shop. He asked me, "Are you going to eat anything?" I replied, " No." The next thing I knew, he brought back a large sandwich for him and one for me. These sandwiches were enormous. I ate half and saved the rest for later. I could have easily eaten both sandwiches. I got a to-go box for the rest of my sandwich and the guy gave me the other half of his sandwich. He dropped me off at my dorm and I never saw him again. This was enough food to hold me until the cafeteria opened at the end of the week.

College was a blessing. I studied psychology and found a good church. A psychology professor took me under his wing and met with me at least every other week for over a year. Looking back, he helped me work through my abuse issues and negative thoughts. Some might call this counseling. He would often ask, "What would you tell this part of yourself now?" I did not know he was walking me through my past experiences, using regression techniques. I changed a lot of my early learning by looking through my present lenses. I learned that being strong and pleasing others hurt me and it was okay for me to express my feelings.

I knew I was at Texas Tech to get an education and to grow spiritually. I played football for two years but did not get a scholarship. It was a difficult decision to not play my junior year. Sports were always a major part of my life, so this was a great loss. While grieving, I had to find my way without this familiar counterpart. I then put more time and energy into church.

I joined a ministry for under-privileged racial minorities in the area. The ministry grew quickly. The predominantly white, affluent church that was hosting this outreach became concerned with the number of under-privileged kids attending their church. I was disillusioned by the racism in the church. I had grown close to these beautiful children who were being left behind. My pastor said, "the outreach needed to stop because there were other needs in our city." I went to church one Sunday and was dismayed as I saw the kids that I cared for being ignored and pushed away. This seriously tainted my view of the church and caused me to question my calling to the ministry. I was hitting a spiritual bottom. Concentrating was difficult, and helplessness crept in. Though I knew these were signs of depression, I had to keep going.

Most of my life I had difficulties due to my poor choices. I was used to having hardship, but this time was different. I was financially, academically, physically, mentally, and spiritually experiencing hardship due to situations out of my control, which felt inexplicable. It was one of those times where if I touched it, it broke. My prayers seemed to bounce off the ceiling and I grew weary of not receiving answers from God. The feeling of loneliness became amplified and cold. I was tempted to "have fun again" by a well-meaning friend. I decided to pray, fast, and continue reading God's Word.

The days were a challenge, driving me to my knees in tears. I sat in a chair and yearned for rest or some peace-- I did not know which. I continued to sit, hour after hour. I forced myself to stop thinking and become quiet on the inside. I then experienced quiet on the inside and outside and was once again standing before God.

In this disassociation experience, I was physically before God and observed a shroud of white light around me. I was aware of God's presence but could not see Him. I was in the presence of angels who were covered by light, but not as bright as God's. I experienced Christ and was present with God. I spoke no words, but asked God everything. He showed me many things, which I cannot articulate. I was at peace - calm and excited at the same time. I went with God to many places yet never moved. This experience could have taken minutes or hours. I was not aware of time.

The next thing I knew I was sitting in my chair. I wished I would have journaled or made notes, but instead I got up and went to bed. I awoke the next morning feeling refreshed. I was restored both emotionally, physically, and spiritually. I put on my running shoes and ran ten miles. I was truly refreshed and, more importantly, my experience of God was restored. Like my earlier divine disassociation experience, this time was mystical and ethereal, truly beyond the world or words. I still get emotional reflecting upon it. I realized from the experience that God has been walking with me from the time I was born.[3]

## Into Ministry.

I returned to school and graduated from Texas Tech in 1985. Before going to seminary, I needed to find healing with my father. I needed to voice my feelings of hurt, fear, and anger from my past. I took time off from work

[3] Years later, once I was a director of a non-profit counseling center in Wichita Falls, I spoke with my grandfather about my spiritual experience that night. He was the most spiritual man I knew; I met with my grandmother about my experience of being in God's presence. I was happy that he blessed it. He later told me, while I was in my mother's womb, he asked God to use me in His ministry in Wichita Falls, Texas. I am so glad he did not tell me early in my life. That would have been a burden that I would not have wanted to carry, especially with my lifestyle. This knowledge crystallized the glimpse God had given me. In hindsight, I am glad I did not speak to him at this time.

to take care of my dad, who was dying of cancer. He was still cantankerous as ever. He cussed and cut me down like he did previously; however, I had learned to set boundaries, and refused to get into power struggles. This was not easy, but I refused to comply with his demands unless he spoke to me without cursing or being hateful.

The first few days of having boundaries were difficult. My dad was bed-ridden and had to go without a lot of things like his beer, food, urinal, etc., until he understood I would not respond to negative behaviors. He finally spoke to me without cursing and in an adult manner. I was able to speak of my early abuse. I spoke to him about how he abused me. I voiced my anger and my fear and pain followed along with the memories. My dad, like every good addict, would deny, rationalize, minimize, or revise history. Instead of arguing, I relayed facts and gave examples. Most importantly, I owned my emotions. He could not deny my feelings. It took weeks to deal with his history of abuse. When he asked me to leave, he told me he was " sorry for trying to make me a real man." I accepted his apology and did not confront his " stinking thinking."

The next day, my dad asked me to get a job and take my brothers with me. I knew he wanted to die alone. I did as he asked: I got a job out-of-state, putting floor and roof joists on apartments. Before I left, I talked to my dad about accepting God as his Savior. He said he was, "not up to it now." When I was leaving the house with my brothers, I told my dad that I loved him. He looked at me and said, "I love you too." This was the only time I remember my dad telling me he loved me.

While working in North Carolina, I got word that my dad accepted Jesus Christ as his Savior. Two weeks later, he died of a massive heart attack. I was sad that my dad died, but glad that he did not have to suffer anymore. My brothers flew home and attended the funeral. I stayed and worked on the apartment, though I did schedule off at the same time as the funeral. I wanted to take time to remember and grieve the loss of my dad.

I found a tree to sit under and began to "be silent" which I learned to do in college. I found it to be a conscious way of looking into myself and dwelling in my temple while listening to my true, authentic self. God met me here. I became silent during the chaos. After about five minutes, I opened with a silent prayer, asking God to bless this time and his guidance in my grief. I began to hear my father's voice telling me what I "should do" and what I "ought to" be. I did not want to give this time over to those old, negative, and hateful thoughts in my head. They poisoned my mind and soul. I had to use deep breathing to empty my mind of my old thoughts-- breathing them out while breathing in God's peace and love for me. As I breathed out the old, I breathed in the new - moving toward my inner sanctuary. I recalled many good times, the funny, joyful times with my dad. These reflections were vivid, like I was there again. I thanked God for my dad and those memories.

I moved from reflecting to experiencing my dad in his glorified state. I really do not remember if my eyes were open or closed when I saw my dad in his glorified state. I knew this person in front of me was my dad. He was so physically different than the last time I left him. He stood before me with jet black hair, looking 25 years younger. He was a picture of health. My dad's eyes were clear while being filled with love and innocence. I told him I loved him, and he smiled with appreciation.

My father's physical change and loving kindness stood out most for me then and now. I am aware that this experience helped me change my old thoughts or storyline. I do not believe I would have experienced my father in his glorified state without forgiving and confronting him earlier with my thoughts and feelings concerning his abuse of me. My father's funeral was perfect, as I sat by the tree, covered in dust and red dirt, among a symphony of nail guns, saws and running engines. I still reflect on this experience today knowing this man of God could never abuse me or others. I am aware of " what ifs" when I reflect on this experience. My experience of a worldly and alcoholic father brought great cost to me, yet my glorified and loving father has brought great peace and healing.

I got to practice bringing truth, love, and healing to my early abused self during a class exercise in seminary. This regressive exercise gave me a window of healing, which I did not know existed. Now I know it as inner child work. This classroom exercise was and is life changing for me and others. It began with my professor asking the class to relax, close our eyes, and be open to experiencing the part of us that we needed to see. He encouraged us to move past our persona or mask, to meet the authentic part of ourselves: the part of us that was pushed down and hidden from others and ourselves. He spoke with reverence as he asked us to think of our safe place growing up, wanting us to remember the color and sounds of our safe place. He asked several questions concerning our safe place, like:

- Did anyone else know about it?
- When would you go there?
- What were you feeling when you were there?
- How did you feel when you were there?
- What made this place safe?

He said, "The first place to look for the part of you that you need to see is in your safe place." He gave us time to think about our play place as children. I remember a fort in the woods by my house. I pictured my lean-to that had 6-inch logs on it. The logs were covered with leaves and pine needles. I could see it clearly. I was aware that I went to my safe place when I was hurt or scared. My older brother was the only one who knew of the fort. It was safe because it was hidden, and my dad could not find it. As I was remembering my safe place, he asked, "Can you remember that safe feeling?" I had a calm warmth go over my body.

As I was experiencing feeling safe, he said, "Once you remember the feeling of being safe, close your eyes. You can now give all your attention to your breathing and allow yourself to use this safe feeling to relax." I thought this relaxation was nice and I planned on taking a quick nap.

I was close to going to sleep when he said, "In your mind's eye, picture yourself outside your safe place." I found myself standing next to the big, dead pine tree in front of the fort. I could see the entrance that was hidden by the fallen pine. I stood there and followed his direction to look to my right and then to my left. Then he asked, "Walk into your safe place to see the part you need to see." I remember feeling hesitant and fearful, which was odd because I did not believe I would see a part of me.

I walked into my fort and it was a lot smaller than I remembered. I could see a little boy sitting with his back to me, in the middle of the fort, digging a hole. He was so small. I was amazed that I could see and be with this part of me. I heard the professor say, "Get close enough to speak to him and let him know you are safe." I walked over to the little boy and said, "Don't be scared. You are safe." I saw him jump because I startled him. This amazed me. I told him, "It's okay." He looked up and asked, "Who are you?" I told him, "I'm you, all grown up." He replied, "That's not true." I was struggling with the same thinking myself.

I was caught up in my own head. This internal experience was odd and a little crazy. I believed I could not step back in time. When the little boy said, "What are you doing here." I was totally caught off guard by his response and did not have an answer. I said, in all my wisdom, "I don't know." I stood there for a long time, then answered, "I'm here just looking at my old fort. I remember playing here a lot. I don't remember digging a hole like you're doing." He replied, "I'm hiding my money from Artie (my older brother)." I looked at him and said, "Well I would hide it too." He said, "You know Artie?" I responded, " Yes, he is still my older brother." He looked at me with puzzlement and asked, " Does he take your money too?" I laughed and said, " Not anymore because I'm bigger than he is now. I don't see him much these days." I could see his confusion and I was not helping much.

I went over and sat in front of him. I was totally absorbed in this experience. I asked the eight-year-old boy what was wrong. He said, "Big Red got out." I knew this was not good. Big Red was our big sow. She was difficult to get back into the pen. My dad would be on a rampage until she was back in the pin and there would be hell to pay if she were not there by nightfall. I had more experience with Big Red and knew how to get her back without chasing her all over the place or spending most of the day looking for her.

I told him, "Don't worry, I know how to get her in the pen." Without hesitation, he asked, "How?" I told him about putting food out and beating the gate for a while. The other pigs would get loud and she would come running.

Then I told him how to handle Dad to avoid getting yelled at or told how stupid he was for letting her get out. I said, "Once Big Red is in the pen you need to stick your head in the front door and tell Dad that she is back in the pen. Then tell him that you are going to check the boards around the pen. He will be happy you are checking something." He said, " That works?" I did not know if he was speaking to me about Dad or getting Big Red in the pen. I replied, "Yes."

I could hear the professor say, "Take some time to say good-bye to him. Tell him if you are coming back but do not tell him you will come back if you are not planning to come back. Ask him if he believes you." I told my inner child I would be back and ask if he believed me. He responded, "I guess." Then I returned to the classroom.

I was not about to share this experience with anyone. I thought this exercise was crazy enough and did not need confirmation from anyone else. There were six of us doing the exercise and they started sharing about their experiences. This experience, even with my education in psychology, was difficult for an East Texas country boy to accept. Many of my peers' stories were powerful. I was the last one to share. I told them about my inner child and the fort. I did not tell them about Big Red because of how real my inner child's reality was during this experience.

I learned more about regression work over the next two years and got plenty of experience, both clinically and personally. I would spend the next two years making time for my inner child. The child within me believed he was not smart. He was neither aware of graduating from high school nor earning a master's degree. He believed and spoke from the old thoughts I worked hard to break.

I wrote a promise to him with my dominant-hand and he responded with my non-dominant hand.

My letter to my Inner Child:

"You need the time to gain a complete understanding. You need the time to play and be played with because you are special. I love you. I hope you will not hesitate when you feel like you need love. Please ask me. I will be there to give you this love. I hope I have the insight to know when you need love, but if I miss you, please tell me. You are a special little boy. I love you deeply and will always be with you."

I then put the pen in my non-dominant hand.

The child within me responded:

"I know you and love you. I love you because you are you. You are a real neat grown-up. You are the best of friends. Please never leave me because I will miss you very much."

I never saw that coming. I did not think the child within me would respond at all, much less with these words. I thought I would have known what "he" was going to write. I did not. Little Wally had his own thoughts and feelings.

**Inner Child Journey.**

I spent time over the next two years understanding how I could grow emotionally, mentally, and spiritually as an adult; but to this day, I have a part of myself with no conscious awareness of these changes. What was even more baffling is that the child within me colors my adult reality. Over years of being a therapist and supervising therapists, I witnessed clients change their inner child's perspective of the world. The adult self was then able to resolve dysfunctional thoughts, feelings, and behaviors.

This inward crossing is the purpose for the book. I learned the conscious mind could know the reasons to avoid something, but still struggle with its past learning. Once my clients spoke to their innermost self, their knowledge and desires changed. I have studied this emotional, or childlike brain for years. The conscious mind (adult self) creates a persona or mask to hide its unwanted feelings and thinking from itself and others, yet these same unwanted thoughts and feelings move the mind wearing the mask. The conscious mind will miss the projected images from the unconscious, which distorts reality and protects its early learning. This childlike, emotional brain creates and confirms its own emotional logic, which makes the projected images the adult experiences appear real.

The scary thing for me is how our childlike brains seek out familiar dysfunctional relationships even though the desired outcome will be missing. I disliked, even hated, my father's behavior, yet without my adult mind's knowledge, I found a partner with these unwanted traits. I passed by hundreds of women without the unwanted traits. The desire to have the familiarity allowed me to look behind the mask of others and move independently of the mask I wore. It is amazing that I found the female version of my father.

## Seminary & Marital Years.

Seminary was a time of hard-won growth. I was in my first year of marriage and beginning a master's program in theology. Oddly enough, this was like mixing oil and water together. I thought marriage was going to be blessed and seminary was going to be like youth camp on the Frio River. I was not naive as an adult; I was truly ignorant. I found out quickly that my expectations were unrealistic, at best.

My expectation of my marriage was that my wife could feel happy, content, loved and respected by me as a man and a minister. Little did I know that my wife, raised in the church as a preacher's kid, would not want to be in the ministry. I thought men and women raised without drugs or alcohol in the home were "healthy and whole." I was ignorant, even with a bachelor's in psychology, of the cost of early emotional and sexual abuse on one's psyche.

I remained ignorant of the cost of child abuse throughout seminary. Ignorance is not bliss; it just creates deeper wounds. I began feeling not good enough, doubting myself and displaying what many would call signs of PTSD again. I broke free of an alcoholic and reclaimed myself and sanity in college to only lose it to a silent killer - a killer that I neither knew nor could see.

I was a man's man. I was educated, hardworking, and had a kind heart. Growing up in a dysfunctional home had some redeeming side effects. I was also accustomed to dealing with physical threats and verbal abuse. Yet, the indirect and passive embodiment of this sort of abuse disarmed me. My wife dressed nicely, had her hair and nails done, spoke politely and was graceful outside our home. Yet inside our four walls I experienced another person.

I knew marriage was going to take work. I believed if I worked hard enough, our marriage would grow. I did not realize this was a mental distortion on my part. The harder I worked cleaning, cooking, and trying to please her, the more I got criticized and judged. What made matters worse was the criticism and judgment was coming from one that did not do cleaning, cooking, or much housework. When I confront her distortion with reality or her lack of a work ethic, I was called an abuser. This was mind blowing at first, but I accepted it over time.

After two years of marriage, I was going to seminary full time, working over 40 hours a week, and doing the household chores. It still was not good enough. I got criticism and judgment inside the home and indirect praise outside. When I confronted this craziness; I was told "you don't love me," or "you're not a minister" or "I hate you and I will just kill myself." I would lose myself with these passive threats and work harder to be a better husband. I lost my boundaries and self on the way to being a codependent.

My internal and external conflict at home was complicated by the fact that I was in seminary which was not like bible camp. I found myself around biblical scholars and theologians. My professors demanded scholarly pursuits. I graduated from the University of Texas Tech and knew how to study. Work on a Master of Divinity took studying to the next level. I struggled with theology, the knowledge of God, because it confronted my rose-colored belief of God and His church. My safe place with God and familiar belief was under attack. I was in crisis once again. I did what I knew: I worked harder.

Working harder was the correct answer to seminary but not my marriage - this approach only solidified my codependent patterns. During this time, I reached a mental and emotional bottom that led me to seek leaving my marriage. I was waiting for my wife to come home to ask her for a divorce when she walked through the door with baby booties in her hand. She was pregnant. I made a vow that night to remain married and to raise my son. Life rocked on and two years later we had our second son.

## Residency.

After seminary, I got into a two-year residency in Dallas, Texas. I hoped things would change in Dallas because my in-laws lived 10 minutes away and could play a balancing role in my wife's life. I knew they would help my wife and health would come into our marriage. Expectation was a way I generated hope during this time. Yet expectations of others were usually met with disappointment. This time was no different.

I worked 60 hours a week counseling clients, going to supervision, and had several assignments due each week. Soon I had great conflict at home due to not being physically or emotionally present. This exasperated any resemblance of normalcy I thought we had in our marriage. What made things worse was I knew I was being mentally and emotionally abused. What I did not know was that she was, too.

She was overwhelmed by me being gone, not helping, and being demanding. Previously, my wife had acted out in more passive ways but now I was "abusing her." This life crisis was a trigger which I was not aware of then. I moved from being her husband to being seen and treated like a perpetrator. As a result, she began medicating with food and alcohol. These were not the tools of relationship building.

In my personal therapy, I said, "She is worse than my dad." I began putting together the pieces with this new self-revelation. I got away from my abusive father and unconsciously married a mirror image of him. I struggled with this image and my codependency for the next 25 years, yet I continued to attend to my inner child. He was growing in wisdom and even getting older.

I began to have greater insight into my relationship in my second year of residency. I was able to diagnose and treat all mental disorders and versed on family dynamics. This knowledge was not power in my situation. I found knowledge to be a curse. I would leave the house to help others get free of addictions, relationship dysfunctions, and mental illnesses, only to come home and live them out.

I used rationalizing, minimizing, and intellectualization to keep these problems from my conscious mind. The use of these defense mechanisms only made the unaddressed issues worse in duration and intensity. I moved more into work because of the positive words of others, my sense of control there, and need to be fulfilled. Little did I know, I was becoming a workaholic. As I medicated with work my wife's compulsive behaviors increased. As it would turn out, I was doing the same behavior my mother did with my alcoholic father. I resented my mother for years for not standing up to my father, for not leaving him or protecting me. And here I was repeating the same codependent behavior "to keep the peace."

I would attempt to please my wife to control her mood and indulges, which only enabled her to continue the poor behavior. Living in a haunted marriage was "easier" than dealing with it. Our marriage was haunted by images of my father as well as the projections of her perpetrator. If this was not bad enough, I became codependent to keep the peace at all cost.

The paradox is I specialized in helping others get free from their past abuse issues and indulgences while having boundaries. I was aware of these dynamics but had a fear of losing my two boys and my ministry as a pastoral counselor. When I spoke truth to her it was minimized and denied. I knew I could not help anyone who did not want to change. I decided to help those who wanted to change.

My counseling ministry grew in my residency and continued when I became a director of a nonprofit counseling center. The illusion of a happy home weighed on me. The more dysfunctional my home life became, the harder I worked to feed both of our indulgences. The more I fed my indulgences of workaholism the more she fed hers. I knew this was a sick cycle.

I did regression work to free my inner child from an alcoholic while consciously living out the learned patterns. I was living out familiar learned behaviors. This learned cycle could only be broken by me taking myself seriously.

As I honored my thoughts and feelings, I began protecting my temple with boundaries. These boundaries also honored her poor choices. These healthy boundaries no longer enabled our mutual dysfunction and broke the toxic relational patterns. The final consequence was a divorce. I have replayed what I would have done differently many times over the course of my 30-year marriage. The answer is, nothing. I could not see myself until I could see and could not hear myself until I could hear. I move from a healer with a wound to a wounded healer. Now, I am a wounded healer with a keen awareness of the journey from a psychological, theological, and personal perspective.

When I look back, I wonder how I lost myself in codependency, i.e., losing myself while making others' thoughts and feelings my god. In truth, I would not be writing about my loss of self in my marriage if not for my editor. Annie is a wounded healer. She confronted me on the "gaps" in my story. She was looking at the missing space of my marital years and asking what happened. Initially I hid from that time because it felt like life lost. Being codependent or a co-addict may be where I missed the mark of God the most in my life. Roads not taken and dreams unrealized are a couple of my many losses.

I know me becoming less than God's best to please another human was a type of idolatry moved by fear. The more I enabled my addict, the greater my fear. My fear stemmed from my love for my boys and ministry. The greater my fears became, the more I enabled. When I got past my struggle against having a healthy self, my fears were silenced.

Today, I know unaddressed fear breeds denial and stops growth. There were years of calm in my life, but this was due to not having a self. Even helping others get freed of codependency did not shake my denial during that time. Denial silently snatched away my hope, dreams, and life. Codependency broke my image on the mirror of my soul. I have met the monster which stopped my own mom from helping or seeing her child being abused.

## A Living Sacrifice.

This book was already written and edited when I had enough awareness and courage to break free of this image of my dad in female form. It took writing this book and doing the exercises to break free of the chains of a thirty-year relationship. I received the same messages of not being good enough, critiqued for not doing enough, and would have all the positivity wiped away due to one negative, often accidental, behavior. I believed if I worked hard and loved enough it would change the messages and the hurtful and unwanted responses I received from my wife. I had grown personally, and my inner child grew up, but I was unaware of living with the shadow of the person who created my wound.

As happens in situations of abuse, I lost my sense of self as a child so I could live. The craving of an addict was relentless on my young soul. My soul was a demand by my father, and I had to forfeit my self-worth to fill his alcoholic desires. I lost most of my childhood by keeping the peace and living in my father's image. I lost my authentic ability to feel and think outside of his sickness. This was the only life I knew since birth.

This book gave definition and a voice to my past healing, yet sadly, it illuminated the fact that I lived with my father's image for years. I lost myself to an image familiar in form to my abusive father. I unknowingly mirrored my art of pleasing on this image of my father. This image became my wife, which called out for the same dysfunction I knew as a child.

One year led into another year of dysfunction as I lived through the eyes of all I had ever known. I was aware of the familiar internal losses and a haunting emptiness, yet still not conscious of the familiar learned pattern of responding that was now poisoning my soul and family. The haunting emptiness was denied, minimized, rationalized, and intellectualized by me. All the while, the losses I experienced as a child were materializing in my adult life. The sad and ugly truth was my children experienced shades of dysfunction and abuse, which I thought I would never allow.

This teaching journey revealed I married my father and watched how I lost myself again to my father's image in my wife. I gradually lost more and more of myself during my 30 years of marriage. As I lost myself, her desires and cravings grew. Her cravings created strife for my two sons as her indulgent patterns increased. The portrait of an addict covered the walls of my house and my soul.

My illness of codependency (modeled by my mother) enabled my wife to continue to indulge. This indulgence medicated her emotions and fed her avoidance of her historic abuse issues. In hindsight, her hidden issues of abuse were acted out on our marital stage. Her hatred, pain, and fears of her perpetrator were projected onto me. She mirrored the image of her past perpetrators on me and this colored our relationship. These projected fragments of her abusers only fed my sick desire to please her at my own expense. Our illusion of a home was only a house of mirrors. The image in the mirror got cracked one Christmas Eve. On this day, many years ago, I could see clearly as I drove home on a dark and lonely night.

The Christmas tree was sparkling with an array of colored lights, like other

Christmases; however, this one was different. As I sat alone in a cold and dark room watching the lights dance upon the ornament covered tree, I had an urgency to regain my own lost peace and joy. This emotional moment moved me into myself, propelling me to hear my own truth. Clarity came through suffering; my heart was filled with pain and loneliness. I could clearly see the emotional, mental, and spiritual cost of living in a house of mirrors with the self-portrait of an addict.

Thanks to this book, written to free others from their past traumas and indulgences, I have found healing along the way. By writing about the cost of defensive mechanisms with suffering, I was able to recognize my own. With a cost of indulgence on the soul, I saw my codependency and started finding ways to free the child within myself. Freedom was difficult and became a hero's journey in and of itself. As with all hero's journeys, I had to do it alone and go through hardships as I fought my villains.

The typical villains were there. They had many different shapes and sizes, but all spoke familiar words to create fear and shame. I feared what others would think about a wounded healer being codependent; I also feared being judged as not spiritual due to the sin of divorce. I know my greatest villain was not wanting to hurt others, especially my children. These villains were deceitful, played tricks on my mind and fed my codependency, but I got to the point where I said, Crazy or Not, Here I Come. This intentional step to break free led me to my heart's true desires and gave me the ability to look through the window of my Soul. I found healing through God's Word, the Holy Spirit, and the exercises in this book.

My storyline is still being written. It is not being written by an alcoholic father, my wife's past perpetrators, or a codependent mother. The author of my new storyline comes from the image of God in me. Through my suffering, I could step away from my fear and shame. My suffering is over. I am free. Free to live, love, and experience life. I am on a new adventure that is filled with hope, peace, and joy. My hero's journey was worth walking through the badlands. Your journey will be worth it too.

# CHAPTER THREE

## EAST OF EDEN

"For I know the plans I have for you," declares the Lord, "plans to prosper you and not to harm you, plans to give you hope and a future." Jeremiah 29:11

**KEY POINTS:**

- You are not alone in your pain.
- There is a way out.
- To get there, begin exactly where you are.

**Reflections:**

- Where are you today? How are you feeling about yourself? Your surroundings? Your past and future?
- This question is a hard one. Stay with it and answer it as you can, even very simply. Respond from your heart and your body, not your head. *Write down your answers.*
- It is impossible to have a complete understanding of all your wounding at the start of this work. These questions, answered today, are the fundamental starting point for moving into deeper healing.
- Keep your "where you are" today notes as your north star throughout the book. Revisit them at the start of each chapter to help map your growth. The questions will afford you more information with the continued exercises in the coming chapters.

## Welcome.

"I shall be telling this with a sigh somewhere ages and ages hence: Two roads diverged in a wood, and I — I took the one less traveled by, And that made all the difference." Robert Frost

You are on a journey to the Soul that will allow you to change your negative traits and habitual and unhealthy, unconscious reactions by becoming conscious. You will re-write your story considering your present truth. If you have relational conflict, indulgences, or a mental "illness" you will need to experience your authentic, God given, self. This journey is difficult because you are a byproduct of "The Fall" and living East of Eden.

The spiritual walk of the journey of healing is difficult because we are all byproducts of "The Fall." In a spiritual sense, we all start our lives living East of Eden. As you read this chapter, your soul is likely crying out in desperation and pain. You are at the beginning of your journey and your own spot East of Eden may feel very dark and threatening. You are not alone, and we will walk back toward the garden together with God's help and guidance.

In the first moments of the world, there was a time in which people were truly conscious; totally present with themselves, their environment, and God. Biblically, the fall of humankind occurred in the Garden of Eden, when Adam and Eve defied God's instructions and ate from the tree of good and evil. This act began a loss of consciousness, or wholeness, that has followed people throughout the ages ever since. This psycho-spiritual tragedy is all our birth right. It is also why reliance on divine support and intervention is necessary when we are lost and hurting outside the garden. As discussed in Chapter 1, we are simply not equipped to find our way back alone.

### Exercise: Connecting with Thyself

*This is not a regression exercise. There are no special instructions included. Answer simply and directly in your journal.*

Making yourself a priority is paramount throughout this work. It is your most important goal. Making yourself important will help you stay in the moment while listening to your authentic emotions. Remember, the Holy

Spirit will bring you wisdom, knowledge, and strength as you place yourself first in a spirit of faith. Gaining wisdom, knowledge, and strength, your self-esteem will increase as you confront your "thinking" of lies and put on God's truth. The Holy Spirit and God's Word will "esteem" you when you cannot esteem yourself. You will learn to esteem yourself to have a healthy self-esteem.

You may fear the deadly sin of pride. Healthy self-esteem is not pride. Pride is an exaggerated view of yourself that leads to conceit, arrogance, and vanity. In contrast, self-esteem is necessary to develop your identity. Self-esteem is confidence in your individual way of mastering experience. Synonyms for self-esteem are self-regard, self-worth, and self-respect. Self-esteem is essential to the formation of a healthy identity.

Do you have a high or low view of yourself? On a scale of 1-10, one being low and 10 being high. What number jumps out in your mind when you think of your value or worth? Make a mental note or write down that number. Then write down all the reasons you think you are amazing, brilliant, beautiful, and wonderful. Just write down amazing and make a list under it of what makes you amazing; then do it with brilliant, beautiful, and wonderful. Circle and underline the reflections that come up which feel most emotionally powerful.

Amazing (1-10) =
1.
2.
3.

Brilliant (1-10) =
1.
2.
3.

Beautiful (1-10) =
1.

2.
3.

Wonderful (1-10) =
1.
2.
3.

Worthy (1-10) =
1.
2.
3.

How many items did you list under those positive attributes? _______

Now write down the negative belief or thought about yourself.
1.
2.
3.

You may find it easier to acknowledge your negative beliefs about yourself. I believe most of your negative beliefs came from others' critiques, which are the heart of other esteem. Are you struggling with other esteem? Does your parents', spouse's, or friends' criticism affect you? Do you have a negative view of yourself when someone else says something negative about you? If other opinions affect your mood or your view of yourself, then you have other esteem. In other words, you think more of them than yourself, which gives too much power to others.
If you are doing these following things, you might have "others-esteem:"

1. Are you a mind reader? Mind reading occurs when you think another person thinks X and will do Y. You will start to defend yourself against X's thoughts or behavior (Y). If you catch yourself doing any mind reading, check out what you are thinking they are thinking. When you mind read, you are wrong 50% of the time and not right the other 50%. People will usually tell you the truth if you check it out.

2. Do you apologize for things you have not done wrong? If you have others-esteem you will walk around saying "I'm sorry" when you have not done anything wrong, you are taking responsibility for something you have not done. It is sad when saying, "I'm sorry" becomes a habit and you do not even realize you are saying it. Apologizing unnecessarily gives others permission to blame you or think you have done something wrong. Do you assume responsibility when someone close to you, like a family member or friend, is angry or "upset?" You are likely questioning yourself, trying to determine what you did to cause it. Others-esteem leads to unwarranted apologies and mind reading. You will not know where you end, and they begin.

3. Do you withhold truth or not give all the information because you fear hurting someone? Perhaps you lie, fearful of their reaction or a desire to create peace. Lies of submission are still lies, and they bring consequences for you and the person you are protecting or helping. If you avoid giving your opinion to others or speaking in groups, you may have "others-esteem." Many label these signs as being codependent. Codependency is having your mood being dependent on what others are feeling and thinking. The key is not the label but to cease dysfunctional beliefs. Others-esteem creates dysfunctional and persecutory relationships.

Preventing dysfunctional "other-esteem" empowers the ability to be more present in the moment. You will come to realize your life has meaning. You will become more conscious and alive. Low self-esteem and others-esteem are reactionary behaviors, which is when you react to something or someone outside of your control. You get lost in the present moment. When you live to please others, it leads to dysfunction. When you refuse to listen to yourself, you will serve something or someone other than God.

Remember, God says let your "yes be yes and your no be no" (James 5:12, NASB). Do not tickle the ears of those around you to please them. This type of pleasing is misguided because it hurts you and the other person. This pleasing is not of God. Your authentic self will speak truth in love. "But speaking the truth in love, we are to grow up in all aspects into Him who is the head, even Christ," (Ephesians 4:15, NASB). It is a part of "growing up" spiritually. It is learning to be Christ-like.

You may struggle with having a self, being in the moment, and living in the present because your normal behavior has been to adapt to others. Adapting is a way of being perfect or strong and not being yourself. In this case, pleasing others would be a relational mutation. While understandable, all relational revisions are inauthentic. Any adaption is a move away from authenticity.

## Exercise: Family of Origin Experiences

*This is not a regression exercise. There are no special instructions included. Answer simply and directly in your journal.*

The mask of the past, also known as the false self, was developed as an adaptive response to childhood trauma and abuse. As a younger person, this mask was a way for you to survive. In my early learning of psychoanalysis, the popular belief was that "masks" were developed to escape a natural personality that was flawed. However, through years of counseling people, I know that there is nothing dark about a person's God given nature. Even living East of Eden, as we all are, God created you in the womb (Psalm 138:13). As a member of creation, you are "good" (Genesis 1:31). Psalm 139:14 says you are "fearfully and wonderfully made."

Today I believe the masks we develop are a method to conform to social pressures and hide past emotional, physical, or sexual abuse. Your mask is like the door to your (soul) closet, which covers all the skeletons in the closet. Are you aware of the suffering your inner child experienced which prompted him or her to develop protective masks? The answer lies within you.

In starting this examination, the most fruitful place to start is often with your family of origin. Begin to look at your family behaviors and beliefs - how did these influence the data hardwired in your brain, even today? You will need to look at your family history and environmental learning and look at how both have affected you. The first thing you may want to do is to look for any genetic history of mental or physical illness, addiction, stress tolerance, or disordered personalities.

You can look at your mother and father's positive and negative traits to gain insight but listen most closely to the negative traits because they have the greatest effect in your life today. Circle and underline the reflections that come up which feel most emotionally powerful.

List the positive traits of your Mother and Father.

1.
2.
3.

List the negative traits of your Mother and Father.

1.
2.
3.

We will be continuing this examination of "who you are" and what that means in the coming chapters. You will most likely find that the reflections you see in the mirror are of your past and are distortions of what is real and true in the present. Your nature is likely past-oriented and based upon the storyline you wrote as a child. Yes, you carry many of your parents' strengths and weaknesses; however, you are also the co-creator of your story.

There are ways to break the chains of your past learning. Odds are that these traits have been passed down from generation to generation. By recovering your inner child, you can retrieve the wisdom and strength of previous generations while discarding dysfunctional beliefs or behaviors. You can change these unwanted beliefs and memories that are millstones around your neck to create stepping-stones for your life.

## Breaking the Chains:

## Connecting with Self & Family of Origin Experiences

It is important to look at the circled or underlined traits in your lists above and reflect upon them further. As you consider these reflections, you may be able to see a pattern between the negative views you have of yourself and the negative traits of your parents. Additionally, you may be able to see that you are drawn to the negative aspects of your parents in others or possess them yourself. Because of the subconscious wiring of trauma, you are more likely to strengthen and use the behaviors you disliked the most growing up.

Being intentional and using your consciousness to retrain your inner child's storyline provides healing. By reconceptualizing your thoughts and feelings concerning your early abuse and trauma, you "can change (and thus, evolve) our brains, [and] no longer fall into those repetitive, habitual and unhealthy reactions that are produced because of our genetic inheritance and our past experiences. You...want to learn how you can use the brain's natural capacity of neuroplasticity, -the ability to rewire and create new neural circuits at any age" (Evolve Your Brain pg. 10 Dispenza D. C. c2007).

Reviewing your unconscious view of yourself and the forgotten aspects of your family of origin experiences is a way to draw material from your inner child. You may be aware of your memories or the emotional responses of your youth while reading your responses. By being aware you can reconceptualize the event, experience, or emotions by using your adult self. In doing so, you are changing your brain.

## About Trauma: The Science

Modern science has proven that trauma exists, layered in both our memories and the actual tissue of our bodies ("The Body Keeps The Score," Bessell van der Kolk). In times of crisis, it often feels like all these wounds are open and bleeding at the same time. It is this sense of emotional engulfment that frequently drives people to despair. However you may currently feel, it is critical to understand that your painful internal places exist at separate points within your body. To fully heal, to finally eliminate experiences of intense emotional flooding, you must cleanse each wound individually, moving layer by layer through your conscious and unconscious mind.

In Evolve Your Brain (2007), acclaimed physician Joe Dispenza states that the unconscious is where, "memories are processed...as feelings. When memories are filtered through feelings, we are unconsciously producing thoughts that are connected only to the past. Having these feelings is to think in the past. This might explain why so many of us recreate the same dynamics, and other recurring circumstances in our life. When we unconsciously feel the same feeling every single day, we create more of the familiar" (475). This is the scientific reason that most people dealing with trauma are problem-oriented and struggle to be solution focused.

Physiologically, your unconscious mind resides in the amygdala. This is the most primitive part of your brain and is designed specifically for survival and self-protection. Trauma experiences encode themselves along this neural network. Because of the drive for survival, these old emotions have their own logic called affective memory. This means that your historic emotions are "thinking" for themselves. Can you imagine what kind of "logic" your non-rational brain would come up with? Here is an example:

*A two or three-year-old child hears loud and angry voices, is left alone, and becomes afraid. Fear is an adaptive, primitive response for a child at this age to best assure survival. His or her amygdala is activated. The fear the child feels then creates a "logic" which says, "I'm alone and will die." In the future, each time the child becomes fearful or hears angry noises, this logic would resurface, triggering fear and the child's past learning that he or she was fundamentally unsafe. The adult brain may know that fear does not equal being alone or dying, but these affective memories may be stronger and have a greater neural network than the adult's rational brain in the life of the child.*

*Remember the game telephone? Where each person whispers a statement in another's ear and then the last person in line states the information they heard. By the time the information gets to the last person, the facts are distorted. The message is nothing like the original one. I first experienced this phenomenon in a sociology class at Texas Tech University. The message was something like, "Our professor found a hooker in her classroom and the police were called. She went to jail." Once it got to the last person in our row, the message was "The professor was a prostitute, and the police took her to jail." Now, consider this with the message being passed down through the emotional lens of your amygdala. The repetition of this same message with the emotions of a two-year-old attached would be like trying to convey truth in a game of telephone while riding a bike on crack cocaine.*

Your primitive emotional "thinking" only gets stronger over the years. Because trauma is stored in a primitive region of the brain, it produces extremely strong drivers of the reactive behavior or "unconscious" states that currently haunt the lives of trauma victims. Consciousness, on the other hand, rests in your neocortex, the newest part of the brain. The neocortex is your brain's motherboard. It is comprised of the frontal lobes, which are its central processing unit. A helpful shorthand is to consider your unconscious mind as related to your younger self, past trauma experiences, and "inner child." Your conscious mind, on the other hand, is most closely related to your adult reality. It produces your most elevated levels of self-awareness. In comparison, it is helpful to realize that your amygdala was fully developed at 8 months of gestation. Your neocortex, however, requires around 25 years of growth to reach maturity (Neuroscience p. 81 Louis Cozolino, Second Edition c2010-2002).

Understanding your emotional experiences and responses can push life along until your mid-twenties is frightening. As a child, you were learning without the brain's physiological maturity or the ability to process and comprehend what you were learning. Your mind was like a blank slate, written on by others. You only had the ability to experience the sensory material and "process" this material emotionally. Perhaps you do not believe in emotional memory or emotional logic. You may believe that you were "rational" or "logical" as an infant or child. I would like you to think about how you were logical, when your brain did not decipher the data you were receiving at the time. Your frontal lobe and the rest of your rational brain were growing and developing. The frontal lobe tells you when, how, and why you needed to do things, while the frontal cortex puts your internal and external experiences into perspective.

As a child, your emotional experiences were remembered through a primitive view of what you experienced. It is like having your emotional historian being a reactive child. Your emotional historian was recording information in a database based on truth or reality. The more the emotional logic is replayed in your mind, the stronger and more frightening it becomes. Then increasing your emotional response or reaction. This continuous negative reactive cycle colors your perspective and beliefs. Causing your past thoughts and feelings to be projected on reality today.

It is the intentional connection of your unconscious mind through your consciousness that serves to heal trauma on a physiological level. As

Dispenza states, "if we can use the frontal lobe and control it, we can know and control our future and ourselves" (Evolve your Brain, p. 348, Joe Dispenza, D.C., 2007). It is exciting to know we have the power to observe - and change - the workings of our minds.

Healing will take an act of your will which is seated in your conscious mind. "The neocortex is the seat of free Will. This is the conscious thought center of the brain…" (Evolve Your Brain-Joe Dispenza pg. 69, c2007). Your frontal lobe is your "supervisor." It is where your executive functioning resides and provides the ability to face your past trauma. If you avoid being intentionally willful about your healing, then your amygdala, where your trauma resides, will increase your unwanted emotions. Consciousness and intentionality are required to disrupt unconscious patterns that flow from past pain to hijack your life.

At the beginning of this work, it is likely you may not specifically recall much of the hurt and sadness that plagues you - it is buried deep in your unconsciousness. However, by taking one step at a time, starting with where you are today, you will heal.

## Managing the Process: Fear

It is important to note that trauma work is almost always connected with a deep sense of fear. If you are feeling fearful at the beginning of this work, that is normal and to be expected. Fear is a universal phenomenon where you find "false evidence appearing real," as noted in much self-help literature. Your adult mind lives in a world of its own personal perceptions and awareness. Its entire function is to keep you physically and emotionally safe. Over the years it has collected a lot of false data to keep all threats - most imagined - at bay.

If you are like most people attempting to address trauma, many of your adult perceptions have likely been hijacked by fear and distorted storylines from your past. You have been mentally rehearsing these negative, fearful states your entire life. Your old, emotional "logic" dictates what you believe and how you behave. The fear of re-experiencing old emotions has likely stopped or challenged your healing process. This fear keeps you a victim of abuse. As such, you act out the thoughts and feelings of the past in your present, projecting that reality onto others. If you do not confront the fear in your life, you will pass it onto others. The pain and abuse in your life will be a generational gift that keeps giving.

As we embark upon healing your past trauma, you should know that you are safe. You will never be asked to go back and relive your abuse as a method to heal them. Our work with your past is focused specifically on reconnecting with the wounded parts of you, your younger self, or "inner child. This is an aspect of your identity where you will receive your most robust healing, once nurtured. Our goal here is to reclaim the child within you, bringing he or she out of scary past times and into the security of your adult existence. While this may sound crazy, it is a method that has proven effective in healing repeatedly in my work with clients.

The first step in connecting with your inner child is to face your fears. Hold fast to the promises of scripture to support you in this. Remember, fear is not of God and must be rejected outright. God says, " Fear not, for I am with you; Be not dismayed, for I am your God." (Isaiah 41:10, NKJV). God wants you to be free of the fear of your abuser. If fear is an active agent in your life, it will snuffle out your thoughts and feelings around the abuse. This suppression is done from your adult mind and has a great cost to your inner child. Your childlike mind will use suppressed emotions to solidify his/her distorted beliefs. Unconsciously, repressed memories will affect your daily life and relationships.

Many of my clients have cried, "It's easier to avoid the pain." Unfortunately, the more you cling to fear as a method to avoid your internal and external conflicts, the more your emotional tension will increase. It is a distressing cycle, whereby the more your conflicts increase, the more you become bound to old beliefs and/or unwanted emotions. Remember, insanity is doing the same thing repeatedly and expecting different results each time. Change requires an act of intentionality. You must consciously choose to confront your fear of your trauma before you can heal from it.

If you moved toward the center of the merry-go-round then your intense emotions, thoughts, or behaviors will decrease. Once at the center, you will feel less physical pressure and have more peace. It is much the same as you approach your emotional pain, fear, or anger from your past wounds. You will hear what you have been avoiding and potentially learn meaning from them. At the center of the merry-go-around, life slows down; you can reconceptualize past thoughts and feelings with your present knowledge.

The need to listen to yourself will take an act of your will. Emotionally, you will want to get off the merry-go-round by moving to the outside to avoid your issues. When you want to get off life's merry-go-round, you must consciously move into yourself. Yes, this goes against what you may think and even want to do. This is the time for you to do regression work and move to your "center." Once you begin moving, you will be on the road of recovery and making progress.

The human mind can rewire itself and evolve while creating its own chemistry. We do not have to be imprisoned by the habitual and unhealthy pain that plagues us. God has blessed us with the ability to renew our minds; because of this, there is also a critical, spiritual element to obtaining full healing as well.

Your inner child learned behaviors growing up to protect him/herself such as being perfect, strong, and trying hard to please others. Such behaviors drive you today. These "drivers" are like wearing a mask that would make others happy or keep the peace. The mask dulls your sense of self, not only deceiving others, but also misleading yourself.

I have clients with abusive spouses; they came into counseling having been verbally, emotionally, physically, and/or sexually abused, oblivious to their own abuse. The abusive behavior is familiar and "comfortable" for my clients. Family and friends cannot help them because they are hiding behind their masks from their emotional and physical scars. These clients spent much of their time being strong, pleasing others, trying hard, or being perfect, believing all the while their masks were "protecting" them.

If anyone noticed or inquired about their emotional or physical signs of abuse, they would lie, thereby increasing the deception. They would pull out their trusty bag of defense mechanisms (denial, rationalization, minimizing, or intellectualizing) as ways of disguising their problems, continuing their self-deception.

One client who lived behind a mask was morbidly obese. She almost ate herself to death. She medicated her emotions with gluttony, losing her self-discipline. Low self-esteem and ever-increasing other esteem almost killed her while she attempted to "please others," or be "okay." Pleasing others did not work. She wanted to lose weight and have "discipline."

## My Story: Elaine

Elaine entered therapy because of pain regarding her weight. At the time, she weighed approximately 255 pounds and was of average height. Reconceptualizing her past negative beliefs with truth was arduous work. Her first two months of therapy consisted of confronting her unconscious web of defense mechanisms. Her historic child-like beliefs distorted her reality.

Through regression work, Elaine slowly developed the ability to look through the eyes of her 11-year-old self. She had difficulty reconceptualizing her past beliefs because her present reality was hijacked by her past. I would say, "Your adult self is looking through your inner child's eyes." We needed for Elaine to work in a different direction, looking through her childhood eyes upon the truths of her adult life. Elaine's present behavior needed to be used to confront her past beliefs and current use of defensive mechanisms. One critical exercise I recommended regarded her mail.

She usually had the mail carrier bring it to her door; doing so was "easier" because her mailbox was past her neighbor's driveway. So, Elaine was asked to discipline herself to walk to get her mail, and she agreed to complete the suggested task. When I next saw Elaine, she spoke of the inability to walk to her first neighbor's driveway without sitting down. She said, "I can't breathe well, and my legs get shaky." I told her to carry a chair.

Her initial fear was of what the neighbors would think of her. She thought and believed she was not "okay" and had to "please others." She was horrified that others would reject her. Early in her life, Elaine learned how to please others by suppressing the painful words other children spoke to her. She had, "always been fat." Elaine finally agreed to walk to each driveway and sit until she was rested. Elaine would rest then move to the next driveway, folding chair in tow. Elaine walked to her mailbox for a few weeks and was excited about her success. Within a month, she could walk to the mailbox without sitting in someone's driveway to rest.

Once Elaine could walk to her mailbox and back, I asked her to walk as far as she could before she had to take a rest. She could then walk all the way back. Elaine was doing great until she began mind reading or projecting her own fears onto others (see Chapter 1). She saw people looking out the window, "to see the fat woman walk." Elaine believed her neighbors thought she, "should keep her fat butt at home." After I encouraged her to ask them what they thought of her walking, she stated, "I was out of my mind" and agreed to continue walking and stop projecting, or mind reading.

Elaine began walking as far as she could and then sitting to rest until she was ready to walk back. She worked up to almost 2 miles one-way and then back again, each time she would move her chair a couple feet further from her house. Elaine was so proud and had lost close to 30 pounds. Then one day someone stole her metal chair. She came into her session and voiced that she had stopped walking because "someone stole my chair." When asked to get another chair, Elaine said, "No, they will take that too."

Elaine believed, "nobody wants me to lose weight," and "I'm tired of being judged." She could not explain these negative beliefs, but Elaine knew others believed these things about her. She constantly read other people's minds and allowed those beliefs to control her. Others' unvoiced opinions were controlling her life. While Elaine had made strides in maintaining her goals, she was willing to give up her goal and happiness based on what she believed others were thinking about her. So, I asked Elaine to listen to what God was telling her and go by that spiritual insight.

She came back to counseling and voiced that God wanted her to have the desires of her heart and not be obese. Then she said, "I guess I should walk again, but I cannot sit on the ground because I cannot get up again." Elaine's fear was that people would talk about her if she needed help getting up. I then asked Elaine to sit on the floor and attempt to get up by herself. She believed it was "stupid." I asked her if she knew why I asked her to sit on the floor. Elaine became sad and said, "Because you want to have a good laugh too." I informed Elaine that I hated she believed I asked her to do this to laugh at her. I then reminded her she was wrong 50% of the time and not right other 50% of the time when she chooses to project, or mind read. She was encouraged to ask me the reason I asked her to sit on the floor and then get up by herself.

Elaine sat quietly for about 5 minutes and then asked, "What was the reason you asked me to sit on the floor and then get up?" I replied, "I believe you can do it. I know that you will accomplish great things by knowing you can get up by yourself." Elaine got up out of the chair and sat on the floor. As she sat on the floor, she began to cry and said, "I haven't sat on the floor like this in years. I cannot remember the last time I sat on the floor with my legs crossed." Elaine had lost so much of her life and happiness to obesity; it was killing her. But the root of Elaine's challenges rested in the compulsion to please others and the belief she knew what others thought about her.

Elaine is like many people who grew up with a dominant parent; in her case, the dominant and "perfect" parent was her father. The difficulty living with a perfectionist is that the "be perfect" measurement keeps moving up. Each time Elaine hit the mark, she heard from her father that, "I could have done better." The message sent when she did not hit the mark as a child was that she, "wasn't good enough," which increased her shame.

Spiritually, Elaine made God in the image of her father. Elaine believed that God, like her father, was critical and domineering. She believed God saw her as, "not good enough." No wonder she medicated her emotions with food. She believed what she thought others thought about her and that God believed the same things as her father.

Elaine was carrying a great deal of emotional and spiritual baggage. She had to clean her emotional and spiritual filters as she journeyed toward her authentic Self. Her journey to lose weight was more to increase her sense of self. She needed to break free of mind reading while developing healthy internal and external relational boundaries. Elaine had difficulty staying present in the moment because she lost herself to a domineering father early in life. Her defense mechanisms were the denial and suppression of her emotions while medicating them with food.

Elaine also had increased difficulty being vulnerable with others because of her previous poor judgment and beliefs about herself. She was eventually able to see God as the Good Shepherd and herself as the lamb the Shepherd came to rescue. Elaine thought herself defenseless but understood the sheep depends on the Shepherd. She channeled her disempowered sense of powerlessness to personal empowerment by learning to be fully dependent on God. Elaine removed her masks of strength and people pleasing, allowing herself to be vulnerable and weak. The best way to achieve a healthy dependency on God is to be weak. I encouraged her to remember to be vulnerable with her friends and God while not engaging in her unnecessary use of defense mechanisms, which hides her from others.

Over time, Elaine began to hear that God was supportive in her goal to walk. She confronted her fear of what others may have thought about her. Elaine was eventually able to roll over and get up from the floor. She said "So, I do not need a chair." Elaine was present in the moment and was empowered and agreed to walk as far as she did with the chair before sitting down to rest and then walk back. Elaine was able to start jogging a few months later. She had lost close to 55 pounds before one of her neighbors called out her name one morning.

Elaine reported that she had just started her run when her neighbor asked, "How far today?" Elaine responded, "Close to 5 miles." She continued, "That when my knees started knocking and I couldn't seem to breathe; time stood still." Elaine was having a panic attack and felt, "like running into the house." Elaine was aware that her fear of not doing well enough and being judged, "kept running through my mind." She noted her neighbor said, "You're doing great. The wind is going to be up this morning. So, take care." Elaine had no response; she said, "I was speechless."

Elaine began hearing truth from others for the first time without the need to defend herself with projecting. She acknowledged she, "could be wrong on what others thought" about her. Elaine was beginning to have a voice for herself and felt encouraged to follow her dreams. She later conceded that when her neighbor spoke to her that morning, she heard her old emotional logic of her dad saying, "Go in the house. You're too fat, little girl." Elaine confronted her emotional logic by saying, "Dad never told me this when growing up."

I encouraged Elaine to write down the positive and negative attributes or beliefs she had as a child. Elaine's inner child was living out her negative beliefs and expected others to have the same responses as her father. Her responses were:

Positive:

1) nice
2) quiet
3) good at school

Negative:

1) fat
2) shy
3) ugly
4) invisible
5) not highly active

Elaine continued running between 4 to 6 miles a day for several months. She had lost over 100 pounds when she made the commitment to train for a marathon. She was constantly asking me why she was not overeating or binging anymore. Elaine did not have a need to fill herself with food because of the joy of running and the praise from others. I told her to tell the chubby little third grader, "about her positive attributes." Now, her list included: "Dedicated, runner, active, disciplined, strong, and nice." Her negative list was, "Still fat." She reconceptualizes her inner child's beliefs with her present truth.

Elaine's first half marathon was approaching in under a month, and she doubted herself. Once again, she struggled with projection and worry about what others would think of her, "trying to run a half marathon." She had retreated into reading the minds of her father, brother, ex-husband, boss, and co-workers, further elevating her doubt and fear. The more Elaine thought about what others thought of her, the lower her esteem fell. She began having more negative thoughts, which increased her compulsive eating. Elaine convinced herself that, "No one wants to see a fat cow running that distance anyway. I probably could not finish it; what was I thinking? I was so stupid."

I ask Elaine to tell her neighbor about her upcoming run before our next session. Elaine came back the next session, "Ready to run" and had hotel information and travel plans. When I asked what her neighbor said about her upcoming run, Elaine smiled and said, "He said, 'that is going to be easier than walking to the mailbox.'" Later, in the session, she said her neighbor commented, "I believe you can do anything you put your mind to. I saw the work you did to get to the mailbox. Once you started running, I knew you had already made it." Again, Elaine could see truth and how wrong she had been about what others thought of her.

She came in shortly before race day and said, "I told my family about the race." Elaine cried when she said, "My dad wants to take me to the race." She did run a half marathon that weekend, and several others before she ran her first full marathon. Elaine's dad was at "every one of them." She found herself by confronting her fears. Elaine stopped trying to read minds, overeating, and being depressed along the way. Months later, I got a card from Elaine that said, "129-pounds off.... I'm happy, happy, and happy and my little girl knows she is special."

Elaine accomplished the core of her regression work through journaling and our exercises together. Allowing her to remember her learned beliefs, which she confronted with her present truth. She did internal dialogue, speaking with her inner child. Elaine remained aware that I look through her eyes more than she looks through mine. As Elaine broke free of pleasing others and having other esteem, she developed self-esteem and a life for herself. She now enjoys a strong relationship with her father and with God.

She married a "strong man I couldn't please" at age 20. Elaine was, "Not very heavy when she got married," and "Way too fat when he left me." Elaine had been divorced for 4 years before she entered therapy. She came to therapy for an evaluation for bariatric surgery. At my recommendation, Elaine followed through with counseling because her insurance would not pay for her bariatric surgery. The insurance company's refusal to pay for her surgery was a blessing. Elaine might not have freed herself if she had received the surgery. She did the emotional and mental work to free her Soul by changing her beliefs and behaviors.

Elaine can now live fully in the moment. She has the tools empowering her ability not to relinquish her personal power to others; Elaine can discern when she shifts into mind reading or working to please others to feel okay. As such, she is now free to be in the moment and present in relationship with others and herself.

## Conclusion Exercise

Can you imagine having a good day but also having negative experiences at work, home, or school? Which experience would you focus on? The overall good day or the few negative experiences? People who have experienced trauma are inclined, as a byproduct of their previous abuse, to hold onto the negative perception due to the emotional charge of the experience, even if the negative experience did not have that much significance in their day. The brain will hold on to negative aspects due to the need to protect itself. Each experience is seen through the lens of the past.

A 10-second experience can color your whole day. You have a good night's rest, see your kids off to school, and everything is going well at work. You go to lunch, and some person you do not know and will never see again, is behind you in traffic. At the red light, you are thinking of a light-hearted experience when he yells curse words at you. You wave as to say, "I'm sorry" when he shakes his head, "NO," shoots you the bird, and goes his way. You go back to work and tell your coworker about it. When you get home, you tell your spouse.

Each time you tell the story, the anger or negative emotion intensifies. As you replay the event in your mind, you re-experience an emotional charge; you are rehearsing the event and giving a person you saw for 10 seconds power over your life. A 10 second experience has amplified by 10,000 in your head. A small negative event has triggered a deeply ingrained fight-or-fight response, prompting old memories of negative experiences with the same emotions. Your inner child is triggered and will replay similar events that carry the emotional pain.

The past is not transforming. If you want to be transformed and transcend your past abuse, then you will need to be "present" and "intentional" with your adult self. You would think this would be easy and normal, being present in the moment, but your brain's hardwiring says different.

**Make a list of brief memories that you had, no matter how trivial, while reading this chapter:**

- 
- 
- 

You may be suffering with life as you live East of Eden. You may have depression, anxiety, or struggle with drugs and alcohol. This chapter may have been clear as mud to you. You want answers to fix your problem and to stop the pain you are in now. Healing is a process of cleaning the lenses you are wearing now. If you are experiencing confusion within yourself and the material you are reading, embrace it. By experiencing confusion, then you are growing. You are taking one set of lenses off and putting on another. The path towards healing may be a little blurry at first but clarity will come as you continue working through the exercises. Keep journaling and talking to your support system.

## Remember

In Matthew 22:37-39, Jesus tells us that we must, "Love the Lord our God with all our heart, with all our soul, and with all our mind." Though often missed in popular translation, Jesus is directing us to love ourselves, our souls, and our minds, and to love God with equal intensity. Although it may feel difficult, commit to loving your body, soul, and mind today - however battered they may feel. These aspects of you are truly sacred, in the exact state they are in, even in your darkest hour.

# CHAPTER FOUR

## THE MINDS PRISM

"Therefore, if you have any encouragement from being united with Christ, if any comfort from his love, if any common sharing in the Spirit, if any tenderness and compassion, then make my joy complete by being like-minded, having the same love, being one in spirit and of one mind. Do nothing out of selfish ambition or vain conceit. Rather, in humility value others above yourselves, not looking to your own interests but each of you to the interests of the others. In your relationships with one another, have the same mindset as Christ Jesus." Philippians 2:1-5

**KEY POINTS:**

- The emotional burdens of our daily lives take the same amount of time and effort as trying to hold a beach ball underwater (gets increasingly difficult as the day progresses).
- Some of your struggles are situational and recent. These are likely in the forefront of your mind.
- Your critical struggles are deeper. They cause tremendous daily emotional maintenance. You are likely not aware you are losing so much to these burdens.
- There is a way to get free of holding these burdens.

**Reflections:**

- What was your childhood like? Who were some of the most influential people in your childhood? What was your living situation like? How does your life today look like your childhood?

- You can change, or modify, chemically encoded negative behaviors from your childhood through consistent and intentional confrontations of your adult mind.
- Keep your "who was I then" and "who I am now" notes as your north star throughout the book. Revisit them at the start of each chapter to help map your growth. The questions will afford you more information with the continued exercises in the coming chapters.
- This space is yours and it is safe.
- There are no wrong answers. All your answers and thoughts will serve to make you more whole as you come to understand yourself more.
- What small and large burdens are you holding underwater right now?

## Welcome.

Your mind is like a prism: it refracts what is shined into it. If you are seeking healing from past trauma, you most likely are walking around with false stories in your head about yourself and your history. These distorted images continue to bring pain and suffering into your life today. Yesterday's illusions are mirror images of past realities — inaccurate projections that cloud the life you see today. The good news is that by using your own mind as a prism to your past, you can begin to properly align and clarify the distortions that continue to haunt you. The prism of your mind will lead you to see the light of reality by revealing your inner life's true color spectrum and experience. The journey of making new meaning from past pain is a pathway of learning which resided internally with infinite possibilities. Your quest begins by looking within yourself for answers. Looking inside your mind will allow you to locate and liberate the self that God created.

In modern society, the pain we experience in life is often responded to with unhealthy detachment. Such detachment occurs from a desire to separate painful emotional experiences from adult awareness. Most people detach themselves from suffering by indulging in external substances to alter their mood. Others emotionally disengage by using self-deception and toxic forms of defense mechanisms. Either way, detachment stems from avoiding your authentic self and masking your emotional distress. Over a period of years, you develop a history of avoidance which creates mask upon mask and an entirely distorted experience of reality. These illusions are a form of deceit your mind has learned with time. They can only be broken by moving inside your mind; using the prism of your mind, or your mind's eye, to re-evaluate. Moving inside yourself and not away from yourself is the key to breaking your illusions of your yesterdays.

The art of healing comes from slowing down your emotions and using your mind's prism. By using the prism of introspection, you will see the true color spectrum of reality. Looking within yourself, you will be able to change the spectrum of what you are projecting, which will in turn allow you to experience what is real. The illusion that you can currently trust what you "see" is a distortion because you are interpreting reality based on your past experiences.

## Trauma & Science: Neural Biochemistry

Your brain tissue is composed of cells that speak and connect through energetic wavelengths. The first step to understanding the distorted thinking of your past is to bend, or slow down, the wavelengths of past learnings. As an example, consider the color white, which we see as "white." White light is made up of all the different colors, or wavelengths, of light. You can demonstrate this by showing white light through a prism, which slows down the refractions revealing all the other colors present.

Many people believe that the prism carries these colors inherently. This is not true; they are the fingers of different energy combined in the light itself. When looking through a prism you will see the color of light that has the longest (red), to the shortest (violet), wavelength. The more the light is slowed down or bent, the more of the color spectrum you will visualize.

The prism of your mind will first see the emotion with the greatest wavelength. The greater your experience of an emotion, the greater the wavelength. The greater the wavelength of your emotion, the more you will see that emotion. As such, your emotional color is based on your history and not on reality. However, the tricky thing is that the light you are projecting appears "white" to you. You will not see the color until you bend, or refract, the light back to yourself through your own internal prism which we will do through a later assignment. This interactive mindfulness exercise will allow you to see what you are projecting and where the projected images originate. The prism of your mind will bend back your projected images to see your authentic self.

Let us say you walk into a room where others are conversing. If you are wearing a mask of projection, you will reflect what you see in them back to them. However, if you are not wearing a mask, then it is likely your inner child is triggered and will project his/her fear or love onto them, which is also an illusion. In turn, if they are wearing a mask, they will reflect onto you what you are reflecting. If they are not wearing a mask, it is likely their historic emotions are projecting on you. The illusion of reality is further distorted. The question becomes, "Do you want to live in a house of mirrors that reflect illusions that you or your inner child is projecting?" Both ways of protecting yourself will lead to chaos or dysfunction. There is a third option.

The third option is to bring your authentic emotions, or self, into the room. This can only happen if you have stopped your projections and your inner child's reactions by deliberate, slow-moving, introspection. "Through introspection and the conscious realization of unconscious compensation, it is possible to transform one's mental conditions and thus arrive at a solution of painful conflicts, one would seem entitled to speak of 'self-liberation.'"(C.G. Jung, Psychology of Religion: West and East, 2nd Ed, 1969, p.491) Carl Jung did not believe in being conscious of unconscious material to achieve "one mind" because "man cannot produce these unconscious compensation at will." (C.G. Jung, Psychology of Religion: West and East, 2nd Ed, 1969, p.491).

Moving within yourself will allow you to walk through your repressed yet authentic emotions. The prism of your mind can stop the color that your inner child is projecting from your unconscious mind. Introspection exercises and regression work will stop you from detaching from the colors your inner child is projecting or the mask you are wearing. By caring for your inner child, you will experience meaning while creating new neurological pathways to sustain him/her.

## Exercise: Using the Prism of Your Mind

*This is a Regression Exercise. In this and all other regression exercises, intentionality. If you are not intentional, your past scripted belief will color your present reality. Intentional, focused, and slow-moving reflection will make your unconscious conscious, while giving you more control, awareness, and esteem.*

You have over a billion nerve cells in your brain. Even as you read the words on this page you are stimulating your brain to learn new information. The following exercise is designed to deploy these nerve cells strategically, especially in your frontal lobe, to create awareness, or consciousness, through subconscious programming. Your frontal lobe is your supervisor, or adult self, that tells you when, what, and how to be. You must use your supervisor to observe your inner child's emotional "reactions." Observing your inner child will begin to break your old chemical memories.

## Exercise:

## Recognizing Your Mental Prism

*This is not a regression exercise. There are no special instructions included. Answer simply and directly in your journal.*

Take one moment to think back to a hurtful childhood experience which changed your life. What did you, as a child, think about yourself after the experience?

List two thoughts you had about yourself after it:

1-

2-

List two emotions:

1-

2-

If you are healthy, without defense mechanisms and/ or defensive strategies, the above question was a trigger for an emotional response which directly went back to the event. Your body responded to your triggered emotions. This body memory (reaction) was part of your inner child's "logic" based on the emotional experience. This reaction made knowing the child's thoughts or "logic" difficult. The ability to listen to your original "logic" is difficult. Now, you know the child's "logic" and emotional state of the event or "secret." Are you willing to bring your adult truth or supervisor into your inner child's experience?

If you are willing to confront the logic and the emotional response of the child within you, you can do so now by telling your brain's historian your present truth. With your adult mind, answer the following questions:

Will you let that happen again?
Can you protect yourself now?
Are you making different choices now?

As you answer these questions you are changing your brain and its "logic."

Now allow yourself to examine the experience. What would you say to that child today?
Would you stand by the child today?
Would your truth be different than his/ hers?
You are changing your inner child's "logic", your brain, and your future.

In "The Neuroscience of Psychotherapy," Louis Cozolino says "the rapid (and unconscious) network of emotions shapes our understanding of the world microseconds before we become aware of our perception. Through simulator mechanisms, our past experiences create our expectations for the future. Implicit, unconscious memories, created in dysfunctional situations years before, can repeatedly lead us to recreate unsuccessful but familiar patterns of thought, emotion, and behavior. Thus, our perception of the world is created based on experience." (2nd, Ed, 2011 p.76 ). It is important to know that Louis Cozolino based this information on actual scientific study of the biochemistry of our brains.

Because we are human, we are more likely to ask for forgiveness for a behavior rather than attempt to change it. Our inclination is to stand firm in outdated beliefs rather than change them. What is even trickier is that we often do not even know we are refusing to fix ourselves or change our emotional filters. As discussed in Chapter 1, our defense mechanisms help us deny, rationalize, or minimize our problems. And if our defense mechanisms do not get in the way of change, then scripts from our childhood about our worth or potential often will. Without a doubt, changing our minds is difficult but it absolutely can be done.

Research shows that your emotions are chemical messengers based on past experiences. These messengers are formed in your amygdala. These chemicals grow in strength and number due to sensory and motor inputs. Your hippocampus, which functions as a type of neural library, will respond to the messages of the amygdala by pulling "books" (memories related to the received emotions). This entire, overly complex process happens in under a second. This is how memories become hardwired and function as a lens to see "reality." I refer to this as looking through the mirror of your soul and not the window of your soul. To be healed, you have must look backward to move forward.

Joe Dispenza says, "Everyone has had a conscious intention to change a habit, and then, so quickly, a sort of mental amnesia sets in and we 'go unconscious,' finding ourselves in the realm of the familiar. We fall back into our mental wheelchairs and behave just as we swore, we never would." (Joe Dispenza. D. C, Evolve Your Brain, 2007 p. 434). He goes on to say, "To change any behavior and modify our hardwired actions requires conscious will and consistent mental and physical practice, as well as the ability to interrupt routines action to override the memory of the body and reform a new set of behaviors." (Joe Dispenza. D. C., Evolve Your Brain, 2007 p 364).

The goal is "revisiting and evaluating childhood experiences from an adult perspective." (Louis Cozolino, Neuroscience of Psychotherapy,2nd ed, 2011 p. 89). By doing so, you will be able to reinterpret in, "a creative and positive way." Revisiting your past childhood experiences with your present knowledge can modify not only your past emotional experience, but also your narrative of these events. Consider the adage, "You can take the boy out of the country, but you can't take the country out of the boy." Many believe this old saying, but do not realize how true it is - how your brain uses your past to create your present reality.

## Exercise: Looking at Your Masks

*This is not a regression exercise. There are no special instructions included. Answer simply and directly in your journal.*

The mask, or persona, of your childhood was needed to make it through the myriad of rules for "safety" in a dysfunctional environment. The only way you could make it was to adapt. To survive, your inner child learned and accepted the dysfunctional rules. These rules could involve pleasing others with a smile. Pleasers give others what they want themselves, while denying their own needs. Or, you may have adapted by being "perfect." Perfectionists focus on control through self-reprimand out of an attempt to keep everything straight. Or you may have learned to be "strong." You learned to not be weak, not to show you were hurt or scared.

Eric Berne called these masks or adaptations "drivers" because they drive, or move, your behavior. The four drivers are to (1) be strong, (2) be perfect, (3) please others, or (4) try hard. These drivers were ways to be OK with parental figures. If you had to adapt to be OK, then the non-verbal message is that you are not OK. What would you feel if you stopped trying hard, being strong, pleasing others, or being perfect? I would bet you would run into the feeling of fear. You will have one or two of these adaptations.

1. Reflect and write down which of these adaptions you learned, and with whom, from your childhood:

    -
    -
    -
    -

Personally, I learned to be strong and not show emotions of sadness and fear. If my dad saw me sad, he would give me "something to be sad about," usually corporal punishment. I learned quickly not to show emotions. "It made it easier," at the time of the abuse and it is still easy to fall into the old trap of avoiding my feelings. I balanced my mask of "be strong" with a mask of "please others."

I did not know how ingenious "be strong" and "please others" was at the time, though they were good survival tools for my inner child. Looking back at the dysfunction of my household, these were the only ones that would have worked. I was strong and sought to please others not out of love, but to avoid conflict. However, these masks cost me as an adult because I could not easily speak my truth and others took advantage of me. I found that taking off the "be strong" and "please others" mask set me free. As a result, I had less suffering.

## Managing the Process: Pain & Suffering

Many people dealing with trauma have repressed emotions from their past experiences. They cannot cognitively reconnect with past pain and must use the prism approach discussed above to deal with their subconscious programming. However, if you can still experience your emotions, or suffering, from the past, you are able to work more directly toward healing. You can create new meaning and conclusions about yourself simply by experiencing or revisiting your earlier suffering. Because you have a pathway through your consciousness, your mind will be able to put suffering into rightful perspective.

It may seem frightening at first, but if you are still able to experience your past pain, spending time with it is important. As humans, we have a deep need to find meaning in our lives, and you can create this for yourself even from intensely negative experiences. Two examples of making meaning from direct experience with pain are Victor Frankl and the Apostle Paul. Frankl was a Jew imprisoned in WWII German death camps. Paul was imprisoned for his belief and ministry for Christ following the crucifixion. Both Frankl and Paul found meaning in and through suffering. RE: WALTER. WE ARE NOT GOING BACK TO RELIVE THE ABUSE. A LOT OF PEOPLE WHO DO REGRESSION THERAPY GO BACK TO WORK THROUGH SPECIFIC ABUSE SCENARIOS. WE ARE GOING BACK TO ACKNOWLEDGE A CHILD'S MENTAL, EMOTIONAL, SPIRITUAL SUFFERING. THE GOAL IS RECLAIM AND RE-EDUCATE THE CHILD.

Suffering, while painful, is a part of life and needs to be experienced directly and not ignored or pushed down. Suffering can be one of your greatest teachers if you are listening and can experience it fully. The truth is that we are all going to suffer at some point or the other, because we all live East of Eden in a world that has missed the mark. Learning how to channel, or use, your suffering is important to create growth. Frankl believed that without the intentional work of creating meaning from suffering, man would fall into despair and hopelessness. By Frankl's definition, "despair is caused by suffering in which the sufferer sees no meaning. Suffering itself has no meaning, but we can assume meaningful attitude toward events that in themselves are meaningless." (The Pursuit of Meaning, 1969 p. 47)

From a spiritual perspective, God will bring meaning to all our pain if we let Him. The apostle Paul found gain and meaning through Christ. In Philippians 3:8, Paul says "More than that, I count all things to be loss in view of the surpassing value of knowing Christ Jesus my Lord, for whom I have suffered the loss of all things, and count them but rubbish so that I may gain Christ." (Philippians 3:8 NASB). The Apostle Paul found meaning in suffering for Christs' sake. Paul was brutally beaten five times (2Corinthians 11:24). He received 39 of 40 lashes because "40 could kill a man" and his oppressors at the time only wanted him to suffer. Paul is proof that meaning can come through painful experiences. Paul's suffering in and of itself was meaningless. Paul's attitude towards his suffering gave his suffering meaning. Finding meaning in your suffering is difficult but being spiritually imprisoned is more difficult.

## Breaking the Chains: Meaning from Suffering

You may not know the fear of lying in bed awake while praying the door would not be opened, the pain of your beaten body sticking to the sheets, or the darkness of being put into a closet for the weekend. Your suffering may have come through critical words of a friend or family member, from the hands of the person you were dating, or in the sterile white room of a clinic. These sufferings in and of themselves have no meaning. The meaning comes through the reason you survived or the growth you achieved through putting your abuse, neglect, or choices into perspective.

*This is not a regression exercise. There are no special instructions included. Answer simply and directly in your journal.*

1. Can you count all things "as gain" - can you find meaning in all the experiences that have caused you suffering? Yes or No

2. If you cannot count all things as a gain, then be specific and list the things that continue to feel like burdens you carry:
   -
   -
   -

The things that are listed above, or the ones you thought and did not write down, are the experiences you still need to face. Your brain "translates past experience[s] into an anticipated future, converting past trauma into a self-fulfilling prophecy of future suffering." (Louis Cozolino, Neuroscience of Psychotherapy, 2nd ed, 2011 p .137) Your inner child experiences are likely the ones you avoid due to the fear of knowing past emotional pain.

## Managing the Process: Fear & The Hebb Theory

"Behold the turtle. He makes progress only when he sticks his neck out."
Anonymous

Fear is an emotion, a chemical messenger that was a byproduct of the fall from Grace. More than any other, fear is the emotion which serves to stop growth and healing. That is one reason that the Bible says, "fear not" 365 times - "one for each day of the year." God knows we cannot grow toward Him while trapped in a mental prison.

Physiologically, fear in childhood is experienced as "unregulated, overwhelming, full-bod[ied] experience." Because the "amygdala is operational at birth, the experience of fear may be the strongest early emotion." Further, strong experiences of fear in early life likely create some of the strongest neural networks in the brain. "Early and traumatic memories can be stored without conscious awareness or cortical [adult] control. They will not be consciously remembered, but instead will emerge as sensory, motor, and emotional memories" (Louis Cozolino, Neuroscience of Psychotherapy, 2nd Ed, 2010 p.247,248).

Not all fear is negative. We all need normal, healthy "fear" to protect ourselves with a "fight or flight" response. In these cases, fear can cause you to do great things. Fear is only pathological when it has control and not you. Signs of fear controlling you can be seen in persistent anxiety, or fear of the future. Anxiety carries daily worry a step further and creates signs of physical and emotional arousal. These signs are hypervigilance, startle response, nightmare, irritability, flashbacks, and the sense of a foreshortened future. Once you begin having anxiety, or these signs, they often run on a repeat cycle.

Fear is self-feeding, like any emotion can be. Your mind and body are not just susceptible to fixation on external stimuli like food, drugs, porn, gambling, etc. Your mind and body are susceptible to becoming "addicted" to familiar emotions, responses that stem from old emotions, or chemical messengers. If you have millions of cells that are "addicted" to a certain chemical message, then you will create this emotion without external causes. There will not be a physical reason to have this emotional reaction in these cases. Your body will send the message to create the needed “hit,” or expected emotional response.

Your hypothalamus, which controls all your bodily functions, will then seek homeostasis. The hypothalamus keeps your body internally regulated. Once stimulated with the messenger of fear it will send a chemical (neuropeptide) to your pituitary gland. The pituitary will send a chemical peptide through your bloodstream to all your organs. These peptides, or molecules of emotion, will go to the receptor sites of the cells. These cells will create a reaction or "body memory." Then this "memory" will send peptides to your brain to stimulate your hypothalamus. Your hypothalamus which created the chemical will make a call to the amygdala. Your amygdala will respond to this chemical message by creating an emotion. You will begin experiencing emotions that occur even without a legitimate external force.

From a psychological viewpoint, this is concerning because you are in the position of experiencing the emotions that likely stem from past bad experiences rather than present reality. Your emotions are firing out of a habit without any reason for the unwanted emotion. I have had many addicts in recovery tell me that they did not use, but they had the familiar feelings and the experience of using "for no reason." This is called a "mental relapse." A mental relapse has the same mental and physical effects as using drugs.

If you experience an emotion or "body memory," you will need to immediately call your support system, journal, and be intentional to go to and keep yourself in a safe environment. This is difficult when you are experiencing a familiar "bad" emotion, like anxiety. When you have anxiety, it increases your blood pressure, insomnia, anger, and isolation. These signs of anxiety can move to overeating or restricting your food intake, depression, alcohol, or prescription drug abuse, to name a few. You may be aware of your anxiety if you do not have it from childhood.

Remember your emotions originate from your amygdala, which has a "mind" of its own. Your amygdala sends its chemical reactions or message that triggers old sensory, motor, and emotional memories. Then these memories, along with your present anxiety or fear of the future, will look through your old emotional logic. Your old logic and memories are unconscious and will color, if not distort, your present reality. This illusion will happen each time you have the emotion of fear. By doing this you are strengthening your negative belief and intensifying your emotional response without knowing it. In a way, you are turning the heat up on the pot of water in which you are sitting.

What makes change even more difficult is that a nerve cell that fires together stays together. The Hebb theory of learning is simply 'neurons that fire together wire together'. This theory has stood up to the test of time. Researchers have found that brain cells that are constantly stimulated become synchronized. Cells or new cells becoming synchronized or in agreement with the old forgotten memories are "in sync" with new cells. The new and old neuron firing pattern will become more effective in their response. Each time these neurons fire they are sending electronic signals that stimulate hundreds of thousands, if not millions, of nerve cells. The new cells that are constantly stimulated become part of the old neural network.

This neural network can be millions of nerve cells that are linked together. The "brain consists of some 100 billion neurons" (Joe Dispenza. D.C, Evolve your Brain, 2007, p. 66). Each time you stimulate the nerve cells they can link with a million other nerve cells. The research of the brain shows that "the neocortex, the home of our conscious awareness, each nerve cell has the possibility of linking with 40,000 to 50,000 other nerve cells... the cerebellum, every neuron has the potential to connect with up to a million other neurons" (Joe Dispenza, Evolve Your Brain, 2007 p. 66). Now you can probably see how easy it is to create an internal or external addiction from a physiological perspective.

The neat thing is that each neuron cell has dendrites that look like a large oak tree. This oak tree has several large limbs and other smaller limbs. These limbs are receiving information through electronic signals. The electric signals stimulate the dendrites that transmit information to the cell. Remember the "cells that fire to together wire together." Now, this may not be a good thing, if you are strengthening your old negative belief or emotional response because you are creating a neuron network that is built on a negative or abusive experience.

Now, the positive news is that when these old cells are not stimulated, the dendrites (limbs) will begin to shrink and pull into themselves. The more you take away stimulation of fear or other overused emotions like shame, guilt, anger, etc. from these cells, the more the dendrites pull in, and the cell will eventually be absorbed into the brain. The cell dies with the old belief and emotions with it. Hebbian learning states that nerve cells that no longer fire together, no longer wire together. The new stimulation (messages and emotions) will create a new neural network. A neural network that is becoming your new extrinsic or conscious memory. The new cell will begin to create a new response and/or expectation.

The belief now is to create a habit: you should do something "21 times" before a new behavior becomes permanent. The stimulation of new cells with new behaviors will take energy away from the old neuro-network. If you do not feed the old cells they will die. This may be the physiological reason for the "21 times" rule and reason you need to do the assignments in this book – they will help you break your old strongholds. Your inner child's hard-wired memories can be identified and dealt with by your adult mind.

Breaking your inner child's learned drivers, by taking time to dwell in your temple will stop the use of worn out, outdated, and overused defense mechanisms. You will stop your dysfunction by confronting and changing the old and putting on the new beliefs and behaviors. Your emotional, sensory, and motor memory will change as you change your beliefs. As you can see, your early learning became the mirror you are now looking through to see "reality". Walking through these learned images will help you experience your authentic reflection. You may reflect on your early learning as Peter Banning did in Hook.

Due to fear, you may have forgotten much of your childhood, like Peter Banning, played by Robin Williams, did in Captain Hook. Take some time to watch the movie if you have not or revisit it if it has been a while.

## My Story: Peter Banning

Peter Banning was a successful businessman who forgot he was Peter Pan. Peter forgot his childhood and that he was once a part of "the lost boys." He "forgot" due to being a workaholic. Peter lost his relationship with his wife, son, daughter, and himself due to indulging in work. Peter was lost and the urgency of his addiction had taken his life.

The importance of Peter Banning going back to the very thing he had suppressed and medicated with work was that was where he found true healing. The heart of the story was when Peter returned to his forgotten memories of Never Neverland. He had to recover the inner child called Peter Pan. You, like Peter, will find that the things that seem urgent now will not be later in your life. The lost moments will speak louder than your meetings, job, calls you must return, etc.

Peter Banning was battling the reality of his childhood. He had to put the fragmented pieces of his life together to get the "Pan." The miracle of finding himself came by finding Peter Pan. He had to endure a lot of trials and tribulations before he found his "happy thought." He first needed to remember Never Neverland and being a part of the "lost boys" before he had the power to fly. Peter's "happy thought" gave him power to fly. Peter Pan had the ability to fight Captain Hook (the image in his mirror), and free himself and his kids from the pirates of Never Neverland. Once freed from Captain Hook's reflection, whom he had become by pushing down his unpleasant memories, he got himself, his family, and happiness back.

If you remember, Peter had repressed his memories of his childhood. He repressed his childhood memories because he was a part of the "lost boys." Now why would a ruthless, successful mergers-and-acquisitions lawyer (pirate) want to remember being a part of the lost boys that were abused by pirates?

You might be aware of the reason you would not want to remember your childhood. In your life, you will find that most people lived in Never Neverland at some point. They too had a period that they were a part of the "lost boys." They, like Peter, worked to forget. He had worked to forget his youth and lost not only himself but became the image of Hook, which he hated. He forgot his own critical questions and answers as he became a successful workaholic. He was lucky that he had Tinker Bell as his guide.

Peter Banning was successful and worked hard to forget his childhood. You will see that everyone has a Captain Hook in their childhood experience. Did you have a Captain Hook growing up? If you did, you may have lost your "happy thought" too. Peter began to let his forgotten past come into his present life, especially at night. At night when his mind was not medicated or distracted by his work, he would experience fragments of his past. He would wake up and see or hallucinate that his house was being vandalized and things went missing.

Peter had to go on the journey to his soul to find his authentic self. Peter put his emotional logic of his childhood into perspective by experiencing the child within him. He brought a new perspective to Peter Pan. The businessman had no knowledge on awareness of what Peter Pan needed to fly. Remember, his happy thought was of his own children being born. The sad thing is his daughter and son became "lost boys" due to his being a workaholic. Peter was repeating what he was doing to his kids and never knew it.

Now you may be like many Christians that would ask God to take your "Never Neverland" away. You may, like Peter, not want to think about or remember your memories of being a "lost boy". God will not take away your memories of Never Neverland or being "lost" from you. Like Peter, you would lose your innocence, spontaneity, and creativity, if God did this for you.

Peter Banning had to deal with his forgotten memories and face his Captain Hook. Peter could find his child within called Peter Pan. He could find the gifts that were pushed down out of his awareness. Peter and Peter Pan were lost and found each other on the journey. Neither one was complete without the other. You will find that you are incomplete without your inner child and you will give the child within you a life that he/she could not have without you. The child within you will give you more life than you could ever give him or her. The roads not taken due to fear and ignorance will keep you captive.

## Exercise: Captain Hook

*This is not a regression exercise. There are no special instructions included. Answer simply and directly in your journal.*

Who or what was your "Captain Hook?' Do you know? If you know who your Captain Hooks were growing up, then write down the names or situations below:

-
-
-
-
-

What were the experiences associated with Captain Hook?

-
-
-
-
-

What were the critical messages?

-
-
-
-
-

What were your authentic feelings at that time?

-
-
-
-
-

What feeling did you use to cover up your authentic feeling at the time?

-
-
-
-
-

## Breaking the Chains: Captain Hook

Many times, my clients do not believe that they have many Captain Hook experiences to write down. They usually come back to the session with a list of names, experiences, or messages they experienced growing up. If you have one name or experience that is OK. If your mind starts throwing out several names, experiences, or messages, then take time to write them down. The time you take will be well worth it. You will find out how important this remembrance is to your growth.

The above list of names or experiences may have surprised you because you are aware of your villain, experience, or message that took your innocence, spontaneity, and creativity away. Your innocence, spontaneity, and creativity were never taken from you. The part of you that experienced the villain is still there waiting to be recovered by you. This part of you is the child within you. Be aware of what age or ages you were when this happened: ______.

You need not know the person, experience, or message because it is not important. The part of you that experienced the hurt is so much more important than the message, experience, or person. It is a necessity to focus on the child that is within you.

Remember that your emotional brain is childlike and will act on any earlier memories that are associated with your present circumstances. As you explore your present circumstances, you may experience familiar thoughts, feelings, and behavior associated with your Never Neverland or with your Captain Hook. If you want to break through your present circumstances, you will need to deal with your inner child perspective of his/her experience in Never Neverland.

If you have no memories of being a lost boy or girl or of Never Neverland, you may have no knowledge of how your early habits have affected your early thinking. We are all creatures of habit, but you can change your habits by listening to your earlier perspectives. You can look back and see your struggle at 28 and it will be an image of the one at 14 and 6 years of age. Yes, your body is older, but your emotional inner child is going by its early learning or schematic. Continually doing the same thing and expecting different results does not work.

Have you heard yourself say things like:

- That always happen to me.
- This is my luck.
- Same shit different day.
- I can count on it.
- This is what happens.
- Different verse but the same song.
- This is Deja vu
- This happens in all my relationships.
- This has happened every time.
- I am used to it.
- Last time I did; it did not work.
- I have seen that coming.
- I knew that would happen.
- Not again!

Now, if you have used these familiar phrases then you might be reflecting your early learning in Never Neverland and getting familiar results.

When you have the names of your Captain Hook's and the ages you were when the experience happened, then use this information about yourself to see if you struggled with old negative beliefs which stemmed from your experiences. This will help you put more of the fragmented pieces of God's masterpiece back together. You will have another line on the page and be even closer to your self -portrait.

You will never know how much you have lost by pushing your Captain Hook(s) and Never Neverland down. You will play out the familiar feelings and outcomes your entire life. You will continue to suppress or repress these, keeping you captive and having you believe you have "bad luck", or a "sign on my back says kick me". You are moving, acting, or playing out your script, or forgotten memories of your childhood. It is important for you to speak to the boy or girl that was beat, raped, or made fun of by others to reconceptualize your inner child's experiences. By reconceptualizing your past, you are reclaiming your child within.

## Conclusion

Here is a list of the key neuroscientific facts regarding healing and the brain to keep in your back pocket as you move forward:

1) "Memory is modified each time it is remembered" (Louis Cozolino, Neuroscience of Psychotherapy, 2nd Ed, 2010, p. 91).

2) "Narratives are a valuable tool in the organization and integration of neural networks prone to dissociation because we can write and rewrite our own stories, new ones hold the potential for novel ways of experiencing. In editing our narrative, we change the organization and nature of our memories and, hence, reorganize our brains" (Louis Cozolino, Neuroscience of Psychotherapy, 2nd Ed, 2010, p.92).

3) "We tend to think of our brains as processing information from the environment, the vast majority of the input to the cerebral cortex comes from what is already inside our brain…In truth, we often have little or no access to the information or logic upon which we base our decisions" (Louis Cozolino,The Neuroscience of Psychotherapy,2nd Ed, 2010, p.135).

4) "neurosciences suggest that an important aspect of love is the absence of fear" (Louis Cozolino, The Neuroscience of Psychotherapy,2nd

Ed, 2010, p. 211).

5) "The emotional mind is far quicker than the rational mind, springing into action without pausing even a moment to consider what it is doing. Its quickness precludes the deliberate, analytical reflection that is the hallmark of the thinking mind. (Daniel Goleman, Emotional Intelligence, 1995, pg. 291)

These are powerful and empowering facts of neuroscience. You can grow new neuron (neurogenesis) cells if you stop your fear-based thinking. Modify your narrative or storyline by telling your story. The new modification will change your brain. You will need to listen to yourself to change patterns of thinking and behavior because you are moving from forgotten (unconscious) memory and not explicit, new, or conscious, memory when looking at reality. First, you will need to confront your fear-based thinking.

Now, just think of your first six years of life. The experts in neuro-cognitive and developmental psychology say you learn 60-70% of your learning for your entire life during this time. What does that say if you cannot remember it? Is this a cruel joke or what? Wouldn't you think you might remember at least half of the 70%? You most likely remember more than 50% or more of this learning, but it is unconscious. This learning is stored and used by you daily, without conscious intent. That is a scary thought if you think about it. You will find that life is much better using all your information that you have gathered instead of living based on your beliefs in your formative years. This information is valuable and allows you to know what is moving you today.

The prism of your mind can bend your familiar "bad" emotions, allowing you to reconceptualize them with your present truth, allowing you to see life's rainbows. By retraining your past beliefs, you can stop living in an illusion of Never Neverland and step into reality. You will be able to take off the old and put on the new self. In Ephesians 4:22-24 states "that in your former manner of life, you lay aside the old self, which is being corrupted in accordance with lust of deceit, 23 and that you be renewed in the spirit of your mind, 24 and put on the new self, which in the likeness of God has been created in righteousness and holiness of the truth".

It is possible to put on a new spiritual self by renewing your mind through its prism.

Self-awareness is work, not a passive experience. Your goal is to be introspective (mindful) while being present. How do you do that? You must raise up the hardwired emotions from below the water line of your consciousness. Doing this by the different types of regression will not only allow you to dwell "in your temple", but to observe your emotions without historical reactions. You will become an observer of yourself. Your hippocampus will allow you to physiologically stand back and observe yourself. You will be able to read "your old chapter," while being able to rewrite what you want to change or strengthen about your story. This will change your unconscious, intrinsic, hardwired memory of your inner child and make a new chemically explicit conscious memory.

## Remember:

You can grow new neuron (neurogenesis) cells if you stop your fear-based thinking. You are modifying your narrative or storyline by telling your story. The prism of your mind can bend your familiar "bad" emotions by reconceptualizing them with your present truth and allowing you to see life's rainbows.

# CHAPTER FIVE

## AS THYSELF

"The whole law is fulfilled by obeying this one command: Love your neighbor as you love yourself." (Leviticus 19:18) Galatians 5:14 NIRV

**KEY POINTS:**

- The words and experiences spoken over you colored your first chapter and storyline
- Creating new thoughts and feelings for your old experiences changes your brain
- Meaning making comes from you taking yourself seriously

**Reflections:**

- Your adult mind was not present when you were a child.
- You can re-write your storyline of your first chapter(s).
- Will you allow yourself to journal to reveal your authentic God given self?

## Welcome.

"Love thy neighbor as thyself."
Ah, gladly would I, Neighbor.
But "Know thyself," the first command.
There is the search and labor.

The "I" of me is a mystery
Deep- hidden from my knowing.
The splendid "You" behind the you
Is like the pre- dawn's glowing.

Can I know you? Can you know me?
Or can we know each other?
The "I" of me and the "You" of you,
How can we find "Us," Brother?

With eyes we search the face, the lips,
For hints and clues in gestures,
The Self concealed yet half-revealed
Within the fleshly vestures.

Not with the eyes, the words, the hands,
Nor intellect's keen probing
Will we discover what we seek,
But in our hearts' disrobing,

The "I" of me and the "You" of you
Will reach with spirit's fingers
To find again that twin hood lost
Whose splendid memory lingers. "
Don Blanding

Your original story about yourself began while you were still in your mother's womb. The script for your first chapter was "in print" by the time you were 8 or 9 years of age; over the years, it has been edited numerous times but remains intact at its core. This early script drives your hard-wired beliefs about yourself, the world, and God.

Early on, you decided:

- if you were ok and if others were ok,
- if the world was safe,
- if you were going to succeed,
- if you were important or others are more important,
- if you could have feelings,
- if you were going to be strong, try hard, please others or be perfect,
- if you are going to be healthy or ill,
- if God is good or not,
- if God existed.

Life's first chapter is important because it sets the tone for your life story. The first chapter is your cornerstone. Some people have the misconception that they make decisions based on what they experience "in the moment." In fact, their first chapter sets those decisions in motion.

The Bible is a great example of how important the first chapter is in a story. The first two lines of Genesis say, "In the beginning God created heaven and the earth. And the earth was without form, and void; and darkness was upon the face of the deep. And the Spirit of God moved upon the face of the waters." (Genesis 1:1-2, KJV). Those initial words are foundational to the Christian tradition and set the Bible's remaining tenor.

In a similar way, many famous and beloved stories develop in a way closely anchored to their first sentences. Consider the following:

- "Alice was beginning to get very tired of sitting by her sister on the bank, and of having nothing to do: once or twice she had peeped into the book her sister was reading, but it had no pictures or conversations in it, 'and what is the use of a book,' thought Alice, 'without pictures or conversation?'" [ Alice's Adventures in Wonderland by Lewis Carroll]

- "I was born in the year 1632, in the city of York, of a good family, not of that country, my father being a foreigner of Bremen who settled at hull. He got a good estate by merchandise and, leaving off his trade, lived afterward at York, from whence he had married my mother, whose relations were named Robinson, a very good family in that country, and from whom I was called Robinson Krueutznaer; but by the usual corruption of the word in English we are now called, nay, we call ourselves, and write our name 'Crusoe,' and so my companion always called me." [Robinson Crusoe by Daniel Defoe]

- "Of man's first disobedience, and the fruit Of that forbidden tree, whose mortal taste Brought death into the World, and all our woe, With loss of Eden, till one great Man Restore us, and regain the blissful seat, Sings, Heavenly Muse, that on the secrete top Of Oreb, or of Sanai, didn't inspire..." [Paradise Lost by John Milton]

Can you see the stories evolving from these starting thoughts? For each, much meaning is grounded in those initial words. Likewise, the power of your early or formative words were as powerful as a burst of thunder on a calm, slow day. The words and experiences spoken over you and your experiences colored the steps of the rest of your journey. Those early images are what you came to know as truth about yourself, even if they were not true reflections and, in fact, were toxic.

## Exercise: Examining Your First Scripts

*This is not a regression exercise. There are no special instructions included. Answer simply and directly in your journal.*

What would the first sentence, paragraph or chapter of your storyline, or script, say?

(1) First sentence:

(2) First paragraph:

(3) Themes from your first chapter:

(4) Who were your first teachers?

If you stop what you are doing and consider your earlier chapters, you will hear the story of your day, year, and life, all the way to the present moment. The good news is that you can choose to accept or reject that old story, but only when you become aware of what was written on that initial slate. To change a story, you need to look at the first chapters of your life's storyline. You can re-write this script based on the new information you are uncovering while doing this work. Doing so will provide new meaning and potential.

By rewriting your early scripts, you change the brain's physiological makeup. Creating new thoughts and feelings for old experiences helps create a new neuronal network. Refer to Chapter 3 for more details on this neurological process. Once you become aware of your scripts and their effects, you can change your storyline and brain.

The writer of Proverbs puts it this way: "You are like a dog returning to your vomit." (Proverbs 26:11, NASB) That is neither a pretty picture nor your desired outcome. If you try to change your present beliefs without changing your early script you will likely fail. Stated another way, if you grew up believing you were ugly, fat, and stupid, looking in the mirror and repeating, "I am beautiful, thin, and smart" will only go so far. Confronting the old thought patterns while highlighting the truth of your life leads to change, and change comes from the inside out. Many of my clients have been empowered to make new choices after realizing they were constantly repeating old behavioral patterns and beliefs.

Who helped you write your script? The first people who helped you with life's storylines were your parents or caregivers. Your parents were your first heroes, models, and teachers; they were almost God-like. They taught right from wrong, what to think/feel, and the morals and ethics that make the world function. Looking back, you would see if they did a great job teaching or were poor teachers of these old truths. The truth is that most parents did the best they could with the information they received from their parents. They simply passed on to you what they had received. Sadly, many parents did not receive a great deal of parenting skills until after they finished raising their children. Only then can they truly reflect on their lives as parents.

Whether your parents or caregivers were loving, normal, healthy, or none of those things, you wrote your earliest scripts based on how you interpreted their messages. You may have made A's and B's and heard your parents say, "You can do better." You may have written a script that said, "I'm not good enough; they will never think I'm okay; or I have to be perfect." How you received those early messages determines how you view yourself today. If your parents were perfectionists, you heard numerous messages to be perfect. Those messages may have prompted perfectionistic behaviors in you because you thought you were not good enough. Message received is not always message sent.

You need to look at your earlier chapters to see if you want to follow those learned beliefs. Eric Berne, the father and creator of Transactional Analysis, developed "life scripts." A life scripts is "an unconscious life-plan made in childhood, reinforced by the parents, 'justified' by subsequent events, and culminating in a chosen alternative" (TA Today, 1989, p.330). Life scripts are the heart of his theory. Berne saw your scripts as how you heard and formulated the transactions of others, both verbal and non-verbal, you received growing up. These verbal and non-verbal messages could be from family members, siblings, or bullies and abusers that were in your life. Those scripts are hardwired into your brain, and you follow those scripted beliefs unconsciously. Your scripts tell you what you are and how you are "supposed" to act. Then you play out your scripted beliefs and get familiar results, perpetuating those scripted beliefs. Your scripts may hide your authentic, God given self.

Editing your scripts is a part of your healing journey to the soul. Many will call it "inner child work," or "regression work," The art of change on your healing journey will be what you make of it. You can be the creator of your destiny or follow old, scripted beliefs. The choice is up to you.

## Exercise: What Events, Experiences or Words Changed Your Script?

*This is not a regression exercise. There are no special instructions included. Answer simply and directly in your journal.*

1. List the events, experience, or words below:

2. Events:

3. Experiences:

4. Words:

5. How did your scripts or beliefs change?

6. How do these changes affect me today?

7. If you received negative messages as a child what would they be?
   -
   -
   -

8. What decisions did you make from these messages?
   -
   -
   -

9. How do your past decisions affect you today?

10. If you went through trials and tribulations as a child; how did your beliefs about yourself and others change?

11. What did you believe about the world after your trial or tribulation?

12. Did your belief in God change?

Every story or hero's journey has an antagonist. The antagonist is one who opposes you or brings evil or opposition into your life. This adversary can be a chronic situation or a long term or brief tempest that brings trials and tribulations; maybe it is even for months and/or years. Difficulties can arise from one word or an experience and/or situation that opposes your moral, relational, spiritual, or psychological health. These situational crises have likely brought conflict, stagnation, or sorrow.

I hope you have eliminated the adversaries in your life; I trust a heroic figure has stepped in when you needed it. Many stories change by heroic means, ordinary circumstances, or meaningful moments; adversaries are overcome or conquered. The dark scene fades away because light brings meaning and hope.

Think about the books and movies you have read or watched. Was there an antagonist? What brought about hope or change? Batman had the Joker, Riddler, and Cat Woman to name a few. For Ann Frank, the antagonists were Hitler and the Nazi army. For Robinson Crusoe, the weather plagued them. The truth of the matter was that the adversary usually brought strength, once processed, or overcome by heroic means. The number one book ever sold is the Christian Bible. God was opposed by Lucifer, who was dealt with by a heroic figure named Jesus Christ, who overcame temptation, his adversary, and death.

Your storyline may not have had a "known," heroic figure to help you fight your adversary. Perhaps you had an unknown heroic figure with the gift of dissociation. If you had a dissociative experience, the cost of your suffering may not be remembered and played out on your present reality. If your parents or family members were adversaries, you may not realize how a change in script might alter your life. It is hard to react, extract, or change your beliefs when you are unaware of the hurt or harm caused by old messages or behaviors given by your loved ones. Look back at your trials, tribulations, and/or traumas to know the messages you received, and the decisions you made to cope with those words or experiences. Give yourself time to revisit these past experiences, hear their meanings, and consider decisions you made at the time. Childhood decisions may be different looking through your present adult eyes or once outside the storms you faced growing up.

Life at 15, 25, or 65 years of age will look different from the life of a 3, 5, or 8-year-old. Just think, if you got one low grade or failed a class in school, you might have thought, "My parents will kill me;" "I'm stupid in math or _____;" "I'll will never learn how to do this." As an adult, you can put these early beliefs into perspective. If you were sexually abused, you might have thought, "I deserved it;" "I did not stop him; I must have wanted it;" "I asked for it." These are distortions written at the time of your wounds. Your newly found insight can help you modify your inner child's present and past realities.

If you choose to do nothing, just remember, your childlike brain will affirm all new information using his/her old information/experience. Having this self-confirming nature is justified to fit your learned beliefs. Previous self-confirming distortions will alter, or color, your present view of yourself and others. Self-justifying will only empower your old beliefs and intensify your "old" emotions. Your "old" emotions will intensify your present ones. Your primitive childlike brain intensifies these distorted beliefs and emotions with its categorical thinking.

Categorical thinking stops all moderation with scripted beliefs. This all or nothing thinking intensifies your script. The lack of moderation increases your past and present emotions, which then color how you experience your present reality. Your inner child's script is taking your present reality hostage. Past scripted beliefs are being played out in your present reality, but this projection of the past can be changed.

Being free is changing your script by using your adult's brain. You can rationally interpret your script though doing so does not mean you are not feeling. You are feeling with your present knowledge and not using your inner child's emotional experience. By performing this inner child work you will change your early beliefs and emotional state of memory.

Early beliefs can be permanent beliefs, yet such beliefs will hamper your future life choices. Early decisions, regardless of perceived insignificance, may create huge struggles in your life. Several factors can intensify your script. Here are some:

- if the perpetrators were relatives
- the length or duration of the trauma
- the younger your trauma happened

- the severity of the trauma
- the amount of support at the time of your trauma.

Such factors will intensify your scripted beliefs, and the unattended wounds may affect life still more in the future. The key is to look at early "decisions" made during or after those experiences.

Remember your childlike brain could not be rational or aware of making decisions. As a child, you made decisions based on your primitive emotional brain's interpretation of all your sensory data. Your inner child had to use what it knew to make sense of the world. No wonder your emotional brain has a self-confirming nature and justifies its belief. Your inner child's survival tendencies allowed you to have time to develop your adult rational brain. Your rational brain was an infant when your emotional brain was already fully developed and active, this is the reason you need to review your scripted beliefs.

Your conscious mind will hear "old tapes." Your old tapes follow your old parental recordings that were internalized by your childlike brain. Remember your emotional brain is learning about the world through your temporal lobe, which gathers all the data from your senses. Aaron Beck the father of cognitive therapy called them "automatic thoughts." Most of your tapes are automatic negative thoughts. These tapes or automatic thoughts are usually from your parental figure growing up. These tapes confirm your scripted beliefs and tear down your authentic self. These tapes will only strengthen your old, scripted beliefs.

Your early decision has been reinforced thousands, if not hundreds of thousands of times since your early experiences. You have whole neural networks built on your emotional and sensory experiences of the event(s). These memories are colored by your emotion at that moment. As a child, your ability to process your traumatic memories was extremely difficult at best. Remember, your neocortex or rational brain's higher learning was still growing.

The experiences written on your blank slate, as a child, can only be interpreted or seen through the lens you were looking through. You could only use the information that you had at the time. This is sad. You are still looking through your emotional brain's lens. These lenses are feelings, thoughts, and old formed beliefs you made as a child. These beliefs can be about esteem, worth, safety, sexual identity, sexuality, trust of others, etc... The list can go on and on. Your early beliefs become harder wired by your inner child's self-confirming nature. Can you see how self-confirming and self-justifying will affect your later decisions, which become more distorted over time.

You are driven based on these old thoughts and impulses throughout the day. Richard Potter in "Authentic Spirituality" says, "Impulses are often reactions to environmental stimuli, whether positive or negative, and the tendency is to act blindly upon impulse in response to the environment. The mastery of impulses not only builds strength of character in the form of will power, but it also puts the individual, not the environment, in charge of her [ his] actions" (p 98).

Remember that your early script was written with emotional color from your amygdaloid and sensory data of your temporal lobe. This became the building blocks for impulsive and reactive behavior. You are responding "blindly" to your scripted beliefs or reacting to your environment. You would be amazed to know how many negative thoughts stem from your old negative messages and experiences.

As human beings, you and I are likely to allow our finite minds to have control over infinite possibilities. You can have infinite possibilities by stepping out of your scripts and into your God given self. The only way you can step out of your script is by using your adult mind. You will need your adult mind to help the child within you identify truth. Your adult deals with reality by using your present thoughts, feelings, and wisdom. Once your inner child looks through your adult's eyes you will experience your authentic self. You will experience a clear vision as you rewrite your script and change your storyline.

When you respond from your Soul, there are infinite possibilities. Are your possibilities limited by your thoughts and perceptions? In "*Creative Mind and Success*," Ernest Holmes (1919) addresses humankind's finite potential *apart from* the Holy. He writes:

"The substance that we deal with, in itself, is never limited, but we often are, because we draw only what we believe." He goes on to say that "Limitation is only our unbelief; life can give us a big thing or a little thing. When it gives us a little thing; it is not limited, any more than life is limited when it makes a grain of sand, because it could just as well have made a planet. But in the great scheme of things all kinds of forms, small and large are necessary, which, combined, makes a complete whole. The power and substance behind everything remain Infinite.

Life is never limited; an ant has just as much life as an elephant though smaller in size. The question is not one of size but one of consciousness. We are not limited by actual boundaries, but by foggy ideas about life and by failing to recognize we are dealing with the Infinite.

Limitation is an experience of the race, but it is not the fault of God; it is the fault of our perception. And to prove this is so, let any man break the bonds of this false sense of life and he at once begins to express less and less limitation. It is a matter of the growth of the inner idea." (pg. 48)

Now the question is, where did your limited view come from: Man or God? I do not believe God has limited your outcomes. I believe that the answer is man. The sad thing is that, as human creatures, our early learning came from our brain's amygdala (feeling center), which received information from your temporal lobe (sensory experiences). This information was based on your experiences and fed your emotional center. Your brain created "logic" before you had the ability to have rational thought through your frontal lobe. This is not taking into consideration the type of words, experience, or events that life dealt you. This would be the script you are going by today. Yes, ninety percent of this early learning is unconscious, i. e., out of your awareness. This is the power of your early storyline or script.

It is amazing how one word, experience or event could change your storyline and foreshadow your future outcomes. Your script change could increase or decrease your life. It all depends on how you interpreted the meaning of the events, experiences, and words at the time you experienced them. I have clients who have early scripted beliefs of "I can't do anything right," "I will never succeed," to "I will die young." They had a tragedy in their life that changed their negative scripted beliefs to positive ones. I have clients who were raped, molested, and/or physically abused who changed their negative scripts to positive ones like: "I will live everyday like it's my last;" "God has a plan for my life, since I survived;" "That's the last time I will be a victim."

These clients, and others, have broken negative scripts like:

- I have no value
- I am alone
- I am a victim
- I am stupid
- I am too thin
- I will never please them
- I am ugly

to scripts such as:

- I am a survivor
- God is with me
- I can conquer anything
- I am not stupid at all
- my body is fine
- I am ok
- I am happy that God made me this way

Now, how did the trauma they experienced change negative beliefs into positive ones? From a clinical perspective, I considered this query for many years. I knew that approximately one-third of those who experienced severe trauma grew from their circumstance. Another third displayed no post-traumatic Stress Disorder (PTSD) after being traumatized. The remaining one-third would suffer from mental and physical illnesses related to the trauma. This did not explain why some of those with a mental illness or negative tapes about their esteem and value got better after a severe trauma. One day, I was being mindful of this question and received an answer from the most unlikely of all people, Bob.

## My Story: Bob

Bob was a short, odd man many misunderstood. He was an active alcoholic with a diagnosis of paranoid schizophrenia. He dressed in his wrinkled slacks, tee shirt, and old overcoat. Bob wore black army boots and a jungle hat. This hat had a string under the chin that let the wearer tighten it. Bob had his so tight it pulled the sides of his hat down over his ears. His hair was greasy and hung down to his shoulders. He and I had a great relationship.

Bob and I met therapeutically for over a year, and his main goal was, "to stay out of the state hospital. There are crazy people there." Bob believed "everyone" wanted to kill him; he heard voices that wanted him to hurt others or himself. Bob had chronic anxiety and severe insomnia. He had a bad habit that was not socially acceptable; Bob talked to himself aloud. He would get into arguments with himself, and occasionally, these arguments would escalate into a screaming match. Bob was aware that people would move away from him, ask him to leave stores, or call him critical names. Bob was also an overly sensitive man.

Bob was in his early forties and looked like a young immature 20-year-old. Before answering my questions, Bob would discuss his answer with himself aloud. Usually, Bob's answers were well thought out once he got to an answer. At times, I waited nearly 15 minutes to hear his answers. Bob drank a fifth of whiskey a day, "or so." Bob was a professed atheist who had no emotional or social support systems. He was aware of, "the Christian lady upstairs bringing cookies and putting them outside my door." This neighbor also gave Bob, "kind smiles." Bob was alone and desperately wanted a friend.

Bob grew up in a house with "alcoholics." Bob's father was "very mean" and often beat him, "for not making "A's" in school, not looking at him "right," and not doing "what he wanted me to do." His mother drank "all day" and told Bob he was "useless, stupid as rocks, a bastard child." She wished he would have, "died at birth." Most weekends found him "put in the closet or sent outside all night until I had to go to school." His parents were "always" this way. Bob got "lucky" when his dad divorced his mom. He was 15-years-old and got to live with his father, who "forgot I was around. It was the best time in my life."

During one session, Bob reported riding his bike. Three men stopped their car and physically beat him. They took him "down some back roads." They put "a bag over my head and would hit me in the face while telling me how they were going to kill me." Bob said, "They got a rope and tried to hang me. They got a rope and tied it to a tree limb. They had me stand on a tire and put the rope around my head. They pulled the tire out from under my feet and quickly ran to their car. They left fast." The rope broke as Bob lost consciousness. He awoke the next morning with a bag on his head and a rope around his neck "in the middle of nowhere." Bob was thankful to be alive.

The week after Bob's last session, I had been pondering how some people break negative scripts of severe trauma. Bob walks in with a broken nose, two black eyes, and severe lacerations on his face. One of his eyes was swollen (like he had an egg under his eyelid). His hair was shorter and not oily. He looked pitiful. I had to hold back tears listening to his story. Bob had an innocence about him that most people never experienced because of his bizarre behavior. Today, Bob was different in a tangible way. At first, I could not put my finger on how he was different because his experience was horrific.

He spoke of being beaten and thinking he was going to die, which also prompted his consideration of the cruel and unusual things his parents had done to him. Bob thought, "I'm about to lose my life and I haven't even lived because of my crazy parents." He became angry when the rope had been around his neck, furious for not changing what he could have changed, wishing he would have accepted love from the good people in his life. When his abusers pulled the tire out from under his feet, he, "smelled cookies and saw my neighbor's face." Bob regretted not speaking to her or knowing her name.

As Bob walked down the back road trying to get home, he said he thought about our time together. Bob said it was "so clear what you were telling me. You were the friend and father I never had in the past. I just spent time talking and not listening. I did not know better. I do now." When he walked down the dirt road, he was aware of today, saying to himself, "I don't have to argue with yesterday." Bob was clear; he was not going to argue with his past tapes anymore. He was going to stop being afraid of dying. Bob's fear, which fueled his paranoia stopped because, "it was peaceful once the tire was pulled out from under me." Bob did not argue with himself aloud again. He stopped hearing voices and was no longer paranoid about others wanting to harm him.

Bob's trauma provided the ability to become conscious and stand apart from his old emotional learning. His childlike emotional brain stopped taking over his rational one. He stopped letting his unconscious, forgotten memory control his present reality. Bob said, "This is the day my parents died," though they died 20 years prior to this event. Bob's storyline changed because of a near death experience. Later, he did inner child work and changed several other scripted beliefs.

You may not have realized your old scripts were manipulating your present life. You may not believe your unconscious mind and emotional brain move your present behavior, coloring your perspective of the world. I hope you will not need a severe trauma to be conscious. Doing the work in this book empowers the ability to examine old life scripts.

Most positive script changes come with a conscious awareness of reality. The process is deceiving because folks often do not realize their experiences are not "real," which is also why you need a support system. Everyone needs encouragement, fellowship, and support; it helps provide reality checks. There may be a church group, a Bible study, 12 Step, or home group with which you could work through this book.

Consider Bob's transformation, it came about through the confrontation with a harsh reality. Had he not been shocked into consciousness by the abuse, he likely would not have experienced his authentic self. The trauma stopped the contamination of his adult rational brain caused by his old tapes and scripts. Bob's rational brain was contaminated by his tapes of cruel and dysfunctional parents and the script of a wounded child. Bob's inner child believed he was broken, insane, and invisible. If Bob had been a Christian, he may have seen God as being cruel and vindictive, much like his parents.

It is difficult to see what is real without fellowship because reality is relative. Reality depends upon who is experiencing it. You and I can "see" the same "reality" and experience it very differently. What is real to you may not be true to your spouse, loved one, or the person right beside you. It is important to receive "reality checks" to help you to see what is "real." Your support system needs to include safe and supportive friends. Such friends will allow you to be vulnerable and authentic. The greater your stress, discomfort, or dis-ease, the more you will need to check your reality. Checking your reality will help you stop the contamination of your adult brain from old tapes of your parents or the script of the wounded child within you.

Reality checks can help alter the old negative beliefs or distortions you have carried through life. Each assignment that concerns your reality will need to be checked with your safe friends and family who know you. Lastly, you will also need to check that reality through your spiritual filter or knowledge of God. You will be amazed at how your friends perceive or "see" you or your "reality." I would bet others will see your reality, behind the mask, as a bit distorted.

## The Importance of Journaling to Heal

Therapists refer to these one-sided thought patterns (scripts) as cognitive distortions. These misleading thoughts limit your ability to experience your emotions appropriately. Journaling is a process that encourages you to reacquaint yourself with the inaccurate thoughts and emotions that have driven your life and perhaps caused great anxiety. To journal well, you will need to use your non-dominant hand (NDH) as it better enables internal mindfulness.

Your life may not be as bizarre as Bob's and you may not repeat your old tapes aloud, but those scripts are still there. You can wait for a crisis or begin to read the first line, paragraph, or chapter by journaling. It will grant the ability to review your present, while exploring your past. Journaling allows you to review your past thoughts and feelings to see what you need today.

You can become the author of your script without going through a crisis. Journaling is so simple; it is hard. You will need:

- to set committed time aside
- to sit down with pen and paper
- to listen to your old memories
- to write down your uncensored thoughts and feelings

As you journal, your awareness will likely increase. The more you hear your emotion, and emotional logic (this is where distortion is held), the greater the likelihood you will know what you want in your present chapter, as well as the preceding chapters. By answering the questions in the previous exercise, you have begun to put words on paper, giving your emotions a voice. Journaling is an active process of discovery that needs to be colored by your emotions. It is not a self-report of your day.

Journaling is not writing about your daily events, schedule, or what others have done to you. You will need to ask yourself how the events, schedule, or other behaviors affected you, hearing your thoughts and feelings about what you are writing. You are on track if you are using "I" statements and if you are not worried about spelling or grammar. This is not an English paper; it is an expression of your heart and soul. Be sure to watch for:

- the use of should, ought to, supposed to, and why's - these are critical parent words.
- the use of "buts," which discount what was said before it.
- use of always, never, cannot, have to, and makes me - these are your inner child.
- lack of emotions, like sad, mad, scared, alone, shame (lack of emotion is a red flag that you are not deeply listening to yourself, rather "reporting" on your day).
- if you write that you "feel that" someone or something will happen then you are thinking and not feeling.

Remember, God gave you emotions because He wanted you to feel them. Your emotions can protect you and provide an abundant life. You will need to experience, listen to, and take your emotions seriously. This might be a reason that God created your feeling center first.

You need to read and assess your journal once a week. Make notes and check for the items mentioned above. Stop old thoughts and feelings by doing this weekly assessment. You will likely experience freedom from old parental demands, expectations, and guilt trips. Journaling allows you to break through your old defense mechanisms and discover your authentic emotion, and this emotional logic.

Journaling can be an emotionally charged experience. If you are writing down your feelings concerning your abuse, spousal infidelity, or life's losses, you will likely experience the emotional energy in your body. When you are releasing the emotional energy, you will be taken back to previous thoughts, feelings, and experiences. You will encounter your inner child's old emotional charged logic, which does not consider the changes in you or your relationships. For this reason, you need to go back to your journal and re-read what you have written, being sure to insert your present adult truth.

Journaling can be cathartic; it helps purge inappropriate emotions and tensions. Some people might even say that catharsis is emotionally healing; yet the healing is putting your painful, anxiety-producing, or rage-filled emotions into perspective. You will be able to use your present truth to confront distorted beliefs. Perspective will come with time because you are focusing on yourself while cleaning the windows of your soul.

Many do not recognize healing as being cathartic. This release, or purging, gives you the power instead of your emotions. Catharsis helps you hear your distorted thoughts, lies, or unhelpful beliefs that move your life. If you go back and check for the above items, journaling will be a release and a means of re-writing your script.

As a child, did you change your mind when someone gave you different information, or when you felt wronged and someone provided, "the right answer?" What did you do when you were an adolescent, and someone gave you concrete data that went against your beliefs? Emotional logic is difficult to refute, especially as your frontal lobe was developing. Your rational brain was built on your childlike emotional brain's self-confirming style of thinking.

Emotional logic comes from the conclusions you drew without the help from your frontal lobe. Your frontal lobe is responsible for your rational logic. Your early emotional logic formed the building blocks for your later beliefs, which some would call biases. These biases stem from your frontal lobe's emotional logic, old beliefs, and/or biases hardwired in your brain. This is the physiological reason for your confirmation bias.

The best university is sometimes the "School of Hard Knocks." The more you are mindful, the healthier you will be. Journaling deals more with the conscious parts of your scripted beliefs, while internal and interactive mindfulness deals with your unconscious: the author of your script, the child within you.

In later chapters, you will take your journaling a step further by learning internal and interactive mindfulness. They will help you experience life without enduring the challenges from the "School of Hard Knocks." Interactive mindfulness allows you to "see" your shortcomings, struggles, and use of inner child's defense mechanisms without hitting bottom. You will recover your soul that has been under attack without you knowing it.

You may or may not have heard of dealing with your inner child or the child within you. You may want to read the small book called The Child Within (Whitfield, 1989) or other literature to gain a general understanding of regression work. No matter what you call it, it is work. Listening to yourself will demand your time, energy, and attention. You will need to make yourself a priority. Yes, you need to make yourself important. You will become a temple dweller and find the relic of God in you. It will be in the form of a child.

## Healing with A Higher Power

Listening to your inner child will be a part of this "becoming" your authentic God given self, free of the world's script, is the closest thing to knowing God in the flesh. You have forgotten the child-like innocence that was free of ambition, pride, and doubt. Your childlike innocence was curious, humble, teachable, and lovable. By living in this world, you have become callused and missed the mark; by hardening your heart, you learned to not cry, chase butterflies, or reach for dreams. You have lost the sensitivity of your heart by protecting it and have forgotten to live in unquestionable faith, unhesitant grace, and *unconditional* love.

The child within you was created for God in grace and with unconditional love. Incorrect images of God may have hardened your heart against this truth. In the process, you created a false self to survive in this world, while your authentic self has been undercover. Brennan Manning in Aba's Child calls this self the "imposter."

One of my seminary professors, Dr. Wayne Oats, referred to the "imposter" as a pseudo-self over laying the images of God present in us. This "pseudo," or false, self covers your authentic self. In *Behind the Mask* Oates (1987), suggested that personality disorders resemble sanity, but are not an authentic way of life. Emerging your authentic self out of the darkness will give you a life. Manning (1998) writes, "The emerging child reminds me I have a face of my own, gives me the courage to be myself, protects me against being like everyone else, and calls forth that living, vibrant, magnificent image of Jesus Christ that is within me waiting only to unfold and be expressed" (Reflection for Ragamuffins, 1998, Pg 274).

Seeing life through your authentic self confronts and conquers the pseudo/false self. Your script is the internal mask that covers your God given self. The mask helps avoid emotions. Your emotions have their own individual message. They have their own wants, needs, logic and purpose in the psyche. Your emotions cannot change into something else just because you would like them to. This masks what your heart of hearts is saying and the true purpose of your emotions. Each time you ignore, suppress, or medicate your emotions, you are denying your true self. You are creating a wall to hide behind.

How many times were you sad, frightened, or angry and did not say anything? In trying to minimize conflict, you hid your true feelings because you did not want to hurt others. Just think of how many times you do this a day, week, or year. By hiding behind the mask, you pushed down your feelings, sacrificing small pieces of yourself every time you denied your emotions. By not voicing your feelings, you are living a lie and slowly developing a false self.

Just imagine being hurt by the words or actions of a friend or loved one: If you are healthy, you will voice the hurt experienced by their words or actions. You will find, by sharing your thoughts and feelings, you are moving closer to voicing what you want and the things you do not want from them. Sharing such feelings and thoughts is healthy. These are the two parts of setting boundaries (1. Identifying your thoughts and feelings, 2. Voicing what you want and do not want) which create an authentic self. This is also a picture of healthy communication, which defines you and allows you to be seen. You are being vulnerable and conscious.

By performing this work, it draws out your authentic, God given self. You will be tempted to avoid the work because it is different, hard, or "crazy." It is tempting to avoid the work by filling the void and acting as through it does not bother you. You may say to yourself, "It won't work for me," "I'm different," or "I've tried everything." If you are saying these statements, you are likely struggling with having a self or having a voice.

The work in this book may be radical in that it tells you to consider yourself while not attributing shame or fear to God. Psychologically, some will be critics of the non-healing aspects of defense mechanisms, which empower you to use your faith to cure the soul. Other people will think working with your "inner child" isn't "spiritual." A few folks will say that linking psychology and theology is an oxymoron.

This book is radical and so is the work. In Latin, radical means "roots." This work encourages you to look at your mental, emotional, and spiritual roots to transform your life. The process will help ground you spiritually and empower you to live fully present. Paul writes in Romans 12:2, "Don't be conformed to the patterns of this world, but be transformed by the renewing of your minds so that you can figure out what God's will is—what is good and pleasing and mature" (Romans 12:2 CEB).

Do you honestly think Paul, under the direction of the Holy Spirit, would tell his readers to renew their minds if it were impossible? This transformative process helps heal the basic goodness of your inner self. Transformation is a process of renewing to become mature or "good." God changes you from the inside out. Psychologically, cognitively, and spiritually, your nature will change.

In Romans12:2, renewing can be rendered renovation of your "entire" mind. The entirety of your thoughts, feelings, and sense of self comprise your mind. Including transformation of habits and potential addictions you may be struggling with now. The transformation is work for anyone, even those people in society who are untouchable and/or worthless.

My suspicion is that when most people feel down, beaten up, and separated from God, they feel as if they are unworthy of God's transformative grace, love, and mercy. Honestly, such thoughts are somewhat arrogant because they suggest you are somehow special in a *bad way*. Ironically, many may think their suffering is "unique," which is simply distorted thinking. As a pastoral counselor, I saw this "uniqueness" in many of my clients.

Those very same clients exercise a strong belief in God and are active in their churches. Why would a spiritual makeover be possible for everyone else and not them? Patients may watch others, who are "worse off," change after they hear stories of overcoming addictions, abuse, and psychological problems. What is happening is that you see distorted images proposing your "uniqueness" when you are looking at your life through lenses of shame.

Self-disgust may have incarcerated more lives, happiness, and hope than any bottle, drug, or sin. In fact, some churches have a history of shaming parishioners, perpetuating Satan's original lie in the garden. Thankfully, some pastors and priests are working to change this approach to ministry.

Look in your Bible for any scripture showing Christ shaming *anyone*; you will not find any. When did Jesus ever push people away because they were unworthy? Christ's life, death, and resurrection were driven by His love for you. Yes, he hated sin because it hurt us and was not God's intention for us. Christ knew that Satan would use anything that was not moderated and twist it into something unhealthy. Shame is one of Satan's greatest triumphs. In God, there is and will never be shame. Christ came so that *all people* might live abundantly (John 10:10, NASB). Shame stops many from stepping into God's redemptive and forgiving grace.

Shame is not humility; it poisons your mind and spirit. If you are looking through the eyes of shame you will further your life script. You will have fleeting moments of transformation, spiritual renewal, and emotional health. You can walk in the darkness of shame or step into God's radiant light of unconditional love, bountiful grace, and total forgiveness. You need to remember what the psalmist wrote in Psalms 34:5: "Those who look to God will shine, their faces are never ashamed" (CEB). Never! End of story!

Yes, these passages are speaking to believers in God. You are clean and worthy, without spot or blemish. Remember that God loves all His children, saved and unsaved, rich, and poor, male, or female. All of them are worth and valuable in God's eyes. *Yet those who do not believe, accept, or cover themselves in Christ's blood will not be given eternal life.* God will not be near anyone who is unclean because He is Holy and not of this world. It is not about you being valuable, it is about God's Holiness. It is like your mom telling you, "You can't go, unless you get a bath. If you bathe, and get cleaned up, then you can go." You going or not going was never about your worth, it was about you being clean or not.

Throughout time, people have struggled with "why" they are "not worthy" to stand before God. For the longest time, I was confused by how people believed that they "should be" able to stand before God without accepting His son's blood sacrifice to cover their sins. I could not understand why others did not understand that they were not God; that the creator of heaven and earth is the One who makes the rules.

Your child-like brain reveals the answer, personalizing all the images and words around it, then confirms this reality repeatedly. Your child-like brain's self-confirming nature cannot moderate while relying on its emotional logic. Moderation is lost to its categorical thinking. Categorical thinking is all or nothing, right or wrong, black, or white, and me or not me. Then your inner child would confirm his/her belief and justify it over and over.

You are re-writing your script and will run into shame or false arrogance which stems from the fear of being hurt and not accepting the alternative: shame. This type of arrogance is not coming from true love for yourself, but from a way to hide shame.

**The Pitfalls of Healing**

- Avoidance
- Time
- Self-Medicating
- Intellectualization
- Effort

Every journey has its pitfalls, and the journey to your soul is no different. True healing of your mind, body, and soul takes courage. The journey is not for cowards. Most people will only take this journey to their soul when they have hit bottom, display signs and symptoms of a severe mental illness, or the body starts breaking down. No one can do the work or take the steps for you. There are many pitfalls along the way, but I would like to point out just a few common ones.

**Avoidance**. The most common pitfall is avoidance. Most hurting people will want to avoid further pain, which keeps them prisoners of that very pain. While it may sound ironic, fear is a powerful motivator when it comes to avoiding this healing journey. Yes, it would help if you had a personal guide, say, a friend who could walk with you on this journey to the soul. Contemporary culture tries to hide weakness, and the fear of weakness fuels avoidance.

You can always call the phone number at the back of the book to get a capable guide. My hope is that you will reach out to other hurting people once you finish this journey. I know you can become a spiritual companion once you face your own fears. A Soul provider has finished the healing journey and helps others walk through their healing journey. You will be traveling what Scott Peck would call the "Road Less Traveled."

## Exercise: Confronting Fear

*This is not a regression exercise. There are no special instructions included. Answer simply and directly in your journal.*

It is amazing how fear can make cowards of us all. You may need to make a list of what you fear facing. Take time to list your fears:

-

-
-
-
-

Here is a list of common fears:

- Fear of finding out memories of hurtful words or trauma
- Fear of the unknown
- Fear of being vulnerable or feeling
- Fear of losing control
- Fear of going crazy
- Fear of this not working

If you are not facing your fears, then you will be acting them out unconsciously in the form of internal indulgences or medicating them with external indulgence.

**Time To Do The Work.** Once you face your fears or step outside of your avoidance, then you will face the second pitfall: Scheduling time to do the work. You cannot do this work in your head. You *must* do it through conversations, exercises, and journaling. Thus, you must make time for yourself, time to be mindful of your own story. Peoples' refusal to make time for themselves is an epidemic. The urgency of the moment gets most of your attention. Most families are two-income families and have children with numerous activities, creating still more urgency. You will not "find" time because it is not lost; you cannot create more. What you *can* do is schedule time in your day for yourself. The sad thing is that most people will spend 10 hours a week watching TV yet will not take 1 or 2 hours to listen to themselves. You will need to make yourself important to do this work.

You will need to stop what you are doing and listen to your thoughts and feelings. Your thoughts and feelings will lead you to knowing what you want and things you do not want. You will learn that you are more important than time, while increasing your meaning in life. Remember, "Be still, and know that I am God: I will be exalted among the nations, I will be exalted in the earth. Jehovah of hosts is with us; The God of Jacob is our refuge" (Psalm 46:10-11, ASV). I hope you will rest in the fact that God is with you, even in your suffering. He will give you peace, strength, and healing. You are not alone. If you allow yourself to "be still" and mindful, you will recover and bring healing to your soul.

**Self-Medicating**. Another danger is medicating with an external indulgence, or addiction. Often, addictions seemingly mask the need to do the work. Numerous clients have self-medicated using indulgences. Yes, this work will help you work through the challenges of indulgences and move toward spiritual healing. You will be tempted to indulge more if your addictions are mood altering because doing so anesthetizes the wound(s). This emotional numbing will impede your self-discovery and healing, yet it will be a part of the healing process. The bottom line is this: Trying to work with your inner child while under the influence may be detrimental.

**Intellectualization.** The next hazard is the belief that "being mindful" is not Christian. Many believe that being mindful comes from an eastern philosophy, and while there are elements of mindfulness in eastern philosophy, in the context of this work, mindfulness refers to being fully aware of your feelings, thoughts, and bodily sensations in the moment. By being mindful, you will be able to be totally present with your story. Being mindful is a learned skill.

Biblically speaking, your body is a "temple." The Greek word *hierón* means temple.

The Greek word temple derived its meaning from the Hebrew word *mishkan*, which is translated, "tabernacle." A tabernacle was a dwelling place or residence for the divine presence of God, per the Hebrew text: "The outward temple is merely the symbol of God's presents, the shekinah. God makes his home in the heart of his people on the church and given place" (Word Pictures in the New Testament, Robertson, c 1931, p.99). If you dwell in your temple by being mindful, you will experience not only yourself, but God. Listening to yourself affords you the opportunity to hear God.

Since, your body is referred to as the temple of God, it is important for you to know the history of the Holy of Holies in the temple before Christ's death and resurrection. In the tabernacle, there were several rooms leading to a room in the center of the tabernacle. The center room was called the Holy of Holies. It was the seat of the Ark of the Covenant and several other spiritual objects that God had ordained. This inner room was to be entered only by the high priest once every year, on the great Day of Atonement. The high priest was above all other priests. The high priest had to be pure before entering the Holy of Holies.

The high priest would clean himself physically and spiritually before performing his sacred duties. The sacred duty was to perform the yearly sacrifice to cleanse the people and priests of their sin. The Day of Atonement was the holiest day of the year for the Jewish people. The priest was to present a blood offering to be at-one with God, according to the mosaic tradition. The blood sacrifice was a form of repentance or atonement for their sins. The blood offering by the priest cleaned the believers in Yahweh from all sin. The Day of Atonement healed their relationship with God. This can be seen in Hebrews 9:1-9:

which states:

"1 So then the first covenant had regulations for the priests' service and the holy place on earth. 2 They pitched the first tent called the holy place. It contained the lampstand, the table, and the loaves of bread presented to God. 3 There was a tent behind the second curtain called the holy of holies. 4 It had the gold altar for incense and the chest containing the covenant, which was covered with gold on all sides. In the chest there was a gold jar containing manna, Aaron's rod that budded, and the stone tablets of the covenant. 5 Above the chest there were magnificent, winged creatures casting their shadow over the seat of the chest, where sin is taken care of. Right now, we cannot talk about these things in detail. 6 When these things have been prepared in this way, priests enter the first tent all the time as they perform their service. 7 But only the high priest enters the second tent once a year. He never does this without blood, which he offers for himself and for the sins the people committed in ignorance. 8 With this, the Holy Spirit is showing that the way into the holy place had not been revealed yet while the first tent was standing. 9 This is a symbol for the present time. It shows that the gifts and sacrifices that are being offered can't perfect the conscience of the one who is serving" (CEB).

The history of God's covenant with the Jewish people was centered around this covenant. The new covenant came through the perfect sacrifice by Jesus Christ. Christ's death on the cross was for your atonement of sin. Jesus Christ was the "sacrificial lamb" that allows you to go directly before God to have atonement with Him. When Christ died, the curtain separated the Holy of Holies from the other rooms of the tabernacle, split down the middle, allowing everyone to enter God's presence without an intermediary.

The Holy of Holies now lies in your temple (body) where the Holy Spirit resides in you. This is the new covenant (Hebrews 8:9) or Good News of the New Testament. I hope you will take time to be mindful and dwell in your temple. You will not only hear yourself; you will hear God's heart for you. You will experience this work as Holy.

**Effort.** The last obstacle is simply this: effort. My clients want to be free from emotional distress, addiction, or broken relationships, but do not want to exert the necessary effort. As a pastoral counselor, wounded healer, or guide all I can do is encourage them to put forth the effort. Honestly, even with effort, things may get a bit worse before they get better, yet you *will* get better with time by doing the work. You will experience great difficulty changing their past behaviors and beliefs. This short-term discomfort will aid in your recovery of the authentic self. If you want to change, you will face obstacles on your way to recovery, meaning making, and finding purpose in your life.

Any discomfort will give you a greater chance to establish meaning in your life. Your search for meaning is among the most important internal drives you will experience as you search for meaning and purpose. Making meaning comes from you taking yourself seriously.

## Finding Your Purpose Through Fellowship

Establishing purpose helps make meaning. You will find that dwelling in your temple and facing fears provides life. You will have no need for outdated defense mechanisms or addictions. When you are aware of your purpose and meaning, you will likely find peace and/or contentment.

Each exercise you do while reading this book will help you gain insight into the wisdom you accumulated over the years. Life experiences put into perspective provide wisdom. Experience is one of the best teachers. The pitfalls and failures of life can be some of the best learning tools. You have used education, training, and mentors to extract the tools or gain the capacity to live life skillfully. You are learning to step out of old pitfalls and script by using your life skills. You have learned these skills throughout your life. Now you can use this wisdom to heal or rewrite your old scripts.

Don Blanding, the author of "Joy is an Inside Job" and author of the poem "As Thyself" was aware that healing is an inside job. I believe this poem is another expression of the inner child work. The search for significance comes in the third stanza:

"Can I know you? Can you know me?
Or can we know each other?
The 'I' of me and the 'You' of you,
How can we find 'Us,' Brother?"

The struggle with finding the "us" is worth the work on this healing journey. This work only comes through "your heart disrobing." Your heart disrobing is soul work. You are listening to your heart while being vulnerable with yourself. This disrobing brings the" I" and "me" together to make "we," which is to say you are integrating the old with the new and becoming one with yourself.

Becoming one is work, but you are worth the time, energy, and attention. You are learning another skill by being mindful. Remember, being mindful is a state of being fully aware of your feelings, thoughts, and body sensations in the moment. By being mindful you will be able to be totally present with your story, self, and God. It will become easier to do with each finished exercise you do. You will be practicing being mindful with yourself which helps being mindful in life. You may have read or have been encouraged to "Be" and wondered what that meant. "Be" is shorthand for being mindful.

I recommend doing this work with a group of friends because of the need for fellowship. I have facilitated several groups and found that support and common experiences create an atmosphere of healing. Group feedback will help you confront your critical parent messages or perpetrators while breaking down barriers that hide your inner child.

While on your journey, I hope you can experience fellowship that is portrayed in the last stanza of "thyself". "The 'I' of me and the "you" of you will reach with spirit's fingers to find again that twin hood lost whose splendid meaning lingers." Fellowship brings empathy from others that helps you confront your shame with truth and love. The most important thing about working in a group is accountability. Remember, you can start your own group and you will find it to be a blessing. I hope you will have this gift of fellowship on your healing journey to find your authentic self.

## Remember:

You can become the author of your script without going through crises. It depends on the light you bring into the darkness of your early chapters.

# CHAPTER SIX

## PARABLE OF A HOME

"They confronted me in the day of my calamity, But the Lord was my support. He also brought me out into a broad place; He delivered me because He delighted in me. The Lord rewarded me according to my righteousness; According to the cleanness of my hands He has recompensed me. For I have kept the ways of the Lord And have not wickedly departed from my God." Psalm 18:18-21

**KEY POINTS**:

- There are no bad emotions
- Accepting personal responsibility is necessary for healing
- Dissociation is a God given way to protect yourself
- Regression is the lens to help your adult mind see

**Reflections:**

- The greatest danger of repressed memories is having them acted out in your daily lives. This is already happening due to your avoidance.
- Make mental notes of your memories while reading the parable.
- Be mindful of times you have dissociated. They will lead to the child within.
- If your inner child spoke to you, would you listen?

# Welcome.

The house wanted to be a home. The exterior was beautiful and inviting; it had bountiful evergreens, accent flowers, and a strong, distinguished front door. It was one of the most special and expensive houses in the area. People would drive by to admire it, and neighbors would complement the house's beauty as they passed by on their morning and evening walks.

The proud house was large - 3000 square feet. It stood above many of the other houses in town and had wood flooring and stainless-steel appliances inside. The house had everything, except it was not a home. In fact, it craved to be warm and cozy on the inside like the smaller ones in the neighborhood that were well-loved by families. Long ago, the house's first owners cursed, fought, and did not maintain the house as needed. The house did not really remember much of those early years.

Winter was on its way, and the creaks in the floor brought a chill over the entire house. The house hated winter. Drivers focused on the road, walkers stayed at home, and the grass and flowers became dormant. It felt alone as the days got colder and shorter. The house had experienced many such winters, more than anyone could remember. So, it would close its white shutters, stay quiet, and try to make it through the dreadful season.

One morning, the gardener put yellow pansies in the flower beds. It was new for the house to have company and beauty in the winter. Each blossom had its own small dot of another color. There was one pansy that was pure white, and somehow it brought all the yellow ones together. The house was curious about that flower from the first time it saw it. This was the first time it had ever seen such a fragile flower. The house knew the flowers might collapse under the weight of the winter snow and ice.

All the pansies were in full bloom when the first winds of winter blew in that year. The white flower constantly talked to the house, but the house refused to speak because it knew the pansy would not last long. The house did not want to get close to such a frail flower, especially during this time of year; however, this did not stop the pansy from talking to the house. The white pansy would talk about the rich soil, sun's warmth, and the beauty of the other pansies. The house stood aloof, knowing it was not going to get close because these flowers, especially the white one, would not be around long.

The house got tired of the pansy asking how she was feeling and hearing how beautiful the day was going to be. The house, in a quick reactive tone, said, "When you get older, you will learn the hard winters of life will kill you or make you stronger." Innocently, the pansy replied, "But if I grow strong, I will only die a slow death like you are doing now." The house closed its shutters and locked its doors.

The night was long, and the hours passed slowly. The house grew tired of the darkness and wished it had never been built. It kept thinking about that one white flower weeping for the house. But the house knew her strength. She had weathered hundreds of cold lonely nights. She remembered many blizzards and white outs that the winter had brought her way. The house knew a "blue-norther" was coming though that night. She could already hear the wind howling and feel the ice and snow slamming against her.

She heard familiar creaks of the floor that brought unwanted thoughts and feelings, or worse, old painful memories lived out once again. She hated her owners' fights, and the pain and fear the children experienced during the night. Those memories all came back during those long days and nights. She would block those unwanted memories with anger toward the pansy. She knew the pansy would not survive the night with all the snow and ice. The pansy would not even get the chance to be strong.

The house awoke the next morning exhausted. She could feel the snow laden on her roof and around her windows. She made up her mind to keep all her shutters closed that day. She did not want to think about what the pansy went through, nor her death in the blizzard. She had a feeling of relief about the pansy dying, which felt odd. The house hoped the dying pansies would not draw attention to her. She was relieved they were gone, though unaware of the reasons.

A few days later, the snow melted under the warmth of the sun. The house opened her shutters and noticed that all the pansies were faced down in the dirt. Their weak stems were covered by the melted snow and dirt. She found herself sad for some unknown reason. She moved her attention back to her daily work. She slept fine that night.

When she awoke the next morning, the house found the sun shining through her windows. She had forgotten to close the shutters. She noticed the pansies bathing in the morning sun. Their colors were more brilliant than she remembered. The white pansy was facing her with a brilliant smile and said, "You left your windows uncovered!" The house was speechless. She finally replied, "I leave them uncovered a lot." The pansy looked at her and shook her head, no. The house quickly changed the topic. "I thought your fragile body would not make it through the harsh storm." The pansy replied, "I was made like a willow to stand up after a storm."

The house gave several reasons she was proud to be strong. Then the pansy said, "Your mortar is cracking, and your bricks are loose. All strong things begin to either break down or collapse after the cracks show up." The house was surprised that she had cracks and did not understand the pansy's statement on breaking down or collapsing, and she was too proud to ask and a little scared to know the truth.

A couple of weeks passed before they spoke again. The house kept her shutters open, day and night, to make a point to the small flower. The house looked out upon the white flower bathing under the warm sunlight as it moved with the light breeze. The house got caught up in the moment as she watched the little flower experience nature. The white pansy felt the house watching her.

Later that day, the house could hear the flower call her. The house responded, "What?! What do you want?" The flower asked, "What is your name?" The house had heard so many names. She remembered being called, "Stupid house," "Damn house," and "Not-big-enough house." As she waited for a response, the flower said her name was "Blossom." The house sat quietly. Blossom asked if her name was Ruth. The house asked, "Why Ruth?" Blossom said, "You're my companion, and Ruth means companion in Hebrew." The house agreed she would be Blossom's Ruth.

For the first time in years, Ruth felt warm on the inside. Ruth asked Blossom why she thought she was a companion. Blossom said, "You kept your shutters open after the blizzard. You experienced me being warmed by the sun. You did not get mad when I confronted you about being too strong and closed off. When I told you of your cracks, you stayed open to me." For the first time in her life, Ruth felt close to something other than herself.

That night the familiar cracks did not have the same effect. The house did not replay or revisit any old words or memories. She felt strangely calm. Ruth thought about what it was like to have her shutters open. She could feel the warmth of the sun and looked forward to feeling the warmth of the breeze around her. The house slept without fears or nightmares. The next morning, she waited for Blossom to wake up.

Blossom awoke with Ruth by her side. They both watched the sun come up and experienced the morning breeze. Ruth shared about all the rooms in the house except the master bedroom. Blossom asked if Ruth had a master bedroom. Ruth explained she avoids that room because it has a lot of bad memories. Blossom replied, "Ruth when you close off rooms, you are giving the past control. For example, I would not be able to be with you now if you kept your shutters closed."

Ruth shared stories about the marks, images and designs carved into the door facing of the master bedroom. The house spent the rest of the day speaking about the awful words, fights, and abuse she experienced in her early years. Blossom listened as Ruth grieved. That night, the house remembered her early years. She never imagined those early words and actions would have the power to influence her today. Ruth knew she was not alone. She felt the warmth of the sun; she had a friend in Blossom. She felt warmth and hope.

Ruth was aware that she was more than those early experiences. They had taken more of her life than they needed to. She sat up all night reflecting on her early beliefs. She had believed something bad would happen if she spoke of previous events. She spoke with Blossom and nothing bad happened. The house remembered the threats of being burned down, and the words that moved her to close her doors, but she did not have the old owners anymore.

The new, calm owners had been with her for years. Ruth realized she had not given them a chance to experience her. She resolved to experience each moment. As she heard the familiar cracks, she rested under the stars, and the wind caressed her with gentle breezes.

Ruth awoke in the morning and allowed herself to experience her full pantry, the new paint, and the new wood covering her floors. The windows in each room were open. The fresh air flowed through her. She moved into each room and brought new life that reflected today. Ruth vowed to bring all the new knowledge of today to any old noises that might trouble her. She was aware of the desire to speak to Blossom and told her of all the changes. Blossom was glad to experience her friend finally living life.

Blossom asked Ruth what had changed in her life that made her so happy. Ruth said, "I stopped living in fear and closing down because I thought I wasn't okay." Blossom inquired, "Do you hear the creaking of the floor when the weather changes?" Ruth replied, "Yes and I hate it." The pansy didn't believe the house, and said, "Ruth, that's crazy. Your boards are shrinking and swelling to keep you from having cracks. The master builder gave you the ability to withstand the harsh weather by giving you the ability to move with the weather. Be it hot or cold. If they were strong and did not move, you would not be standing today." Ruth had never thought of the sounds being a strength. The house only remembered them in times of severe weather because she thought she was breaking.

Ruth asked, "What do I do when the boards cry out?" Blossom replied, "They are not crying out; they are celebrating life and their ability to move. I allow the wind to move me right and left. The wind can take me to the ground or raise me up. I just trust God's design. I trust the sun, winds, and weather. It all gives me life. You need not stiffen or brace against yourself to fight the winter; you are designed to withstand it and celebrate how wonderfully you were made. You were made from great pines, once they were great tall trees. Now they are part of you. Your windows were once sand. The air that moves you, the moisture that fills you, they give you life. If you fight it, you will truly break." Ruth thanked Blossom and moved inside away from the window.

Ruth moved past the paint, sheetrock, and wood. She found her spirit was not in these things but was also a part of them. The house celebrated what made her Ruth. She found the nails, wood, and bricks were only a part of her. She became one with the things around her and the things that moved her. She found that she could not hear the groaning of the wood but could only experience being alive with sound. The house was not standing *by* Blossom but was *with* Blossom. Ruth was a part of something greater than herself. She was with and a part of God. She could celebrate all things and be hopeful in all things because she was more than those things. She found herself lost in laughter and praise. She experienced peace beyond her understanding. She knew and was known by God.

The house was going to tell Blossom about her experience, but realized Blossom already knew, because they were one. Ruth realized she had a Soul that was a part of herself and God. She celebrated for the sake of celebrating; she praised for the sake of praising. The house never literally moved, yet she was free to expand and contract. She could not wait to experience her dwellers, rooms, and weather. She was now at home.

In this story, Ruth made the unconscious wounding within her conscious, and in the process, she experienced her emotions. If you do not integrate your emotions, you will not experience self-control or self-awareness. Emotions color all pictures both internal and external. In layman's words, emotions are the feelings that move you. "All emotions are, in essence, impulses to act, the instant plans for handling life...the very root or the word emotions is more, Latin verb 'to move' plus the prefix 'e' to connote 'move away,' suggest that a tendency to act is implicit in every emotion" (Daniel Goleman, Emotional Intelligence, page 6 c 1994). Emotions generate action and/or movement.

Emotions left unharnessed by your cognitive ability will become reactions. You may react based on old forgotten memories or on primal emotions. When you react, you are emotionally moving away or towards something, real or perceived, outside of yourself. This gives this "something" or "someone" control over your actions. If you grew up getting your hand slapped every time you reached for a spoon, later in life, you may reach for a spoon and unconsciously pull back your hand or drop your spoon, if someone else reaches at the same time. This reactivity can control your life outside your awareness.

In the Minds Prism, you learned that the amygdala is the feeling center for the primitive, or emotional, brain. The evolution of the primitive brain created the rational or "new brain." Your new adult brain is housed in the neocortex. All the new brain's circuitry is built on the wiring of the emotional brain and limbic system. The emotional brain is a contained unit, working in concert with your new brain. In addition, I would suggest that you also have the emotional mind of your inner child, as well as the rational one from your adult. Therefore, your inner child is a contained unit working through your adult brain. Remember, however, emotions fuel the motion/impulse in your adult mind and inform it of old forgotten memories.

Bear in mind that having self-control and self-awareness is not the process of controlling your thoughts. Managing your thoughts is important, yet the process of self-control and awareness is about controlling the emotions. The amygdala contains your emotional memories while your hippocampus puts the memories in context to create emotional meaning. Further, these memories need to be examined and put into perspective. If you lost connection with your amygdala, there would not be any personal meaning. If you want to know what moves you, go through your emotional rolodex. If you do not deal with what moves you, your rational mind will be hijacked by your historic emotions and the emotional logic they contain.

When you are listening to and dealing with your emotions, you move through the library of your mind: the hippocampus. Most people avoid and medicate the emotional brain. You may not want to deal with painful memories. Moreover, you may hate giving them control of your life. What makes experiencing your emotions important is your amygdala can create its own memories without your conscious awareness. "Anatomically the emotional system can act independently of the neocortex.... Some emotional reactions and emotional memories can be formed without any conscious, cognitive participation at all" (Daniel Goleman, Emotional Intelligence, page 18 c 1994). Pay attention to your emotions and their memories to remain steadfast.

## Exercise: Connecting with Your Emotions

*This is not a regression exercise. There are no special instructions included. Answer simply and directly in your journal.*

To heal, you must listen to your emotions or feelings that influence your early script -- all of them. You can have many emotions. Here are some with their common derivatives. Circle those you feel most of the time.

Then draw a line under the one you avoid, medicate, or suppress.

- **Happy:** festive, relaxed, calm, complacent, satisfied, serene, comfortable, peaceful, optimistic, joyous, content, ecstatic, enthusiastic, glad, pleased, grateful, cheerful, excited, carefree, playful, elated, jubilant, thrilled and emotionally lighthearted.

- **Sad:** depressed, hopeless, dreary, dull, moody, sulky, defeated, pessimistic, melancholy, despairing, miserable and emotionally low.

- **Hurt**: Upset, disappointed, and emotionally heartbroken.

- **Angry:** annoyed, enraged, irritated, frustrated, grumpy, angry, indignant, hostile, furious, and emotionally irate.

- **Afraid**: fearful, threatened, frightened, timid, cautious, concerned, apprehensive, alarmed, anxious, hesitant, scared, petrified, terrified, and emotionally worried.

- **Loving:** accepting, passionate, understanding, sharing, affectionate, and emotionally warm.

- **Interested**: eager, intrigued, absorbed, excited, enthusiastic, intent, earnest, fascinated, and emotionally content.

- **Guilt:** Guilt is an emotion, and it is also a thought process. It is an awareness or acknowledgment of doing something wrong, usually followed by shame without right action.

- **Confident:** calm, secure, empowered, independent, brave, loyal, courageous, respected, and strong.

- **Doubtful**: distrustful, uncertain, hesitant, insecure, dubious, bored, suspicious, and skeptical.

- **Shame:** uncomfortable, embarrassed, humiliated, dependent, jealous, envious, distant, evasive, stubborn, impulsive, cruel, preoccupied, powerless, helpless, humble, shocked, and disregarded.

Self-control is an aspiration in our society. If you are looking for self-control regarding your mental and emotional health, relationship, or indulgences, then you will need to first have self-awareness. *Believing you are self-aware and suppressing your emotions does not lead to self-control.* By avoiding your historic emotional suffering, you are giving something or someone control over your life. Who are you giving control? By giving up control you cannot overcome addictions, emotional, and mental disorders. You must go through the heart of the matter, your emotions, and your emotional logic.

Do you know when you are speaking, listening, or protecting your heart, you are speaking from your inner child? Your heart cries out to be seen, heard, and loved. Hopefully, you will see, listen to, and love all that makes you who you are. When you are listening to your inner child, you will be able to experience your intuition, common sense, and your "sixth sense." These are not a purely adult emotional process. Be aware of what moves you and listen or feel that which pushes you along: your emotions.

People who say they do not make emotional decisions are mistaken. Your personality is stored in your neo-cortex and driven by your inner child's brain. As such, listening to your adult mind *and* your inner child's emotions is paramount when making decisions. Obviously, you do not want to make wholly emotional decisions without using your adult reasoning. Many addicts are moved by emotional decisions. You need to listen to your heart with your adult reasoning to become one-minded. It would scare me if you made a strictly rational decision. Not that your rational decision would be wrong, it just would not be entirely correct. To exercise self-control, you must walk through the door of self-awareness – awareness of both your inner child and adult mind. When you listen to the percussion of your feelings you will begin to know what you genuinely think.

Guilt and shame may lead you to believe you are a terrible person. Perspective is a part of awareness that leads to healthy self-control. Are you looking through the perspective of your adult self-esteem or your inner child's guilt and shame? You can walk through your emotional shame or guilt and find that you made a good decision and did not do anything wrong. When you process your emotions, in context of memory, you may see that you did well and are okay, allowing you to confront this guilt or self-blame.

For the emotional decision makers who do not assume responsibility, it is difficult to recognize that the assessed blame was misplaced. Accepting personal responsibility is necessary for healing or mental health. Most who are under-responsible can move through their emotions and activate their conscious minds. If they can experience sorrow for past actions and take responsibility for them, they will be able to stop blaming other people or circumstances in the present while putting the past into its appropriate perspective.

## Exercise: Naming Your Emotions

*This is not a regression exercise. There are no special instructions included. Answer simply and directly in your journal.*

Look through your emotional lens at the feelings you earlier circled. These are your possible rackets, or familiar bad feelings that were acceptable to feel growing up. Now look at those feelings you underlined. These are closer to your authentic emotions. Focus on your underlined words for the following exercise. Write them down, sit with them, and let them have energetic space within you. For example, if you underlined "sad":

Listen to the messages that come from being sad then write them below:

-
-
-
-
-

Then, as you feel sad, and hear the messages that go with that feeling, be aware of the memories that arise with that familiar feeling. List the memories below:

-
-
-
-
-
-
-

**Example**: sadness

**Messages:**

- I cannot do anything right
- I will always be a failure
- I hate myself

**Memories**

- my dad telling me the house was not clean enough
- mom telling me that I need to stay home from prom because of my grades
- I had an abortion when I was 15 years old

It is important to journal on each circled or underlined word. You will gain more self-awareness and control by doing the assignment.

What is the "truth" from your adult brain after this exercise? Do you believe you cannot clean the house? Do you believe that you have never succeeded, or you are worthless for a having an abortion? If you still believe these lies, then you need to ask yourself two questions that will put these acts into perspective:

1) What would I say to my best friend or my child if he or she were going through these memories and having these beliefs?
   -
   -
   -
   -

-

2) What would God say about my beliefs?
   -
   -
   -
   -
   -

I hope you experience God's grace and forgiveness. If you have asked for forgiveness, He remembers your sin no more. (Hebrew 8:12-17). I hope you see that your friend's or child's worth is not based on a couple of mistakes or poor parental choices. As you experience God's grace, perhaps your beliefs will change, which will also alter your inner child experience.

In the "Parable of a Home" above, Ruth found her Soul. Ruth was over-responsible. She assumed responsibility for things which were not her fault. She made only "rational decisions," and had been abused. She gained freedom by experiencing her emotions and memories. Truth came by opening her shutters and not suppressing her despair and fear. By experiencing her emotions, the house could stop indulging in her shame, despair, and fear. You, too, will find that true introspection will demystify your early learning while bringing a sense of rest to the innate cry of your Soul: the longing you seek with God.

Avoiding your past suffering leaves you fractured. The Soul is connected more to your (primitive) child brain than your (rational) adult brain. The closer you get to your authentic, emotional self, the closer you get to God. This journey through your emotions, wounds, and past experiences needs to be put into God's perspective while remembering that God demonstrates unconditional love. You will find, like the pansy in the parable, you can blossom and become whole. This healing and health can lead to healthy self-control. Dealing with the emotions you underlined will lead to healing.

It is difficult to understand how your negative thoughts stem from repressed feelings and distorted memories, but they do. Your underlined emotions will keep you captive if you suppress or medicate them. These emotions are the ones that propel these feelings. You can create life if you are willing to listen to them and put them into perspective.

For further context: Some of my clients have been psychopaths or sociopaths. They were "normal" people who used and abused others to meet their own needs. They were generally well-dressed, educated, and charming. Their challenge was a lack of conscience. They had great rational brains but were disconnected from their emotional brains. They could not feel normal sadness, sorrow, fear, regret, or any other emotion. They had the ability to act sad, scared, and angry, or act out other emotions to get their needs met. Still, they could not experience genuine emotions. They had great problems experiencing their souls.

I think psychopaths serve as great examples of the cost of being emotionally disconnected. It is odd that some people work so hard to avoid feeling or having certain emotions. When you medicate or suppress your emotions you may become pathological. It is counterintuitive to believe you are healthier when you are not feeling your emotions.

If you want to experience God, you must be connected to your emotional brain. Think of God's essence. His essence is love. Love is experienced in your old primitive brain, the emotional one. You cannot experience love fully without your emotional center.

## Being Conscious

The goal is for you to become fully conscious, yet being in and aware of the present moment is not strictly a rational process. Being conscious is a mystery in and of itself. Being conscious is a delicate balance of being rationally and emotionally present in the present moment. A good example may be intuition, which is often considered the purest form of thought and emotion. "Intuition is often considered to be the highest, purest form, surpassing even reason and inferential thought. Intuition refers to an extremely specific and long-acknowledged way of knowing. In epistemology-the study of ways of knowing-intuition is often considered to be the highest, purest form, surpassing even reason and occurs before any thinking takes place" (Gerald G. May M.D. Will and Spirit. Page 25 c1082). It is the ability to experience, sense and/or know something before it happens.

Many believe the rational brain is the seat of your soul. Personally, I am not sure where the soul ends or begins. I believe it is neither in your new or old brain. The seat of your soul is a delicate balance between your adult and inner child. It is neither rational nor emotive; it is both. The problem is that your emotional health gets ignored, pushed down, or medicated. You are not alone in ignoring your emotional brain; it is a cultural challenge.

Consciousness is difficult to define because it is a cultural invention rather than a biological function. Being conscious can be used to refer to conscious thoughts about yourself and the environment, while self-awareness is being introspective apart from your environment. Another way of explaining awareness is being intentional with self-examination. Being conscious is fluid and can be molded to fit several lines of thought. If you will recall, consciousness is a state of being aware of the self and environment with your true rational and emotional minds. When thoughts and feelings come together in the brain, they form a sense of self that you know as "I," or self. Being conscious begins with a self that is aware, or better yet, possesses "a knowing." Knowing would be your awareness and intuition working as one. Knowing is informed by your thoughts and feelings simultaneously to create movement. Sadly, many are not as conscious as they think.

Most of your mental activity are routine behaviors that are based on your inner child's early learning which are not conscious. If you are medicating your emotions with any mood-altering substances or activities, avoiding your feelings and thoughts, or using defense mechanisms, you are not in your adult mind. Avoidance, medicating, and defending keeps most folks from learning of their inner child much of the time. You need to be in your adult mind to be self-aware and be self-aware to have control. This does not consider the fact that much of what you "see" is based on your faulty beliefs – beliefs stemming from thoughts, feelings, and experiences gathered in and through your childhood. Your emotional brain carries these memories and beliefs to your rational mind. If you are not aware of your emotions, you will not know whose thoughts and feelings, or behaviors are moving you today.

When you are aware of your childhood emotions and beliefs, which originate from your early experiences, you may find you disagree with the conclusions you made growing up. You may have been neglected and believed, "I will always be alone," or "I don't matter," or "I want to die." If you are being introspective or self-aware, you can use your adult mind to disprove this to your inner child that experiences the fear of being neglected. This is easier said than done, your emotional brain is still childlike in its thinking. Your childlike mode of learning was/is self-confirming, suppressing, or ignoring any memories or facts that would undermine its belief. Your emotional brain will move toward things that support it.

"The beliefs of the rational mind are tentative; new evidence can disconfirm one belief and replace it with a new one – it reasons by objective evidence. The emotional mind, however, takes its beliefs to be absolute, and so discounts any evidence to the contrary.... Feelings are self-justifying, with a set of perceptions and justifications all their own" (Daniel Goleman, Emotional Intelligence, p.295 c 1994). Self-confirmation and self-justification make it hard for your rational, adult mind to convince your emotional, childlike mind of anything different or new.

The key is to become aware of your inner child's feelings, thoughts, and beliefs and bring perspective from your adult mind. It will take patience and time to change your childlike mind. This process will lead to self-awareness and self-control for your adult and inner child, which will lead you to your heart's true desire. "The heart's desire is the will of the Soul and is not usually an entirely conscious phenomenon. The will of the Soul is triggered when the heart's desire becomes conscious intention" (Richard N. Potter, Authentic Spirituality p.74 c 2004). You may refer to your conscious intent as being willful. This willfulness comes from your Soul's heart of hearts. You may call this God's will for you.

Blossom, in the "Parable of the Home," was conscious, self-aware, and present in the moment. She was aware of the breeze and sun. She experienced the weather and moved with it. She was aware of her faith in God, which she modeled for others. She was a friend and companion to Ruth. She allowed herself to see past Ruth's beauty and strength to her cracks and pain. Blossom did not allow her emotions or suffering to control her but spoke from her heart. Her emotions informed her steps, which gave her wisdom. Blossom was a pansy with awareness of other pansies, the house, and her environment. Blossom neither avoided nor used defense mechanisms. She owned her feelings and thoughts with Ruth.

Blossom is a good example of being present. Presence can be seen in many ways. While I was training to be a pastoral counselor, I was encouraged to be present with my clients. It took several years to learn to be present with myself and even longer to learn to be present with another person. It is so difficult to explain, let alone teach the art of "being" with another person. You are learning to be present or mindful of yourself. You cannot be truly present with someone else if you are not present with yourself.

## My Story: Darlene

Darlene is a small, thin, fragile six-year-old little girl who shows signs of schizophrenia and has been diagnosed by a psychiatrist as psychotic. I have been seeing her for several months. She has the gift of presence, which most people do not see in her. She is an old soul. She has knowledge far beyond her years. She will not take her antipsychotic medication and her parents and doctor are afraid she will break with reality. She reminds me of a white pansy in a field of weeds. She came to my office for her session.

Darlene: You are wearing boots today, Mr. Walter.

Counselor: How are you doing, girl?

Darlene: Girl is fine.

Counselor: Well, how have you been?

Darlene: Been fine, but everyone else is mad.

Counselor: What are they mad at you for?

Darlene: You know. Are you worried?

Counselor (*I knew that they wanted her to take her medications*): Well, I hate that everyone is mad at you.

*(Darlene was right and I knew it. I did not have enough data to say she did not need medication, but I did not think she needed it. She was right about me being "worried"*

*because her parents would pull her out of counseling with me and put her with someone that believed the way they did about her condition and medication.)*

Counselor: You are right again. Darlene, I believe you have a strong gift for *knowing,* which scares others and sometimes you can feel the presence of people and things that are not seen by others. You are right. I am worried.

Darlene: (*looking at me with a childlike innocence and her eyes fully present with me*) You are right. They would get me to talk to someone else. I want you to talk for me.

(*I did not voice this out loud to Darlene. She knew.*)

Counselor: What do you mean, "Talk for you?"

Darlene: You know. I am sorry you are feeling so scared. Just tell them what you think!

Counselor: If I encourage them to give you medication and tell them that you think you know what others think and feel, you will be ok with me telling them?

Darlene: You will not do that? You have moved a lot of your books out of here.

(*This little girl had a knowing that was tied to being totally present with others and her environment. She had a God given gift of discernment with a prophetic voice*)

Counselor: I have moved about 10 or more (*books*). I will speak with your parents. How do you think that will go?

Darlene: I do not think they will like it much. They do not want me to know what they are not telling me.

(*Darlene gave me valuable insight. I did not know that their conflict was her knowing what was in the room. I thought it was about her being psychotic.*)

I think you and I are the same, kind of. Tell mom that too.

Counselor: I will tell them that you have gifts. Your gifts are a lot more supernatural than mine. So, I will call them in here. Is that ok?

Darlene: I like it. Do you know other kids have "knowing's"? They do not talk about it.

(*I called Darlene's parents back and told them that their daughter was exceptional and had a strong presence that most kids have but are usually squelched by their authority figures. I told them I have worked most of my life to learn how to sharpen the very gifts their daughter has now. I told them that she was strong and will not believe what others think about her truth.*)

*Both parents were about to say something.*

Counselor: Just wait a minute. I believe your daughter needs help to contain these gifts. She will not give you feedback on what she knows unless you want her too.

(*After about twenty minutes of answering their questions, I ask them to leave so I could check in on Darlene*)

Darlene: I do not think they will like it much. They do not want me to know what they are not telling me.

Counselor: I know that you did not say that. I know you have gifts, and you need to know how to control them. I am sorry for not asking you. So, do you agree?

Darlene: You are not sorry. You know that they would have got mad at me.

(*Again, she was right because I knew her parents wanted to break in and tell her that she is sick. I did wish I would have asked her if she would agree to ask them first if they want to know*)

Darlene: I want to play with a bear. (*a stuffed animal in my office*)

Presence is the art of relating to the presence of the environment around you while being aware of your own feelings and thoughts in the same moment. Most people are like Ruth, in the Parable of a Home. Few are present like Blossom and Darlene. "The reason we live life so dimly and with such divided hearts is that we have never really learned to be present with quality – to God, to self, to others, to experience and events, to all created things" (Jim Branch, c 2006, March Crina Wjederkenr Blue Book p.29). The first step in being present is to be conscious.

## The Awakening

Time rolls on, it does not matter if you survived life's wrecks or are currently getting out of a burning car. The world tells you to put on your face and be happy. The mask of happiness is expected and well received in our culture.

You can make yourself more important by acting perfect, strong, or pleasing to others. Like the home, you may have learned to be perfect and not show your cracks. Perhaps you learned to be strong, never showing your weakness. You may keep your shutters closed to protect yourself. It did not work for Ruth. Closing herself off only kept her haunted by her past and insulated against new relationships. You may find yourself on autopilot if you have learned you must be strong, perfect, or pleasing others to be okay.

The game of life continues saying, "no rest for the weary". It does not matter if you are a part of the walking wounded. No one knows your pain and suffering. You were once desensitized from the haunting memories until you no longer had strength to keep your mask in place. The sociable suited mask is no longer big enough to hide your suffering. You just want to isolate and be left alone. Then the awakening occurs, you wake up having flashbacks, anxiety, or depression of your childhood abuse, haunting your present function. Intrusive thoughts or nightmares may increase your struggle. You want the memories of the abuse to stop.

You understand why Ruth had her shutters closed. Even reading this could trigger memories or flashbacks to your early abuse. You do not want to remember or feel your old fear, pain, or shame. You may think it is crazy to confront your hurt, fear, shame, guilt, loneliness, or other unpleasant emotions. While the desire is to be strong, you may also realize that resisting the experience is not helpful either.

In *The Language of Emotion*, McLaren (2010) writes:

"If I resist the emotion and turn towards avoidance and distractions. I actually began to suffer --maybe not in the moment, when I'm watching too many videos, playing to many online games, or eating too much chocolate -- but when I put my distractions aside, where am I? It is a few hours and a few hundred calories later, and I still have not dealt with the original emotion. Will it return with more insistence next time, or will it burrow itself down further into my psyche? Whichever thing happens, the original emotion is in a less healthy position, my awareness has been pulled away from it, and I've set myself up for emotional imbalance I may not be able to address the next time it appears. If the emotion rockets back out with more intensity, I suffer. If it represses itself so I cannot find it, I suffer. If I resist the original discomfort, that discomfort increases the intensity until I am in full-blown suffering.

My distractions do not make me more capable or more aware; they just take me out of commission for a while. Though I may experience a sad sense of fun in my distractions of choice, the discomfort remains, my resistance increases, my emotional agility decreases, and my suffering is certain. It is as if I am placating an upset baby with a toy rather than helping it learn and grow." (pp.85-86)

While avoiding, your emotion will resurface, discomfort remains, agitation increases, negative thoughts increase as your arousal and anxiety intensify. Your suffering is internalizing. A counselor would flag these as signs of Posttraumatic Stress Disorder. You are traumatizing yourself. Your unwanted and avoided emotions of the abuse are now controlling you and your working memory. "Working memory is an executive functioning par excellence in mental life, making possible all other intellectual efforts, from speaking a sentence to tackling a knotty logical proposition" (Daniel Goleman, *Emotional Intelligence*, page 79 c 1994). Your repressed emotions of your early learning or dissociated experiences are now overwhelming your rational brain's prefrontal cortex, where present feeling and historic emotions meet.

When anyone has their innermost being hurt, their soul aches. The painful memory is quickly suppressed by the adult mind. The greater the emotional charge of the unwanted emotions, the more likely you will suppress them. The memories are not conscious, but they still influence your mind, and therefore your body. *Inner child work is the recovery of repressed memories that are unconsciously affecting your mind, body, and soul today.*

There are great dangers with repressed memories. You will find that your current situations and relationship issues are not the main issue; the challenge is the forgotten memories that manifest themselves unknowingly in common daily activities. You cannot be free or victorious until these "unknown" memories are acknowledged and addressed consciously. Your inner child's mind is made up of repressed memories, experiences, and knowledge of which you have no adult awareness.

The only way to gain control is to be aware of what moves your inner child today. Regression is the lens to help your adult mind see. While I realize the last thing you desire is to revisit your pain and fear again by speaking with your inner child, regression is not about reliving your past emotions and/or abuse. This inner child work allows your adult self to experience the child within you who is hidden and desires the memory of abuse to stop. By loving and nurturing yourself this will stop past child abuse memories, listening to your inner child's thoughts and feelings while sharing your truth today. This process allows you to bring the unconscious into the conscious, lessening the "craziness" of life.

Now you may think that listening to your old wounds sounds like "psychobabble." What you are calling "psychobabble" is your soul trying to communicate. When you are at the crux of your pain, shame and/or fear, as I was on Christmas Eve, you are also at the center most part of the authentic self. Examining yourself will help you hear your authentic emotions and thoughts. These thoughts and feelings will lead the way to your freedom from all abuse, neglect, and addictions. If you are a spiritual person, doing so will lead you where God dwells in you. If you are a Christian this is where you will hear and experience the Holy Spirit of God. Listening to your Soul speaking allows you to know and be known while experiencing God's Love.

## My Story: Judy

"Judy" was a client experiencing increased anger with men. She had a poor self-image and was your "normal college professor." She spoke of her uncle with such anger. I asked her about her uncle. "He is a deacon in the church. You know, one of those bible thumpers. He coached all his kids' sports, and he is a cyclist."

Do you see him a lot? I asked her. "No. I try not to be around him," she said. Judy's tone was getting more condescending and sharper with each answer. She noted, "The last time I was around him was about 10 years ago at the family reunion. He continues to be a jerk (present tense). I mentioned she had not seen him in 10 years, how is he still actively being a jerk to her?

Judy sat up in her seat, and with anger in her voice said, "When I was nine and at the reunion, he called me on stage. And in front of everyone called me, his 'dumpling' and everybody laughed." Judy was getting louder and louder with each word, as if she were yelling at me. She continued, "He told everyone (pause) how big I was getting. Then he put me down. I cannot believe that he would do that to me or anyone. I hate him for that."

"Did he call you his 'dumpling' before this reunion?" I asked. Judy said, "Yes, he would come over a lot to get me to play softball or volleyball. He would ask me to go to church about every week." I pointed out, "He sounds like a good guy that loved you." Judy leaned forward in her chair (I thought she was getting up to leave) and said, "How can you say that? He called me fat in front of everyone. Everybody laughed at me. Mom and dad both were telling me I was getting fat and to not eat too much at the reunion. Then he tells everybody how big I was getting. I hate him."

Judy's mother and father were alcoholics, and most would consider them dysfunctional by any definition. They were critical of her not being perfect. Judy was exceptional at everything but, "never good enough" in their eyes. She grew to believe that she was not okay. She was a brilliant professor who felt, "stupid and fat." Judy learned to not feel her emotions by working. She would work "12 to 14 hours a day" to distract herself from hearing her emotional brain. Years of not listening to her emotions became toxic. She displaced her anger toward her father onto male students, her husband, and pastor. The pastor referred her to me. Judy wanted to learn to be happy and not to be angry.

Judy did not understand how her child-like emotional brain worked. She did not know that her emotional brain learned by associative memory because it was not logical or objective. She associated all her shame, pain, and anger with her uncle. He was probably the healthiest person in her life. Her emotional brain heard, "dumpling" and associated it with "being fat." The self- affirming nature of the emotional brain used past hurts to increase the hurt and shame of those moments. Judy "forgot" how her uncle was always there for her and loved her. This reality was unseen by her emotional brain. She began indulging in anger and work to maintain emotional safety.

I asked her to call her uncle and share her anger and what she experienced with him. Judy agreed to call her uncle but had a lot of ambivalence about doing it. Judy came back to the next session "shocked." Judy could not believe she had believed that her uncle was so cruel. She reported that her uncle, "cried on the phone." She had forgotten not answering his phone calls or going to events and parties that he invited her to. "He thought I was on drugs or something," she said.

Judy's child-like emotional brain began listening to her adult brain's logical and objective views. Her adult brain was processing the data in logical ways, not looking through the old lenses of her inner child's, self-confirmation, and self-justification that kept her hurt and angry. She began to journal her feelings and process them more objectively, and the transformation was unbelievable. She experienced peace and kindness. Judy worked less and increased her time at home and church. She began having her college students journal and created time for them to talk to her. Her inner child and adult brains began to function as one unit; she had found her authentic self.

If you want to be free like Judy you will need to stop your external indulgences like alcohol, drugs, sex, pornography, food, and work (to name a few); you need to become aware by listening to your thoughts and feelings without self-medicating. If you want freedom from internal indulgences like doubt, despair, pride, envy, and boredom, you need to listen to your inner child's feelings and thoughts to find freedom. If you want to experience your glorified self, then you need to listen to your heart speak. This inward crossing will lead you to peace and joy that will pass all understanding.

The journey to the Soul, while daunting at first, is so much easier than losing yourself gradually over time. It will stop any addiction and break any stronghold. The pestilence of time is not the cure of the soul. Time can allow all wounds to become septic. Life's burdens will become lighter when you are consciously aware of the parts of you that live in distortion. You will experience a self that is selfless and full. You will not strive, but overcome; you will not be hungry, but be full; you will not be gradually emotionally dying but feel life at its fullest.

Your inner child cannot be healthy and whole without your adult awareness. You need to be consciously aware of your feelings. You need to know the difference between your present reality and your past one, to be free from past teaching influences and/or abuses. The process of healing is looking back at your old emotional wounds while remaining grounded in the present.

This is the reason that many refer to this type of healing as regression work. If you insist on seeing life through your adult lens, you cannot retreat to an earlier emotional age which makes it difficult to change your old emotional logic. Inner child work allows your adult self to re-associate with the dissociated child part of you, allowing you to see your inner child's feelings, thoughts, and beliefs that move you today. Your inner child needs to look through your eyes during this work. The sad thing is that you are already looking through your past lens and being re-abused without your knowledge. This is the reason that you need to stay in the present reality, in your adult mind, and not your inner child's.

If we were talking about a mistake you made last week, last month or even last year you would love a "do over." Most would love a redo because, "hindsight is 20/20." You would have said, done, or believed this or that differently. Most would love the chance to change their words, behaviors, and beliefs. Yet, when you confront a history of abuse, poor choices, or less than stellar behavior, you may think it is hopeless. If thinking it is hopeless is not enough, you will become more afraid of emotions that seem "too big" or insurmountable, which is a lie.

Such lies come from the father of lies, Satan. If your belief system does not include Satan, then emotions that are "too big" are a form of self-deception, which empowers your past abusers. You will stay a victim instead of becoming a survivor. Living through your old feelings and beliefs without an awareness of doing so, your abusers will continue to affect you emotionally, mentally, and physically. You will avoid by indulging in those things that will give you temporary relief. Sooner or later, you will attribute your abuse, addictions, and deterioration to the people around you and God. Deception will not only affect earthly things, but heavenly things, this is true hopelessness.

You may or may not be hopeless today. You may be like the walking wounded and can keep your mask hiding your depression, anxiety, and or loneliness. Knowing your early storylines, where your Never Neverland was and your Captain Hook that hurt your inner child. Like Blossom in The Parable of the Home you will need to reach out to your Ruth by writing with your Non-Dominant Hand (NDH) to give your inner child a way of speaking to you. You will need to be able to bring light to your history of darkness, loneliness, or fear by writing with your NDH.

Realizing what you heard as a child could still harm you may be challenging. Your primitive brain "learned" from life's negative experiences. Those negative experiences are like weeds, they need to be pulled up by the root. By confronting the negative thoughts, it will stop your inner child from planting more weeds and cultivating them by its self-confirming thinking.

The inner child brain has a deterministic view of the world. Bringing your adult brain into the picture can differentiate between the flowers of free will and the weeds of determinism. In the upcoming exercise your rational thinking brain will bring an understanding of freewill through your dominant hand. Your emotional primitive deterministic brain will use your non-dominate hand. As you do this exercise, use your dominant hand to write the questions and answers.

Your inner child's logic may be that of a wounded or adaptive child. You are giving words to your unconscious thoughts and feelings. If you know where you lost your innocence or when you were wounded, you will get a clear picture of the child's belief. If you grew up adapting and slowly lost your authentic self, then you may get answers that need more clarification. Hearing from your inner child is a positive sign, which will help your wounded inner child's healing. This part of your journey is not construed to invite you to relive any abuse. Instead, the goal is to communicate with the younger part of you that was hurt or scared.

Remember, your inner child does not know your story once the dissociation happened or repression or created separation. You have knowledge and experiences that will be healing for your repressed memories and/or the dissociated part of yourself. You are the only one that can attend, nurture, or teach this child the truth. It is important to remember that you can have knowledge of healing or great spiritual wisdom, as an adult, but it will not be healing if it is not communicated with your inner child.

Writing with your non-dominate-hand (NDH) is an internal conversation that allows you to reconceptualize your past abuse with today's truth. This conversation will bring healing to the child within you. By performing the work needed, this healing will change the reflections in the mirrors around you, images projected from your past childhood beliefs, and the carried pain, shame, and fear of your heart.

## Exercise: Regression with Your Inner Child

*This is a regression exercise. Please note the following special instructions:*

- *Before regression work, move to a quiet place where you will not be disturbed by unexpected noises or activities.*
- *Answer prompts with both your DH and you NDH. Your DH represents your rational, adult mind; your NDH will bring forward the voice of your inner child.*
- *You may "draw a blank" on several prompts. This often happens when the inner child has not been listened to before. It will take time to establish trust. Keep taking positive action steps by continuing to attempt the questions.*
- *"Blanks" also occur when the mind creates an amnesic event around disassociation. You can work through this with additional time and attention to*

*the inner child.*

- *You will need support while doing this work. Have your therapist, minister, or other professional ready and available should you begin experiencing too much distress, either before, during, or after regression work.*
- *This work is best done with a supportive friend who will help build confidence and encouragement for your inner child.*

Allow yourself to get in a quiet place and do this NDH hand exercise.

You know what your inner child needs and wants from you. You may know where the dissociation happens, the age, and safe place of your inner child from the previous exercises. This is the time you get to bridge the dissociation gap created by your trauma. You are going to ask your inner child questions with your dominant hand (DH) and listen to the answers coming from your NDH and see if you believe your truth.

Stop and ask your questions that contain your present truths with your dominant hand (DH), the one you write with, then answer with your NDH. Trust your answers to be truthful. You can use these example questions, which also contain truth, or create your own questions to create healing for your inner child.

1) Little child, do you know I will not judge or critique you?
   DH-
   NDH-

2) Little child, do you believe I will keep you safe?
   DH-
   NDH-

3) Little child, how do you feel now?
   DH-
   NDH-

4) Little child, how old are you?
   DH-
   NDH-

5) Little child, do you trust me?
   DH-
   NDH-

6) Little child, do you know I will take care of you?
   DH-
   NDH-

7) Little child, where are you at now?
   DH-
   NDH-

8) Little child, do you think I will come back and talk to you?
   DH-
   NDH-

Performing this interactive mindful exercise may be more dynamic than your other exercises but can be the biggest gift you will have ever opened or given yourself. You will know if this writing and time with your inner child was meaningful if you moved past your historic negative view by making emotional contact, or if the child within you is no longer alone. I have had several clients use automatic writing to break their cycle of depression, anxiety or heal their corroded value or esteem, which opened the door for healthy self-love to themselves. They found healing by finding their child's innocence, spontaneity, creativity, and value. It was amazing to watch them defend themselves and set boundaries to protect the inner child when they had not done so previously.

These clients began to empathize for and with themselves. Empathy is a fertile foundation for any meaningful relationship. Once they learned to empathize with the child within, they could confront old beliefs. They began changing their thoughts and feelings toward themselves. It was amazing to see clients who hurt themselves, got lost in alcohol, or tried to fill the void with sex stop indulging and begin loving themselves. Their transformation came from the inside out. They changed their hard-wired beliefs about themselves by engaging the child within them.

This is one of many steps on the hero's journey. Your journey to the soul will be totally unique. Perhaps your inner journey thus far has been uneventful. Perhaps you are asking questions like, "What's wrong with me?" "Why didn't I hear from my child?" Please remember there is nothing wrong with you. The child may remain hidden due to not feeling safe.

You may need to ask yourself, "Would I be a safe and loving adult for my child within?" Take time to evaluate your environment to know if it is safe. Are the people around you safe? You will know internally what your answer is concerning your safety. If your inner child was sad or scared, then you are closer to healing. If your inner child spoke to you in this exercise, then that is a good sign that safety exists.

You may have. "Drawn a blank" while doing this exercise. You may say, "I asked the questions, and I didn't have one answer that came from my non-dominant hand." If this was your experience, you may have blocked listening to your inner child due to fear of facing past abuse issues. Blocks are normal if you have not been listening to yourself.

Here are several reasons for blocks.

- fear of the "unknown"
- a core belief that you should not exist or be important
- history of dissociation
- use of external indulgences
- increasing shame
- over use of defense mechanisms
- if you or the environment is not safe

These are reasons for "drawing a blank." If you experienced "nothing," continue taking steps on your journey.

Most of you will experience the child within you by doing this exercise. Your NDH answers are usually from the part of you which experienced the trauma or negative messages – the part of you that was protected through dissociation. Your inner child was the part that has been walled off by defense mechanisms, indulgences, or dissociation.

If your NDH wrote loving and insightful words, then you experienced your free child. This free child was dissociated from your dysfunction, trauma, or abuse. Some may call this part of you a wisdom figure. Do not be alarmed if your free child was younger or older than the time you experienced your trauma or abuse. Trauma of any degree can create dissociation by your adult or free child from your adaptive child.

Dissociation is "Segregation or separation of a group of mental processes so that their normal relationship to the rest of the personality is lost" (Benner, 1985, p.318). Separation or disassociation from an experience is literally instinctive; your mind separates itself from the body's experience of reality. Meaning, your sense of self leaves the body. If you disassociated, then your sense of self could be outside of your body during the unwanted experience. While your mind is outside of your body, usually from the vantage point of being above or from the sides, your dissociated self-watched the experience. When the threat (trauma) was "over," you re-associated with your body. The dissociated part that left your body may have amnesia of the event which means your free child or adult self would also have amnesia of the event while your adaptive or wounded child would remember the experience.

Like Ruth in the parable of the home, you may have amnesia, which is a partial or total loss of memory, a barrier used by your psyche to protect your free child and adult minds. Meaning that you will not likely remember the event from which you dissociated. Again, this amnesic barrier is a protection of your adult self. Dissociation is a God given defense that allowed you to survive dysfunction, trauma, or abuse. It is nothing like denial, rationalizing, minimizing, or other blind spots we carry. You spontaneously dissociated due to a need to survive. Protecting your mind is a gift, not a curse. You may find that your inner child, who went through the dysfunction, trauma, or abuse, may feel abandoned by you due to the dissociation.

If you dissociated, the wounded child carries your old memories and feelings, and may not know you. For this reason, you need to take time to listen to your inner child's story. Taking time to be patient and nurturing. Do not defend or try to "fix" your inner child because he/she is not broken. It is important for your adaptive child to be heard and attended. If you are listening to him/her, you may be the first person to hear about or be told about your history of dysfunction, taking a huge step toward healing. Remember, the goal is to reclaim this pushed down part of yourself by listening to his/her thoughts and feelings.

Your adaptive child, the one who learned to be strong, be perfect, please others, or try hard, needs nurturing. Your adult self can give your adaptive child the love, attention, and knowledge he/she desired by opening the window to your soul, changing all the images projected on the world around you. Your adaptive child will begin to see through your adult eyes, and you will stop looking through his/her eyes. Ruth began to look at her history of abuse and broke through "be strong" and "please others" drivers. She now hears life in her cracks and leaves her shutters open.

During my hero's journey, I experienced the essence of God. I found my inner child was hidden from my adult mind and used the defense mechanisms of suppression and repression, indulgences of alcohol, and God given dissociation to keep the dysfunction of my youth hidden from myself and others. Only through my hero's journey was I able to see what I was projecting onto others and believing my own self-deception. My inner child was wounded from the dysfunction and abuse of my home.

My inner child had little knowledge of my adult self. I had more awareness of him because I did not have the same thick amnesic barrier. I dissociated several times during the physical abuse from my father. I remember watching him yell and swing the belt that hit my body, dissociating from my body, which protected me from the severe physical and emotional pain. Many professionals believe an amnesic barrier will follow a dissociative experience. Some of you will have dissociated and have no memory of the trauma or abuse due to the amnesic barrier that exists.

I had little amnesia of my abuse growing up, which made my regression work or the hero's journey "easier." Even though I had memories of the experience seen through dissociation, my inner child had little knowledge of me and his life after the dissociation due to the amnesic barrier. Once my inner child learned my truth, he had a clear understanding of his value and knowledge of truth concerning the dysfunction of his childhood. As I experienced more of my inner child, I experienced more of my God given self or free child. My free child has given me a true picture of God while experiencing His unadulterated grace, mercy, and love. I no longer saw his grace, mercy, and love through my child's eyes.

It will be important for you to trust and know that you are not alone on this journey. Psalm 34 was a valuable truth on my journey. You need to trust the guidance of this book and rest in your support system. If your fear increases after a regression exercise, call a therapist in your area; set up a Skype session with one of the resources given at the back of this book, or speak with your pastor. This work is not for cowards.

Finally, I recommend doing this work with a friend because of the need for fellowship. You may bear your pain in isolation behind the walls of loneliness. "These walls that are intended to protect us from further pain only makes us prisoners of what we cannot, or will not, feel.... Communication is vitally linked to our bodies and is probably the single most important force that influences our health or lack of health, trauma and addiction" (Dayton, 2000, p.185).

You need the support and common experience to create a healing atmosphere. The feedback will help you confront your critical parent or perpetrators while moving through your inner amnesic barriers. Fellowship brings empathy from others that confronts your shame with truth and love. The most important thing about having support is the accountability of breaking the cycle of isolation that leads to the repression of your feelings. Charlie Whitfield (1989), author of several books on discovery and recovery for adult children of dysfunctional families says, "To heal our Child Within we have to share it with others" (p.95) You will find healing and blessings by creating your own support system.

**Remember: Regression Work Summary:**

- Before regression work, move to a quiet place where you will not be disturbed by unexpected noises or activities.

- Answer prompts with both your DH and you NDH. Your DH represents your rational, adult mind; your NDH will bring forward the voice of your inner child.

- You may "draw a blank" on several prompts. This often happens when the inner child has not been listened to before. It will take time to establish trust. Keep taking positive action steps by continuing to attempt the questions.

- "Blanks" also occur when the mind creates an amnesic event around disassociation. You can work through this with additional time and attention to the inner child.

- You will need support while doing this work. Have your therapist, minister, or other professional ready and available should you begin experiencing too much distress, either before, during, or after regression work.

- This work is best done with a supportive friend who will help build confidence and encouragement for your inner child.

# CHAPTER SEVEN

## SELF IMPROVEMENT NECESSARY (SIN)

"He who did not spare his own Son, but gave him up for us all--how will he not also, along with him, graciously give us all things?" Romans 8:32, NIV

**KEY POINTS:**

- As a Christian, God will never leave you nor forsaken you due to your sin.
- Sin does not mean you are evil; it means you have missed God's mark for you.
- Discipline or boundaries comes through honoring others' good and bad choices.

**Reflections:**

- Which of your sins keep you away from God?
- Which sin do you not forgive?
- As a believer in Jesus Christ, have you experienced God's true love and forgiveness?

## Welcome.

"Sin is a willful choice made by human creatures, and disfigures our esteem, social connections, and relationship with our Creator. In effect, it prevents our love of God, one another, and ourselves." Scott Hamilton

If you grew up hearing that SIN meant "self-improvement was necessary" to be happy, would you have a different response or reaction to this word? I feared the word "sin" for many years. I accepted Christ as my savior when I was eight years old, yet I still believed as an adolescent that if I sinned, I would be condemned by God. The Baptist church I attended taught that sin separated believers from God and God hates sin. I knew I was sinning more than I wanted to admit. I was waiting for God to condemn me to hell for eternity. Boy, was that bad theology. It took me years to spit out that poison from my early learning and knowledge of God.

It was my second year at seminary when I realized sin was a word that meant "missing the mark" (Romans 3:23). Paul uses the Greek word *hamartia* when referencing "sin," which means, "missing the mark" (Thayers Greek-English Lexicon of the New Testament, 1889, p.30). This meaning gave me a totally new theology. You see, I grew up shooting targets using BB guns, rifles, slingshots, and bow and arrows; I had missed the mark thousands of times. Then again, that did not stop me from shooting my guns or bows. I still practice today. I worked hard at aiming small and missing small.

When thinking back to my past on shooting targets, I remember my first recurve bow, a 55-pound bear bow. I could barely pull the string back in sixth grade. I had more problems hitting the target because it took all my strength to pull back the bow string, and still more strength to hold the string's tension while aiming at the target. Hitting the target was my goal, or at least was the goal for the first 10 to 15 shots.

Somewhere between the tenth and fifteenth missed shot, I became so enraged, I threw my bow about 70 feet. I said a couple of choice words and walked away. A couple days earlier I was so proud of that bow, but I had enough of missing the target. What added insult to injury was not only did I miss the mark, but also the target; I had to chase down and find each of my arrows that missed the target. After losing two of my arrows, I decided I had enough of my bow.

What made matters worse was my dad watched the entire episode. He was notorious for breaking my BB guns and burning my sling shots when I did not take care of them.

At that moment, he probably had good reason to burn this bow based on my actions. My first thought was, "oh *&^%." My second thought was. "Let him burn it, I really don't care." I would have helped him light the fire. While I did not want to hear what my dad thought, I knew I would hear it anyway. Before I could walk away, he yelled, "Go get that damn thing." I began to walk toward my bow, and the next thing I heard was, "Leave that Mother F**ker there!" I was ok with that decision because I was finished with target practice.

As I began heading to the house, I heard him call my name to come and talk to him. Which was the last thing I wanted to do, but not going was not an option. I walked over there, still boiling on the inside for not hitting the target. "Sit your ass down and think about it," he said. I did not want to "sit down and think about it." Around my house this meant being grounded to that chair, until I was told to leave. I was never told this rule, but after two or three whippings and hearing, "Where in the hell do you think you're going?" I put two and two together. This time, I sat down for about thirty minutes just stewing. Then he had me go get him a beer, which helped the situation. It gave me a reason to get up to release some tension.

I was around 11 years old and a little rebellious. I knew I needed to get away because the "silent treatment" did not do much for me. When I got back with his beer, he asked, "Well Robin Hood, are you finished with your bow?" Now usually this was a no-win situation for me because I knew I was in trouble either way. Still fuming, I replied, "Yeah, I gave it up for lent." I knew this was not the right answer but at the time, I really did not care. He sat back in his chair and began drinking his beer. After what seemed like an hour, he said, "That bow is a good bow and the man that made it was a good man. If you want to hit that target it will take a lot more misses."

Now, I did not realize my dad was trying to give grace while teaching a lesson. "I don't mind missing the target. I just hate chasing the arrows," I whined. After a moment, dad said, "Bullshit. You can't stand missing the target." I must give him credit; he was right about missing the target. He said, "Well, Robin, you can cry over all your misses or you can start by moving closer." Now, I had not thought about that option. I was probably 30 yards from the target. I got on our pitching mound and put the target where the catcher is normally in position. It just seemed logical at the time. I was thinking all this over when he said, "I would try 10 yard shots, if I missed a couple, I would stand on the damn thing if I have to and shoot it." Now looking back on things, this was one of the most valuable lessons and likely the most grace-filled memory I have of my dad.

As I got up, from the chair, I went to retrieve my bow and arrows. I decided to stand ten yards from the target. I hit the target with three out of my four arrows. That fourth arrow was shot over the pine tree, because I could not hold the string back long enough. I did not care about that fourth arrow because I hit the target three times. Looking back this was a valuable life lesson that helped me understand grace and sin.

God wants me to aim towards His will and not my own. He knows I will miss the mark and sometimes the target. I may miss the mark more than once, twice, or even three times, but God does not judge me for missing the mark, God does, however, encourage me to move closer to Him. I have sinned and missed God's mark a lot. I occasionally miss God's target totally. When we are missing the mark, I think God is asking us to "move closer."

God wants us to walk by faith and not by sight (2 Corinthians 5:7). God was neither angry at me nor did He shame me. I can just see him smiling and saying, "move close enough to hit the target." I am amazed at God's grace and unmerited favor for me. He does not want me to miss His mark because He loves me. Unfortunately, favor does not have the same meaning in our society as it did in the early church. If I told you God has unmerited regard, support, and approval of you, what would you think of this kind of favor? The bottom line is that God thinks highly of you. This kind of "favor" cannot be earned because it is "unmerited." I was freed that day in seminary. I know that Self Improvement is Necessary (SIN) for me because God wants the best for me and knows I will improve as I draw closer to Him, even when I miss the target. God grieves when I hurt. Self-Improvement is Necessary (SIN) for me to grow in faith and to be able to hit the mark.

You will occasionally miss the mark, maybe even the target, often yet; I trust doing so will move you closer to your target. If you are judging yourself, then you are likely moving away from your goal, which will decrease the likelihood of succeeding tomorrow. When you experience God's grace, you will move closer to your target; the closer you are, the greater your chances of hitting the mark. I hope you will look at your behavior because your inner child's thinking may fool you and have "stinking thinking" or be living from scripted beliefs. These learned beliefs about sin can move you away from your target while feeling increased shame and guilt.

My old scripts concerning sin were written by the church and an alcoholic father. Neither taught me much about God's unconditional love, grace, or mercy. Sin was an abomination against God and brought damnation. I viewed God as a judgmental, malevolent (mean), and punitive. Sin separated me from God and would bring punishment. I believed punishment was eternal damnation in a lake of fire. These scripted beliefs created fear and shame. It is important for you to assess your inner child's beliefs concerning sin. You need to ask yourself the following questions:

## Exercise: Examining Your Sin Script

*This is not a regression exercise. There are no special instructions included. Answer simply and directly in your journal.*

- What did I believe sin was while growing up?

- What were the consequences of my sin?

- Who were my role model(s) of God?

Your childhood theology is likely still running in your head, even today. Sin is not complicated; it is missing God's mark for you. It is out of love that God wants you to hit the mark. When you miss the mark by sinning God says, "Move closer." If your childhood beliefs are informed by this type of unconditional love, then you are blessed. How did you practice hitting God's mark? The key to hitting the mark is to look at your behavior.

Your behavior will speak louder than your words and will help you hit the mark more times than you miss. I had to literally move closer to the target when my internal critic was screaming, "I should be able to hit it from here." If I would have listened to my critic, I would have left my bow and never hit the target. I learned my true goal was to hit the target and not to be a great archer. On the other hand, my expectation was to hit the bull's-eye and not the target, and that got in the way of accomplishing my goal.

During my junior year at Texas Tech, I decided to take an archery class. On the first day of class, I noticed all the students standing at the furthest line from the target. The teacher noticed everyone behind the back line. This line was approximately thirty yards away from the target. He told us to put down our bows and to retrieve an arrow. We were then to walk to the target and stick the arrow in the bullseye, the red, center-most point of the target, before going to sit down. Then class began. The teacher taught us how to put an arrow on the bow string, close our eyes and visualize our hands on the bow, drawing the bow string back, holding the string on our anchor point, releasing the string with our fingers, and watching the arrow hit its mark.

After visualizing the arrow hitting the bullseye, he had us move closer and walk through all the steps again. He knew everyone was mentally shooting their bow from the back line. He had everyone walk to the frontline and said, "Look at the target." He went through the fact that most people will be more focused on the bow and arrow and not focused on what they were shooting at with the bow. Each of the circles measured 6" in diameter; he pointed at each one until he got to the bullseye. He said, "the bigger the target the bigger the bullseye" and "the closer you get to the target the bigger your target becomes." There was truth in what he said about the target and hitting the mark.

God's mark must be a huge target because God is huge. I know the importance of getting close to the target to hit the mark. I know how frustrating it is to miss the target, but I neither beat up myself for missing the target, nor do I throw my bow anymore. I hope you will stop, close your eyes, and visualize your target. Be aware of what you want for yourself and the child within you and what God wants for both of you. If you run into judgment about missing the mark, then you are listening to bad instruction. I hope you know this judgment or condemnation is not from God. This judgment is from your past critics and their beliefs about God. An easy way to not get caught up in your "crazy thinking" is to look at your behavior. Your behavior will highlight truth.

Presently, I ask my clients about their spiritual, mental, and emotional goals while on this healing journey to the Soul. Over and over, similar patterns have emerged. Sally was my first client. Her spiritual goal was "to have 30-minute quiet times each day;" her emotional goal was, "journal three times a week." Sally said, "I got mad because everyone interrupted me" when she was having her quiet time. Sally did not follow through with her emotional goal because "I didn't have time."

Mike's spiritual goal was to, "read a chapter a day from the Bible," and his emotional goal was to, "not look at pornography." Mikes' spiritual excuse was, "I didn't have time and couldn't stay focused." His emotional excuse was, "I looked at pornography the day I left, so I didn't think about my goal anymore because I blew it."

Arlando's spiritual goal was to, "pray every day before I go to work." His emotional goal was to "spend time talking to little 'Lando'." Arlando's spiritual excuse was, "I didn't have the time." His emotional excuse was, "I had too much going on." Are you seeing a pattern?

While time received the blame, it was not the problem at all. These clients used defense mechanisms of blame, minimizing, and rationalizing while making something else more important than themselves.

The truth was, they avoided their assignments and then unconsciously lied to themselves. They all figuratively threw their bow and mentally walked away. They were judging themselves and felt shame because of their perceived failure. I asked each of them to move closer to their target. Sally was to have a five-minute quiet time and to journal one line a day. Mike was to read one verse a day and not look at pornography one day during the week. Then, Arlando was to pray for thirty seconds a day and to speak to little Lando once a day.

The following week all of them hit their target several times. I could have looked at several spiritual reasons and psychological factors for their "failures;" but I chose to have them move closer to their target. Mike's happiness, joy, and relief were written all over his face. He had five days without looking at pornography, and Arlando's excitement was the same when little Lando, "spoke to me a lot." Yes, I believe their past beliefs and behaviors got in their way. Their defense mechanisms were covering their truths. I kept my eye on their targets and helped them to do the same. Their behavior told the story, so I changed their behavioral goals.

I remember what it was like to think I was Robin Hood when I had never picked up a bow. It is important to look at your present behavior to find out more truth about yourself. You might be living in denial without knowing it. You are not aware that these lies, driven by your early learning, will keep you from achieving your goals. Your behavior will lead you to your behavioral truths, which gives you the ability to confront your adult awareness. Like it or not, your actions speak louder than your words. You might be like the apostle Paul "I do not understand what I do. For what I want to do I do not do, but what I hate I do" (Romans 7:15 NIV).

Paul's choices and behavior bothered him. Paul's behavior or deeds were speaking truth that grieved him and God's heart. Paul used his "thorn in the flesh" (2Corn. 12:7 NASB) to get closer to God. In his writing to the church of Corinth Paul says, in vs. 8 "Concerning this I implored the Lord three times that it might leave me." And in vs. 9 "And he has said to me, 'My grace is sufficient for you, for power is perfect in weakness.' Most gladly, therefore, I will rather boast about my weaknesses, so that the power of Christ may dwell in me." Vs. 10 "Therefore I am well content with weaknesses, with insults, with distresses, with persecutions, with difficulties, for Christ's sake; for when I am weak, then I am strong" (2 Corinthians 12:8-10 NASB).

We are more like Paul than we realize. Christians hide their thorn(s) due to fear of judgment from others. Paul learned "when I am weak, I am strong." He was not proud of his weakness and "implored the Lord three times." (2Corn. 12:8 NASB) Paul most likely prayed more than three times about his weakness. Three was a whole, perfect, and complete number that represented God. Paul was speaking to those who knew that "three times" would be a meaningful and complete number to God. Paul was pulling out all the stops, so to speak. He knew God's "grace was sufficient."

You may struggle with a behavior that misses God's mark or an indulgence that takes you away from God, but just remember, God does not move away from you. God's love is steadfast (Psalms 36;5, 86;15), unconditional and will not be taken away. Lamentation 3:22 says, "The steadfast love of the Lord never ceases; his mercies never come to an end"

(Lamentations 3:22 ESV).

Hebrews 13:5 NASB says, "I will never desert you, nor will I ever forsake you." I find the word "never" to be a long time. Many pastors and parents hint or threaten that God will turn away or will leave you because you have sinned against Him. This is not true! The book of Hebrews is confronting the Jewish Community and the leaders of the church, the high priests, that were following the law of Moses and not the teaching of Jesus (Hebrews 3:1), "NEVER will I leave you; never will I forsake you."

Hold on to this, especially if you have missed God's mark. God is love. God is your loving Father or daddy. God will discipline you, as any loving father, because He loves you. Remember, this is discipline and not punishment (James1:2-4; Proverbs 3:11-12). The book of Hebrews deals with God's discipline by saying, "you have forgotten the exhortation which is addressed to you as sons," My Son, Do not regard lightly the discipline of the Lord, nor faint when you are reproved by him, for those whom the Lord loves he disciplines, and he scourges every son whom he receives. It is for discipline that you endure; God deals with you as with sons; for what son is there whom his father does not discipline" (Hebrews 12:5-7 NASB). God's discipline is love based, just as you discipline those you love.

If you love your children, spouse, or friend you will give them responsibility for their behavior, and later, holding them accountable; a form of discipline, which is needed to increase responsibility. Having no accountability will harm you or those you love. Proverbs 23:13-14 (NASB) says; "Do not hold back discipline from the child, although you strike him with the rod, he will not die. You shall strike him with the rod and rescue his soul from Sheol." This strong emphasis of discipline comes across as punitive punishment, which is drastic. Discipline will "rescue the soul from Sheol." Some scholars believe it is a realm of hell that extends to this plain of earth dealing with the "realm of the dead" (*The Interpreters Dictionary of the Bible*, Vol. 1, 1962, p.787).

Notice the "soul," or the seat of your innermost being, is rescued. I strongly dislike physical abuse. I could even say I hate physical abuse or harming children, or anyone else. You can "strike," singular tense, and still provide discipline. Discipline is not punishment or abuse. As it states in Proverbs 13:24 (NASB), "Whoever spares the rod hates their children, but the one who loves their children is careful to discipline them." Rod in Hebrew comes from "Shebet," which literally means stick. A stick was used for punishing, riding, measuring, or walking.

The rod, or *stick* of discipline, as noted in the Old Testament, could help you move towards your personal goals or spirituality. Your measuring stick needs to be God's discipline. This discipline comes from love, not anger. Have you ever seen anyone beaten or disciplined by one *strike*? It takes great control for a parent to discipline with one strike. The parent will need to educate and speak to the child to make the strike count. Can you imagine how much control it would take to use the rod only once?

It is important to recognize that this strike was with a "rod," which is not done with the hand. The Psalmist was intentional about the rod, which is neutral. Your hand, open or closed, is personal and has a greater ability to hurt your child or *loved one* emotionally and mentally. I am using loved ones because I have had several men and women who strike their spouses, believing it to be righteous because they are "saving the souls" of their spouses. If you read the above statement and believe that there is a righteous reason to strike your spouse, then you are "missing God's best."

Recently, I have seen more physical abuse of men by their wives than I saw in my first two decades of clinical practice. When I spoke with the wives about their abusive behavior, these women justify, rationalize, and minimize their physical assaults, just as their male counterparts had done for years. Again, Proverbs 13:24 refers to children not spouses.

The "child" in this scripture would be less than 12 years old. In ancient times, a boy in the Jewish culture was no longer considered a child after twelve years of age; they were men. If you remember, Jesus' first documented conflict with his parents (Luke 2:41) was when he went into the temple and did not tell them. Going to the tabernacle was one of the first rites of passage for a Jewish boy which meant he was no longer a child. Even in our culture when a child turns thirteen, they are no longer a child but an adolescent.

The psalmist was speaking of "rescue his soul from Shoel," which speaks to an eternal or spiritual realm. As a child of God your Soul is precious and holy (1Peter 2:5). Your soul is your innermost being which God filled with the Holy Spirit and redeemed through Christ blood (Ephesians 1:7). God wants your Soul, the seat of your affections and will, protected with discipline. Your Soul or spirit is made up of thoughts, feelings, and experiences which make you who you are. Your Soul is your mind, logic, and emotions. Yet, it is more dynamic than your beliefs or personality.

Your soul's essence is to relate to God. Spiritually it is your Holy of Holies. From a somewhat secular view, in "The Care of the Soul; A Guide for Cultivating Depth and Sacredness in Everyday Life" by Thomas Moore, Moore says: "There is nothing neutral about the soul. It is the seat and the source of life. Either we responded to what the soul presents in its fantasies and desires, or we suffer from this neglect of ourselves. The power of the soul can hurl a person into ecstasy or into depression. It can be creative or destructive, gentle, or aggressive. Power incubates within the soul and then makes its influence move into life as the expression of soul. If there is no soulfulness, then there is no true power, and if there is no power, then there can be no true soulfulness" (2009, p. 129).

This "source" of life is God. Your Soul is more than a source of energy for life. Your soul's "Essence of Life," has the need for discipline from God. It is the desire to be filled by something greater than itself. Your Soul is untamed and needs direction. It wants and craves meaning but does not know how to get there by itself. I know you may not understand or even know what your soul needs. If I were to ask you, does your Soul need direction? What might your answer be? Would it be a yes or a no? You might say yes, it wants direction but not discipline or correction.

If you are going in the wrong direction, how would you want to be corrected, educated, or disciplined? I believe, like all children we need discipline for stability and security. You need it too. You need yet may not want discipline. Discipline directs self-improvement which is necessary for growth. Your inner child needs and craves discipline, and you will need to provide discipline for the child for mental growth and spiritual wellness.

If growth is your destination, will you get there by going in the wrong direction? The answer is no. Then, why is it hard to get education, rebuke or discipline for your wrong choice or direction? The answer is, your Soul needs, craves, and wants to be happy, whole, and complete while not knowing how to get to your destination. Your soul was separated from its maker due to the knowledge of good and evil. Freewill has a choice. This choice is a split in the road between heaven and hell, good and evil or natural and the supernatural.

The soul was and is not prepared for this knowledge of good and evil. For this reason, God told Adam and Eve not to eat from the Tree of Knowledge of good and evil. This knowledge was neither bad nor the problem. The problem came with the choice called Freewill, which was used to eat from the Tree of Good and Evil. Eating of this fruit gave Adam and Eve awareness as to how to gratify themselves that was not of God. Unfortunately, they were unaware of the consequences of evil. Because of this choice, they started to hear, see, feel, and experience all desires from the flesh that were not of God.

Lucifer who is known as Satan. Yes, the demonic (Satan) entered the world. I never liked the word demonic because it sounded scary. Demonic does not mean demon possessed or following Satan. It means the behavior resembles the characteristics of a demon or evil spirit that is not of God. Missing God's mark allows us to use defense mechanisms, internal and external indulgences/addictions to hide our God given self. Our authentic selves are covered by critical messages, old negative tapes or thoughts that are not of God. Yes, this creates the feeling of shame and fear that is not of God. Are they demonic? Yes, they all take you away from your innocence and security that was covered by love or from God. The Fall created a separation from God due to the knowledge of evil.

Through this separation, the soul gained knowledge and had emotions that were neither of nor from God. Because of this separation from God, the soul was left with a void that could be filled with the desires of the flesh. Mankind's desires of the flesh left the soul in search of its creator. This will be true for your soul today. Proverbs 13:4 says," The soul of the sluggard craves and gets nothing, while the soul of the diligent is richly supplied" (ESV translations).

This "wisdom literature" speaks to how you need to feed the soul. The above passage will be the same for a believer and nonbeliever. This literature brings wisdom to guide and direct your paths for better choices and to bring biblical wisdom for your soul. One difficult part in Missing the Mark will be hearing you are Missing the Mark. The "sin" of being a" sluggard" gets you nothing, while being" diligent" in pursuing God will get you "richly supplied." This literature will give you direction and will become more powerful as you experience the Word of God and not your so-called natural "cravings."

When your soul was not filled by God or His love, there was a strong craving to fill this void. In Galatians 5;17,18 it says, "For the desires of the flesh are opposed to the [Holy] Spirit, and the [desires of the] Spirit are opposed to the flesh (godless human nature); for these are antagonistic to each other [continually withstanding and in conflict with each other], so that you are not free but are prevented from doing what you desire to do. But if you are guided (led) by the [Holy] Spirit, you are not subject to the Law (AMP). Growing up in the flesh (not God) you filled the void of your soul and mind with desires of the flesh. Your soul was created in the image of the sacred and holy which was created from the beginning in the image of God (Genesis 1:27). As a Christian the void was filled by God's Spirit, yet the work of cleaning out all your inner child's learning will take your discipline.

The care of your soul will need discipleship from its maker, God. It will be important to remember: "But knowing their thoughts, he said to them, 'Every kingdom divided against itself is laid waste, and every city or household divided against itself will not stand.'" (*Matthew 12:25 AMP*). This division is knowing what you need to fill your Soul, i.e., good versus evil or desires of the flesh versus God's will.

There will be a split between the image of God and man. The split has created conflict for you mentally, emotionally, and spiritually. The spilt will make your life difficult. You will neither know the road to take nor will you want to be told you are on the wrong road. You will do everything in your power to avoid your inner child's shame and fear while craving structure and discipline. If you want knowledge of how to attend to the sacred you must be open to God's direction and reproof. The key will be to discipline, educate, correct and/or teach yourself and others how to honor your soul.

The root word for discipline, in Greek, is *Paideia* derived from the root word *paidos* means child in Greek (p.473.) All children need discipline, instruction, education, correction, and exhortation. God sees you as His child and wants to teach and praise you. Discipline needs to be a positive and not a negative. Discipline does not need to scare you; it is God's unconditional love for you.

It is not an accident that God calls His children, "joint heirs of Christ," and uses *Pias* as the root word for discipline in the Greek. In the Old Testament, the Hebrew word used in Proverbs 23:13 is *Musar*, meaning discipline and correction. In the New Testament, the root word *Pias* or child in Greek shows the heart of God and the context for the word. Discipline comes from being God's disciple or child. You need to be taught and corrected without being harmed. You need to hear the cries of your heart while experiencing your Heavenly Father's Love. Thus, you will begin to look through the window of your soul.

At one time, I would have seen the "rod" of reproof or discipline as abuse. I grew up hearing the familiar phrase "spare the rod and spoil the child." I received abuse under the flag of spiritual correction. Many children grew up with parents that abused them physically and spiritually due to poor theology. This abusive type of "discipline" scared me too. I thought not sparing the rod was normal based on my experience of my father. Later, I found out his discipline was called abuse. God's discipline and reproof has *never* left physical or emotional marks on my Soul. The sad thing is, my sin had natural consequences that hurt me and grieved God.

God grieves, like any loving parent, for a child that gets hurt breaking the rules. As a child of God, you need to know that it hurts Him when you are mistreated. You may have been hurt by spiritual authority figures at home or in the church; this would fall under spiritual abuse. "Spiritual abuse can occur when a leader uses his or her spiritual position to control or dominate another person. It often involves overriding the feelings and opinions of another, without regard to what will result in the other person's state of living, emotions or spiritual well-being" David Johnson and Jeff VanVonderen, *The Subtle Power of Spiritual Abuse* (Minneapolis, MN: Bethany House Publishers, 1991), 20-21). Spiritual abuse "is performed through some 'spiritual' means and damages a person spiritually" (1991, p.13).

A lot of spiritual abuse happens with words and is not physical in nature. Scripture misuse is used to manipulate your behavior or to discount your thoughts and feelings. A spiritual wound can keep you from experiencing God's best for yourself. Spiritual discipline is not abuse because it edifies and builds you up.

Discipline and correction are necessary for growth. They teach you how to feed and care for your Soul. Caring for your inner child will require you to listen to your desires, feelings, and thoughts as you take God's discipline and/or instructions seriously. You need to hear the cries of your heart/Soul while experiencing your Heavenly Father's love. Looking through God's Word allows you to see through the windows of your Soul, helping you deal with your present reality while becoming mindful of your current thoughts and feelings. Unfortunately, even as a Christian, you will look through the mirror of the soul that was filled with the desires, teachings, and experiences of the flesh. It will be difficult to be aware, present, or holy looking through the lenses of your past.

Healing of your Soul is derived from allowing spiritual discipline to come through God's Word, the leading of the Holy Spirit, or through proclamation of God's Word; you will become aware of yourself, others, and God. The hunger for the Divine and not the flesh intensifies (Psalms 119:20; Isaiah 26:9). If you filled your temple with the Divine, your Soul would rest.

Jesus said," I *am the way, and the truth, and the life. No one comes to the Father except through me." (John 14:6 ESV)* If your Soul is cleansed by Christ's blood you will know the way to His Father. As a Christian, you filled your Soul's sanctuary with the Holy Spirit. You have the direction of the Holy Spirit and the Word of God. His word will direct your path and fill your Soul. As a Christian you have a greater chance to look through the windows of your Soul. Yet you will still need discipline to know how to direct your choices concerning good and evil in your life.

Evil comes through the "father of lies" (John 8:44) and truth comes from God. True freedom can be found in God's Word. Jesus said," If you continue in My word, then you are truly disciples of Mine; and you will know the truth, and the truth will make you free." (John 8:31-32 NASB). Being free spiritually can be a springboard to heal mentally and emotionally. Understanding the difference between truth and lies is difficult because we live in a world that has missed the mark.

I had a client say to his wife, "I can't do different if I don't know different." Several years later, I saw this same couple in a family session with their son who turned to his dad and said, "I can't do different if I don't know different." Is it not interesting how the inside workings of the family transcend down to the children? Discipline allows you to "know different." It depends on your teachers that instructed, educated, and directed you growing up. You may not have heard of sin because it has been cloaked behind other secular words.

In our culture the words for sin have been replaced by "emotional problems, addiction, negative thoughts or struggles." What is the reason for the changes? Sin became emotional problems, addictions or struggles to take away personal responsibility and accountability to God. Sin is not a four letter or dirty word. Christ concord these problems or sin.

My seminary professor, Dr. Wayne Oats, believed sin was not used in our society because sin was a religious term and linked to God. This is sad because behavior problems, struggles, and/or indulgences take God out of the healing dynamic. These behavioral problems are problems with the heart, attitude or habits that cover the Soul. I will refer to these problems as sin. They miss God's mark for you and Self-Improvement is Necessary (SIN). The key is to understand the nature of the healing power of the Holy Spirit and God's Word. Sin is following fleshly desires and not God's desires for you. Fleshly desires create consequences, missing God's best for you.

Placing your sin at God's feet will decrease behavioral problems and struggles. These sins of the flesh can be "healed" by three God given virtues: faith, hope and love. The greatest of these virtues is love. Love yourself, your neighbor, and your God.  It is possible to be freed from sin but will need God's help to be freed from your indulgences and struggles. Being freed can be seen through the eyes of obedience. Obedience is another scary word for most people.

Most of my clients think obedience is scary especially using it in God talk. Obedience to God is an act of faith (Romans 1:5,16;26). Faith, in what is said, in this case, in God's Word. Obedience in Greek is *hupakoé* which means "compliance or submission" (Thayer's Greek-English Lexicon of the New Testament, 1886, p.637). Compliance with God's Word will purify your Soul. I love 1 Peter 1:22 & 23 which says," Since you have in obedience to the truth purified your souls for a sincere love of the brethren, fervently love one another from the heart, 23. for you have been born again not of seed which is perishable but imperishable, that is, through the living and enduring word of God" (NASB). Is this verse saying, "obedience to the truth purified your soul?" The Truth is in believing in the "living and enduring Word of God" and is "imperishable."

Ask yourself, have I been compliant and obedient to God's Word? If you have dysfunctional behavior, emotional issues, and overuse indulgences, then you may struggle with the issue of obedience. Even reading the word may make you feel judged. You may want to rebel when you hear words like obedience or submission due to your past authority figures. It is normal to not talk about your sin with others.

I wish there were another common word for "sin" like poison, bump or hick-up. Just the association that you may have when someone says "sin" is judgment and condemnation. What image/face would you put on God with the word sin? I believe the most recognized verse in the bible is John 3:16 and the one most missed is John 3:17 which says; "For God did not send his Son into the world to condemn the world, but in order that the world might be saved through him" (John 3:17 ESV).

Now you may want to hold in your heart, "For God did not send his Son into the world to condemn" me. The sacred is a love letter and not a seal of death for those that "believes in him (Jesus) should not perish but have eternal life" (John 3:16 ESV). This is a sacred and holy gift from God. The only thing called for is your acceptance or faith in Jesus Christ. He came "to save" your life: this does not condemn you. You may want to hear God's Love when He speaks of sin. God Loves you so much, he sent His Only Son to die for you. That is love, not condemnation.

My client, a recovering methamphetamine addict, totally believed that God loved him. He told me "the best road map to God was sin." I gave his theology some thought and asked more questions. I asked him the next week what he meant by "the best road map to God was sin?" He smiled and said, "if my right is wrong then I know left is right. I just turn left when my right is wrong in God 's." He had his way to God and made the path simple. I do not believe his path would have been so simple if he feared being condemned for his sins. He did not throw his bow and walk away from God, he turned and moved closer to his target.

Simplifying your sins by performing the opposite of obedience to God's Word will lead you down a path of destruction and result in death. Obedience to God's Truth will purify and bring healing for your Soul. Now, if you have a past filled with "sin" or you are totally "corrupt" you will be purified, cleansed and forgiven of all unrighteousness, if you believe Christ died for your sins. You can also stay healthy by being obedient to God's Word or Truth.

It is amazing how arrogant we are as humans when it is concerning the holy. I had clients who would constantly tell me what was wrong with the Bible. They neither believed nor accepted the Word of God on God's terms. They would accept parts of God's Word, while telling me what parts they would not accept because it meant they had to change. Instead, they wanted God to fit into their own image and expectations. They did not want to accept His expectation. Here lies the problem. They could not be obedient to God because it was on their terms. This usually created tension, defiance, or a power struggle with God. Anytime there is a power struggle both parties lose.

You are freed or cleansed from ALL sin and unrighteousness by accepting Jesus Christ, God in the flesh, as your personal Savior. In Roman 6:22, 23 (NASB) Paul says, "But now having been freed from sin and enslaved to God, you derive your benefit, resulting in sanctification, and the outcome, eternal life. For the wages of sin is death, but the free gift of God is eternal life in Christ Jesus our Lord." Now if you have accepted Jesus as your personal savior, you are "freed" and "sanctified." Does this sound like condemnation or love for you by your Heavenly Father? Having this "free gift" comes "in Christ Jesus our Lord." The small preposition "in" is the key, which cleanses you, without punishing you from all the time you have missed the mark or sinned.

Let us go back to the small "in" of Romans 23, it created wars with other nations and religions. It is "in" Christ Jesus, not anything or anybody else. This really sounds judgmental and exclusive, doesn't it? It sounds exclusive because it is "in" Jesus, and not in Buddha, Ala or John Smith. You may not want to accept the power of living in Christ due to your love for others and/or you may not want others punished for believing in other gods or do not want to judge those with different spiritual beliefs. Exclusivity can cause many to hide their belief in God or reject God all together.

It is difficult to access God or spiritual healing if you are denying His Word. Many Christians will create deception by denying, compartmentalizing, or rationalizing their knowledge of God because of this exclusivity, and they are afraid of condemnation of non-believers of Christ Jesus. Disbelieving others will be punished by having eternal life in hell.

Remember, you are "in" Christ Jesus." "In" Jesus, you are freed and cleansed from all unrighteousness. It will be difficult to be a disciple if you are not "in" Christ; it would be even more difficult to have obedience to God's Word without accepting that Jesus is the way, truth and life. How do you get to God without being "in" or going through Jesus Christ? You do not.

This is not judgement but resting in God's Word. There would be more believers in Christ if God's Word were more inclusive. It is not inclusive of other ways to get to God because God's redemption comes only through Him. There was only one creator and one way to conquer sin and death. If there was another way God would not have sent His only begotten Son. He would not have become flesh and blood to become a sin offering.

Many believe Jesus was God incarnate or God in the flesh when he was on earth. I ascribe to this belief that Christ will bring healing on a supernatural level. The supernatural brings God's power and healing into the natural. To bring the supernatural in to the natural only comes through Christ Jesus because through Christ you will bring God's power in your life and the Holy Spirit into you. The Spirit of God will comfort, intercede, and bring fruit of supernatural healing into your life. This *Soul Food* will be dealt with in the next chapter.

Once you are "in" God, He will never abandon you. The gift of having healthy discipline from God does not need to embark on fear of abandonment. God will be patient, long suffering, and kind in his Love (Romans 2:4). He wants to hear your pains and fears because He loves you so much. You will need to face your fear of God to experience Him fully. Remember, "There is no fear in love; but perfect love casts out fear, because fear involves punishment, and the one who fears is not perfected in love" (1 John 4:18 NASB). God says "fear involves punishment" and is not of God because God cast out all fear. God's essence is love and has unconditional love for you.

## Punishment versus Discipline

As a child, you may have been punished and not disciplined. Punishment is being penalized, mistreated, or abused. Jesus is a good example of being punished. Jesus suffered abuse for acknowledging that he was the Son of God and the "I am the I am" which is saying he was God. In the Gospel of John, chapter I and 14:1-14, there is good testament to this fact. He was also a sacrificial lamb sent by God to die for your sins. Jesus was accused in an illegal trial before the Sanhedrin (Matthew 27:1-4) and given a death penalty. Leaders of the church were performing true spiritual abuse. Christs' punishment was being nailed on a cross and suffering death by conquering sin and death.

He suffered the nails of punishment as we all do. Christ endured spiritual punishment to set us free of sin. Your emotional, physical, sexual, or spiritual punishment came at the hands of others and was no fault of your own. Your inner child may have experienced nails of punishment by loved ones, sexual abuse by a family friend or bullying at school or work. These types of nails hurt you mentally and emotionally. The cost mentally might have led to self-doubt, distrust of others and false guilt. The emotional cost was usually hurt, fear and shame.

The child's memories of the nails can be haunting and usually the adult medicates with indulgence, self-defeating behaviors, and automatic negative thoughts. Each nail can take life and happiness away from you by creating mental disorders and physical illnesses. These sins of others may have moved you away from your target. You too may have thrown your bow. Lift your veil of denial, rationalizing and minimizing, and you can heal those wounds. The inner child and your adult self can find healing from a natural and supernatural source, removing the nails of injustice by being aware of your past punishment.

No wound can heal if the nails are still buried in your heart or mind. You can live life like you have no history of your nails of abuse. This lie will stop you from living healthy and being whole. Your inner child will act out being wounded, while the object in your wound is ignored. When you acknowledge the injustice, you can pull out the foreign body that created the wound.

The deepest wounds can be suffering injustices at the hands of well-intended people. The greater the love - the greater the wound of the injustice. The result of this injustice may have led to severe depression, PTSD, anxiety disorders or use of indulgences. One of my clients said, "I don't need enemies when I have people that love me controlling my life." The key was the controlling.

Discipline, instruction, or correction comes through honoring other's good and poor choices. Guidance and instruction take time, energy, and attention, which many parents do not perform today. It is easier to say, "Do what I say, not as I do." "Shame on you." "I don't want to hear what you think." Then they give severe corporal punishment to create order. Hearing critical words or actions causes you to lose yourself.

I hope you do not minimize your inner child's abuse because it was not "really bad" or "others had it worse." Minimizing and rationalizing are not of God. These are ways to deceive yourself while avoiding removal of the nails of injustice in your life. God cares about your paper cut and your amputations; He loves you with all His heart. Your heavenly Father knows the hairs on your head, and they are numbered. In Matthew 10:29- 31 it says, "Are not two sparrows sold for a cent? And yet not one of them will fall to the ground apart from your Father. But the very hairs of your head are all numbered. Do not fear; you are more valuable than many sparrows" (Matthew 10:29-31 NASB).

I hope you experience or know the love of God; this love is not mystical. It was modeled by Christ and revealed by the one who created you. Romans 8:1-4 says, "Therefore there is now no condemnation for those who are in Christ Jesus. For the law of the Spirit of life in Christ Jesus has set you. For what the Law could not do, weak as it was through the flesh, God did: sending His only Son in the likeness of sinful flesh and as an offering for sin, He condemned sin in the flesh, so that the requirement of the Law might be fulfilled in us, who does not walk according to the flesh, but according to the Spirit" (NASB). Your inner child needs to know neither you nor God will condemn the childlike logic of experience.

God will have "no condemnation" when you bring your struggles of pornography, workaholism, gluttony, or other sins of the flesh to Him. That is a promise from God. Condemnation is the heart of punishment, fueled by judgement, and love is the heart of discipline fueled by mercy. Punishment closes the window of the Soul for your inner child and opens the door to shame and guilt, while discipline opens the door to integrity and character. It is important to know that Christ's sacrifice confronted all legalism that gave authority to the law.

The Spirit of God through Christ's sacrifice has "condemned sin in the flesh." Christ's sacrifice conquered all sin of the flesh. Meaning sin and condemnation of the flesh is finished for Christians. Now, if that does not give you and the child within your freedom from your historic fear of being condemned by God nothing will give you freedom or peace. If God does not give your sin power what is the reason you give sin the power to shame you? Doing so divides your inner child and God.

Fear of God's condemnation may stem from what you were taught as a child by your Pastors, Priests and Rabbis. They may have preached that sin will separate you from God, or worse, will lead to damnation by God. This would be true for those that reject God's salvation through His Son, Jesus Christ. If you continue reading in Romans, keeping the context of this chapter, you will see Romans 8:38, 39 says: "For I am convinced that neither death, nor life, nor angels, nor principalities, nor things present, nor things to come, nor powers, nor height, nor depth, nor any other created thing, will be able to separate us from the love of God, which is in Christ Jesus our Lord" (NASB). Nothing will "separate" you from the love of God. It is sad that many parents teach their children to fear God's judgment, condemnation, and punishment, especially if they are Christians. Many parents teach of an angry and vindictive God to control their children. This would be labeled as spiritual abuse and would leave many scared of God.

Are you able to hear an angry tone in these verses? What could be missing is the tone of the story because the words are clear. Remember, scripture in the old and New Testament was passed down from generation to generation in an oral tradition. The stories had tones and the experience of the story tellers' relationship with God. The tone came from the attitude of the one that is telling the story. The words like obedience, submission or sin had a story with them. You may have read the Word of God and felt judged or you may have heard the attitude of those that taught you and not the tone or compassion of God.

Can you hear compassion or judgment? You may be hearing judgment based on your old emotional experience and the inner child's emotional logic. Those nails of injustice will color your view of compassion or judgment. Bring this truth to your inner child by journaling and dwelling in your temple through regression. These forms of being introspective will give you the ability to clean the emotional lens of your soul by bringing your present truth to your inner child. You will be able to stop your old emotions of hurt, fear, and shame from coloring your present view of yourself, others, and God. Giving you the ability to make your own choice about yourself, others, and God.

It is difficult to differentiate between punishment and discipline if you grew up receiving punishment. You believe it to be discipline. How would you know any different? I did not know the difference until I consciously reflected on my discipline growing up by taking time to reflect on my history of punishment by my abusive father. He was neither a good model of discipline nor God. I had a client, Matt, that had a similar story. Matt's discipline was normal for his father and mother.

## My Story: Matt

Matt was a little boy struggling with school and was "out of control." Matt was almost 10 years old and a little "chubby." Being a little overweight is normal for little boys and girls getting close to puberty. Matt had "great parents." He continued talking about his mom and dad, and then his tone changed when he started speaking of his problem with wetting the bed. Matt would wet the bed and his dad would whip him "hard." His dad took this a step further by making him put his sheets out in front of the house where all his friends could see "how lazy you really are." "He calls me pissy pants when my friends come over." When Matt would forget to do his chores, he would get his "butt busted." Matt had low self-esteem due to his guilt and shame.

Matt came in wearing long pants on a day the temperature was 103. Matt was "cold." Matt told me he got "busted" for being "lazy." I asked Matt, "What was the reason you were busted and what were you busted with, last night." Matt replied "I think a coat hanger. I was pulled out of bed and do not remember." I asked Matt to show me the marks that a coat hanger would leave because that was not normal discipline. Matt raised his pant leg, he had red whelps with blood leaking out of some of them. I told Matt I was glad that his dad only hit his legs. He looked at me kind of stunned. "What?" Matt stood up and lifted his shirt which had the same weeping red marks on his back and one on his neck. I asked Matt to go get his mom and dad in the waiting room. I informed Matt that he needed to stay in the waiting room. Matt asked, "Did I do something wrong?" I told Matt he was a super kid and of course he did not do anything wrong. Matt got up and left to get his parents.

Matt's parents came in and the first thing his dad said, "Can you fix that boy?" I replied, "Matt is a great little boy and quite normal." His Dad was shocked, and his Mom smiled as she turned away from her husband. I let them know Matt's weight gain was normal for a child starting puberty. I informed them that I did not know if the bed wetting were a problem or a symptom of a problem, but it could be fixed. His Dad looked curious. His Dad sat up and asked, "How can I help him because discipline doesn't work? He is head strong."

I told them that bed wetting was a non-voluntary act. Kegel exercises strengthen the sphincter muscles that start and stop the flow of urine. He would need to change some bedtime behaviors such as not drinking liquids

30 to 45 minutes before bed and urinating before bedtime. Dad said, "That's it?" I told them we had a bigger problem, and I could tell both were visibly concerned. They both responded in unison, "What?" I told them that I knew they loved Matt and would do nothing to intentionally hurt him, but the fact that Matt was suffering from what was called Post-traumatic Stress Disorder, or PTSD.

In the Diagnostic Criteria of the DSM-1V there are several signs of PTSD, which are:

- re-current and intrusive distressing thought about the event
- re-current distressing dreams of the event
- acting or feeling as if the traumatic event were recurring
- intense psychological distress at exposure to internal or external cues symbolize or resembles an aspect of the traumatic event
- physiological reactivity on exposure to internal or external cues symbolize or resemble an aspect of the traumatic event

Persistence avoidance of stimuli associated with the trauma and numbing of general responsiveness as indicated by three or more of the following:

1) effort to avoid thoughts, feelings, or conversations associated with the trauma
2) effort to avoid activities, places or people that arouse recollection of the trauma
3) inability to recall an important aspect of the trauma
4) marked diminished interest or participation in significant activities
5) feeling of detachment or estrangement from other
6) restrict range of affect (e. g., unable to have loving feeling)
7) sense of a foreshortened future

Persistent symptoms of increase arousal as indicated by two or more of the following:

(1) difficulty falling or staying asleep
(2) irritability or outburst of anger
(3) difficulty concentrating
(4) hypervigilance
(5) "exaggerated startle response" (p.209-211).

Matt had problems with fear, worry, sadness, anger, and feeling alone. He felt as if people were looking down on him. His low self-worth was complicated because he had decreased trust in others, especially his dad. Matt had behaviors such as self-harm to himself and aggression at school towards peers and authority figures. I informed mom and dad of Matt's thoughts. He had increased dread of going to sleep with intrusive thoughts during the day. Dad quickly moved to Matt's poor grades. Dad was educated about Matt's intrusive thoughts, which decreased his interest in school and sports.

The last thing highlighted was Matt's detachment from himself and others, along with his restricted behavior having a narrower range of emotional expression than would be expected. Matt's Dad was inquisitive about the reason for his son's PTSD. He was informed that it was because of his punishment on his son. His punishment for Matt's wetting of his bed was abusive. Matt's Dad was in disbelief. He could not believe he caused his son's trauma. Matt's dad had authentic sadness and sorrow. "I only wanted him to grow up. I did not want his friends making fun of him." I informed mom and dad that Child Protective Services would be called, and dad would need to agree to therapy. Dad was visibly upset and agreed to therapy.

Matt did the Kegel exercises and stopped drinking fluids 45 min before bedtime. His enuresis or bedwetting stopped completely. He could tell his dad about his hurt, scare, anger and shame during his dad's 5th session. The signs of PTSD had already begun to cease. Matt and his dad were educated on discipline. Matt was surprised to know that his dad had the same problem with wetting the bed growing up. He was punished by his Dad in the same ways. His Dad had increased shame for his own bed wetting which he medicated with alcohol. Matt's Dad did not know he was abusing his son; yet, Matt had all the signs of PTSD. I saw him about 12 years later; he was doing well.

Many people believe that Posttraumatic Stress Disorder is only from going to war. Most of my clients that suffered from PTSD were sexually and physically abused, yet you may have signs due to "normal" punishment. Remember, I had the same signs of PTSD as Matt when I was fired from my job.

If you, like so many others, had "good parents," you may have been punished and did not know of the emotional, mental, and physical cost because it was "*normal*" to you or you "deserved it." The cost was the same, no matter if your parents were good or bad parents. If chaos was "normal" then you will look and expect chaos, creating emotional and mental costs to your quality of life and to those around you.

Discipline, not punishment, adds to your stature and does not take away from your life. Remember, discipline comes from the Greek word *Paideia.* Its root word is "child," which means "to instruct" in Greek. Discipline is meant to build you up while educating and to speak truth in love to edify or build up others. In Ephesians 4:15 it says, "speaking the truth in love, we are to grow up in all aspects into Him who is the head, even Christ" (Ephesians 4:15 NASB).

"Growing up in all aspects" is from speaking truth in love which is a form of discipline. If you:

- heard screaming, yelling or profanity
- received a physical spanking that left bruises, marks, or broken bones

Or

- received words that tore at your heart like stupid, worthless or slut, then it was not

discipline. This was verbal, physical, and emotional abuse. This type of "discipline" tore at

your value and self-worth. It was punishment.

If you are aware of your inner child's past punishment, you can guard his/her heart and soul now. You will likely use your inner child's historical learning on yourself and others if you do not change it. As you do inner child work you will want to use healthy discipline, while speaking truth in love. It is easier to speak truth in love to the child within you because of your knowledge and awareness of your historical feelings and thoughts.

Discipline is necessary, even now, because you are experiencing the child within you. It is important to not keep the same punitive approaches that you learned growing up because it only creates more harm for your soul, re-affirming that the world isn't safe for you or your inner child. Reviewing your inner child's old messages or tapes is a necessity to confront them while replacing punishment with healthy instruction.

What is the real truth? You will hear and know discipline from God's truth. In 2 Tim 3:16-17 it says, "Every scripture inspired of God is also profitable for teaching, for reproof, for correction, for instruction, which is in righteousness. That the man of God may be complete, furnished completely unto every good work" (2 Timothy 3:16-17 ASV). You will also have the Holy Spirit which will "guide you into all truth" (John 16;13) and "even [know] the depths of God" (1 Corinthians 2:10 ESV). This is spiritual healing for all wounds yet need to be applied by you to your early learnings.

Your old beliefs color your present truth. Comparing your old beliefs with scripture is vital to know if you still have some negative beliefs or old bent nails of punishment. The Holy Bible is not to take away from your life, but to give it. The Scriptures are to give you protection, correction, and direction. Sharing your early beliefs or present reality with your support system will assist in showing truth because not all punishment is so easily identified.

## Prayer of Memories

You may desire to say this prayer of memories to clean your Soul and fill it at the same time. You will need to stop and get quiet in a silent place. Listen to the words and the heart of this prayer. Look at your heart and give God your pain and suffering while your Soul fills with Gods peace, love, and joy. You might find yourself being held by Jesus as you are holding the wounded part of yourself. Being active in prayer will move your spirit and shake your Soul. I pray that the Holy Spirit will hold you and guide your heart. Be mindful as you dwell in your temple and experience yourself and God.

# PRAYER FOR HEALING OF MEMORIES (INNER HEALING)

*By Robert DeGrandis, SSJ*

"Father, I thank You for Your Son, Jesus, who died on the cross not only for me sins, but for my fears. I thank You that Jesus is the same yesterday, today, and forever, and that He wants me to be completely whole: spirit, soul, and body.

Lord Jesus, I ask You to walk back through every second of my life. Heal me and make me whole. Go back into the third and fourth generations and break harmful genetic ties.

Jesus, you knew all about me, even before I was born. Thank You for being there as life began. If fear or any other negative force was transmitted to me as I was in my mother's womb, set me free from those things. Thank You, Lord Jesus, for being there when I was born, and loving me. (Some came into this world not being loved and not being wanted, and they felt such rejection. Lord Jesus, from the very beginning fill each newly born child with Your precious love.)

Lord, walk back through every second of my life during those early years. (Some were separated from parents because of sickness or death; some were born into large families and did not receive the love that was needed). Lord Jesus, go back and fill every void, give the love that was not received. Remove every hurt. Take away all fears - fear of darkness, fear of falling, fear of animals, fear of being lost. I thank You, Jesus, for setting me free and healing me.

I pray, Lord, that You will take my hand and walk to school with me. At times, I felt so shy, so afraid to leave home and go into new situations. Jesus, there were times I felt embarrassed at school. Would You please take away those memories? When I was treated harshly by a teacher, or I was hurt by classmates, please heal those hurts. (Some fears entered during those first school years like the fear of speaking in public, or fear of failure). Thank You for healing those hurts and setting me free from those fears. I thank You and I praise You.

Lord Jesus, I thank You for my mother. (For those who did not have the love of a mother, fill that void, that empty place and give them the love that was needed). I ask You to stand in between my mother and me and let Your divine love flow between us. I ask forgiveness from my mother for any way I have hurt her or failed her, and I forgive her for any way she hurt or failed me.

Lord Jesus, I thank You for my dad. (For those who did not feel the love of any earthly dad, please give them all the love they needed but did not receive). Stand between my dad and me. I pray that Your divine love will mend any broken relationship. I ask forgiveness from my dad for any way I hurt or failed him, and I forgive him for any way he hurt or failed me.

I lift my brothers and sisters up to You. Where there were feelings of competition, jealousy, or resentment, I ask that Your healing power and love mend every broken relationship. I forgive each brother and sister for hurting or failing me, and I ask their forgiveness for hurting or failing them.

Thank You, Lord for being there in my teenage years when I was in Junior High School and High School. There were new problems and fears. As each painful memory is brought to my mind, I pray that You will take a spiritual eraser and wipe the pain from mind. Take away any feeling of humiliation, embarrassment, guilt, fear, or failure. (Some have been teased because of race, looks, size or poverty and they were wounded so deeply). Let each person know You loved them as a special, unique individual and that You were there in every situation.

As each of us started to leave home there were new fears, frustrations, or hurts. (Some wanted to go on to college and were not able to, others were not able to enter the profession they had dreamed of, and they felt such disappointment). Jesus, please heal every disappointment and every hurt.

Thank You for being there as we entered marriage. (For some it was such a beautiful, new beginning. For others, it was a nightmare). Jesus, please take away every hurt. I pray that You would stand in between my mate and me (and if there has been more than one mate, please stand in between each one) and heal every hurt. I am saying to my mate, I forgive you for hurting me and I ask your forgiveness for hurting you. Lord Jesus, through Your divine love, I thank You for mending every broken relationship, and wiping away every painful memory.

Thank You for our children. Take away any feeling I have of failure or guilt as a parent. When I punished unwisely or was too possessive with my love, when words were spoken in criticism or anger; I pray You will heal any hurt that was caused, I ask for their forgiveness and forgive them for hurting me.

Lord, during those terrifying times of accidents, those times of sickness or surgery, I thank You for being there. I ask You now to take away the horror, the fear, and the trauma I felt. Thank You for being there during times of sorrow. I thank You for taking my hand and walking through the valley with me. I thank You for lifting the burden; I thank You for taking away my sorrow, my grief, and my mourning. I thank You for giving me Your joy and Your peace.

Now, Lord Jesus, thank You for walking back through every second of my life up to this exact moment. Thank You for healing me of all my hurts, my painful memories, and my fears, and for setting me free. Thank You for filling me with Your love. Help me to love myself. Help me to love others. But most of all, Jesus, help me to love You, for this is my desire. I thank You for giving me joy and peace. Thank You, Jesus. I thank You for going way down deep into the darkest recesses of my mind and cleansing me.

I thank You for healing my emotions, my mind, and my memories.

I thank You, Jesus, for making me whole, and I give You all the praise and all the glory.

In Your Name, I pray. Amen."

You will need to sit and journal what thoughts, feelings and experience you gave to God. Be mindful, of the effect God has on these experiences while cleansing your Soul. Be aware of God's presence replacing your pain and sorrow. Your inner child might not want to believe it is possible to be clean from the nails that pierced the heart and mind. You may go back to the "darkest" places out of habit of indulging in it. Stop and **FACE God** by Fleeing the thought or temptation, Acknowledge God's Word; taking Captive your thoughts and Enlisting the Holy Spirit. This will help you be aware of the light and healing. Do not recreate what God has already cleansed. Be mindful to step into God's promise, light, and love.

You are experiencing your authentic self when you are in the light because you are a child of the light (Ephesians 5;8). Your Soul has been cleansed by God. Do not believe the lies of your internal critics or script which was developed in the flesh. Leave the lies and the yoke of slavery with God and accept His truth while making it your own, resulting in a process of healing. Satan, the Father of lies (John 8;44), will come your way because he wants to corrupt your mind and steer you away from Christ and His gospel (2 Cor 11:3). It is important to remember you are "not wrestling with flesh and blood [contending only with physical opponents], but against the despotisms, against the powers, against [the master spirits who are] the world rulers of this present darkness, against the spirit forces of wickedness in the heavenly (supernatural) sphere" (Ephesians 6:12 AMP).

Satan is compared to a roaring lion that wants to devour you (1 Peter 5:8). He wants you to live in fear and shame. Fear and shame will keep you from moving closer to your target. He will tempt you with your internal or external indulgences (Matt 4:1; 1 Thess 3:5) which hides truth with past lies. You will need to rebuke, and resist Satan and he will flee (James 4;7). You have the power to rebuke and resist Satan because you are a child of the Highest God.

It is important for you to move closer to God's target even when you miss the mark. God's best is waiting there for you. It is easy to move away from the target when feeling fear and shame. At times, you may find it difficult to not throw your bow because you miss the target more than you hit it. I hope you hear God say, "move closer my child."

If any one of the common people sins unwittingly in doing anything the Lord has commanded not to be done, and is guilty, When the sin which he has committed is made known to him, he shall bring for his offering a goat, a female without blemish, for his sin which he has committed (Leviticus 4:27-28 AMP).

You might be asking the question, "Where was this loving God when I was being hurt and abused? Or "He did nothing to stop it." Unfortunately, I have heard this from many of my clients. Please remember, God never abandoned anyone while they experienced any form of abuse. He honors free will and was sickened watching the abuse happen.

## My Story: Sam

Sam is a good example of how journaling can identify early developmental and spiritual problems while healing early learned beliefs. Sam worked through her distorted spiritual beliefs which were modeled by her authoritarian father. Sam could help her inner child recognize her value and experience God's love through journaling with her non-dominant hand. After building a relationship with her inner child, Sam wrote a love letter from God to the child within her. She could bring her present knowledge of God's love and apply it to her old, distorted beliefs.

Sam was a 42-year-old female client who was suffering from clinical depression. Sam's depressive signs were no energy, concentration, or libido. She had increased appetite and need for sleep. Sam reported "praying all the time" and "waiting on God to heal me." Sam came from a "military" family and her dad was "Patton." "He ran a tight ship." Sam reported decreased memories before third grade.

She had a great view of God from her Adult self, yet constantly thought that God was going to "chastise" "judge" or "punish" her. Sam knew God was loving, yet she had increased fear of a God. Sam questioned the reasons she had these "crazy" thoughts of God leaving her, which created anxiety. She was encouraged to journal with her non-dominant hand. The non-dominant hand drew out her early emotional experience and its logic. She was to ask the question with her right, dominant hand. Her dominant hand was her higher learning or adult-self, and answered the question with her left, non-dominant hand. Sam was asked to trust herself in asking her questions.

Here is what Sam journaled with her non-dominant hand writings:

1) Why are you scared of God? "I don't know."

2) Are you scared of God? "Sometimes, kind of."
4) Tell me what you mean. "Dad gets mad and says I'm too much trouble."
5) Do you think you are too much trouble for God? "Sometimes."
6) Do you know that God will never leave you or criticize you? "Dad does and he whips me hard and sometimes I pee, and he gets madder."
7) I am so sorry about you getting whipped by your dad, but God is bigger and will not whip you for peeing on yourself or be mean to you. He is not like your dad. "Are you sure?"
8) Yes, I am sure. Please trust me, and I will tell you more about God. "OK. I never did break dad's mirror. "I know you didn't. Mike did." "Dad whipped me and called me a liar."
9) I remember. But God knows the truth and was sad you got whipped, so many times for it. "Really?"
10) Yes, and dad was wrong. I think God would be mad at dad. "I am."
11) That is ok. I got to go but will you talk to me again? "Yes."

Sam could not believe what her inner child had written her. Sam constantly said, "I didn't know what she was going to say next." "I had forgot how hard dad was on me." The mirror, I got whipped for everyday until I said that I had done it. Then I got grounded from my bike all summer for lying. Boy I was mad." Sam continued writing with her non-dominant hand. Sam continued telling her 7-year-old self about the loving God she knew, while allowing her inner child to know that dad's discipline was abuse or severe punishment.

What Sam thought was normal discipline and her dad running a "tight ship," had colored her images of God. Sam became aware of her abuse and early beliefs by spiritually dwelling in her temple. By doing regression work with her non- dominant hand, Sam could bring truths to her inner child. Sam's present truth was the healing ointment for her old emotional wounds. Sam hungered for God's comfort and healing, but her foundation was built on the belief that God was condemning, punishing and punitive.

It is important to decipher if your emotional filters received discipline or punishment. Discipline adds to your life with healthy learnings, while punishment creates a foundation of fear, shame, and guilt. Your childhood experiences of your parents may be the expectations you place on God. Remember, you are not judging your parents, but remembering what you experienced growing up. The experience of discipline will be remembered, while the experience of punishment will likely be suppressed and acted out without your awareness.

So, stop, look, and listen to your emotional experience before age six and write them down. Trust what you think and feel.

## Exercise: Examining Punishment

*This is not a regression exercise. There are no special instructions included. Answer simply and directly in your journal.*

Did you experience discipline or punishment? Circle one

What types of discipline or punishment did you experience?

-
-
-

What were the emotions and beliefs about yourself and God that came from the discipline or punishment?

-
-

Did you experience the nails of injustice by others? Yes or No
By whom?
Are you suffering from fear, shame, or guilt? Yes or No

Sam wrote a letter about her beliefs in God to her 7-year-old inner child. "Stop worrying my child. I have loved you before you were born. I made you and love you so much. I know that your dad loves you. But he can never love you as I love you. I love you my little girl. I felt the belt, switch, and hose on your back. You will never be hurt by those things by me. I will love you with love, grace, and guidance. Come to me and rest in my arms. Stop worrying. You are beautiful in my sight, even your dry humor I love. I will never leave you. You can rest my child. Please know. I love you. Sincerely, God."

Sam wrote this letter several times until it said what she believed God wanted her inner child to know. Sam's new song for herself was "Forgiven" by Skillet. She broke the chains of her past by looking behind her mask. Sam hid behind the mask of perfection and pleasing others. Sam's weaknesses and fear of rejection were hidden from others; she thought even God did not know her fears. She broke her script by taking off her mask and making herself important. Sam was unaware of her early emotions and her beliefs. Sam's script or early belief about her dad colored her adult relationship with God, allowing her to know her inner child's thoughts or feelings.

Has your life and image of God been based on your old hurt feelings and experiences? You can check your spiritual lens by writing what you believe God would say to your inner child. Allow yourself to write God's letter to your inner child.

## Exercise: God's Letter to Me

*This is not a regression exercise. There are no special instructions included. Answer simply and directly in your journal.*

If your letter has any condemnation of your Soul in it, then you are not experiencing God's grace and love. You will need to rewrite "God's letter" to yourself.

You will hear the old teachings or tapes in your mind while journaling or writing with your non-dominant hand, becoming aware of your expectations that you are placing on God. Your expectations come from the attitude in which you were taught. If you are expecting to be judged and sent to hell for being a sinner, then this will color your view of God; especially, if the tone of the one that taught you was angry, fearful or pessimistic. Past spiritual mentors or role models may have feared, which skewed God's "good news." The tone, attitude and expectations of your past instructions had a great impact.

I hope your inner child will experience a loving God through your teaching. You will start to look through the window of your Soul and not its mirror/reflection. The child within you will be able to look through your eyes and not the colored lenses of others' expectations and beliefs about God. You will need to take your colored lenses off first to experience the God who came, died, and rose in three days for you. A God who wants you to prosper in all areas of life. I wish you could experience God as a loving father or faithful friend.

Spirituality is experiencing the Holy in ordinary and sacred things. My story of God says, "God loves my ordinary life and delights as He experiences life with me. God makes me important and not my experience. He cries when I cry, laughs when I laugh, and gives me gentle discipline when I am not listening. He reaches out to make the ordinary extraordinary." Hopefully, you will experience the Holy as you tell your story to your inner child. The result for both of you is like experiencing a loving Father or Daddy.

## My Story: Susan's Story

Susan was a 56-year-old obese woman. Susan had been in counseling for over 6 months. She came to counseling due to her depression. Susan's depressive signs were decreased energy and concentration, increased anhedonia (no joy or motivation to do meaningful things), insomnia and increased appetite. Susan had no plans to kill herself, "but if I didn't wake up it would be ok." Susan had "good parents" and did not know why she was so depressed. Susan spoke of her husband, Junius, as "a good man and a Godly man." She was asked to make a list of her verbal, emotional and physical marks left by her parents. Susan brought back her homework assignment the next session. Susan walked into session and sat in a different chair, one that faced the door and was shaking her head as to say no.

Susan said, "I don't know what to think."

Counselor- What are you going through Susan?

Susan - I did that homework and it hit me in the face. I had no idea (*She pulled her journal out of her purse and opened it. She laid it facing down on the table*)

Counselor- Are you going to share what you wrote?

Susan- I pulled it out, didn't I? (*pause*). You can read it (*Susan grabbed the journal to give it to me.*)

Counselor- Will you read it and tell me your thoughts as you go?

Susan- I guess I will. You do not want to take time to read it. (*Susan is using a defense mechanism of projection to "protect" herself*). The marks are (Susan did not use past tense) You are not smart, pretty, or athletic as your sister or just fill in the blank.

Counselor- Those are hurtful words. Sounds like they left emotional marks.

Susan- They left a pit of darkness. I was not aware of my mom and dad telling me that before. No wonder I quit basketball and track. No wonder I did not go to college. No wonder I eat like a pig because I will never be good enough

Counselor - Are those messages true?

Susan- Yes, they are.

Counselor- So you were not smart, pretty, or good enough to play basketball?

Susan- I was not as good as my sister. I could never beat her in basketball. She was always smarter, faster, and happier

Counselor - You were twins?

Susan- No. She was two years older than me. She was a four-year letterman and in the top 10 of her class

Counselor- No wonder you never beat her. She was not only older, but good at what she did too

Susan- Yes, she was something special. My parents would always compare me to her. Over and over!

Counselor- Was that fair?

Susan- No. (*Pause*) No it was not fair (*Susan began to experience truth*) she was two years older and I would have never beat her. I wish we were twins.

Counselor- So you would have kicked her butt.

Susan- I think, I would have. (*Susan began to be sad and wiped away tears*). The sad thing is I believed God thought I was not good enough too.

Counselor- I do not understand.

Susan- I did the last part of the exercise and wrote that I should honor my mother and father and not to think too highly of myself. That is not true.

Counselor- No I think God was sickened by those messages and that you beat yourself up. I believe He is happy you know the truth

Susan- My parents took me out of honors classes, basketball, and track because I was "too stressed." How stupid. I do not get it. (*Susan keep shaking her head as to say no and crying for several minutes*). They confirmed that I was not ok by punishing me that way. How could they have done that to me? No wonder I gained weight like a pig and heard that I was" lazy" or "too stressed" all my life. That is not fair I just needed some support, understanding or guidance.

Counselor- I am so sorry for all your losses. It is nice that you are seeing truth.

Susan- I am not lazy and I am not too stressed. I am going to start running and lose this weight because this is not me, never has been.

Susan began listening to her authentic self while learning to love her-self. She started her "new life," as she referred to it, after that session. She trained to run a half marathon and lost approximately 55 pounds. Susan finished her first half marathons before a year had passed. Susan made a list of "new truths" and followed them daily. Susan's mental and emotional wounds were healed by her present truths.

Susan's parents did not discipline her at a time that she needed them too. They took control in a loving way which was later seen as punishment. Punishment is one exerting their will over another even if it is viewed as the right thing or comes from love. Susan's marks were not left with a belt. Susan's marks were by the words and actions of her parents. Susan's parents' words and actions took a toll on her emotional and mental state.

## Remember:

God's discipline, not punishment, adds to your life and does not take away from it.

# CHAPTER EIGHT

## SOUL FOOD

"1 Corinthians 3:16-17 Do you not know that you are God's temple and that God's Spirit lives in you? If someone destroys God's temple, God will destroy him. For God's temple is holy, which is what you are."

**KEY POINTS:**

- You are not alone in your pain.
- There is a way out.
- To get there, begin exactly where you are.

**Reflections:**

- Where are you today? How are you feeling about yourself? Your surroundings? Your past and future?
- This question is a hard one. Stay with it and answer it as best you can, even very simply. Respond from your heart and your body, not your head. *Write down your answers.*
- It is impossible to have a complete understanding of all your wounding at the start of this work. These questions, answered today, are the fundamental starting point for moving into deeper healing.
- Keep your "where you are" today notes as your north star throughout the book. Revisit them at the start of each chapter to help map your growth. The questions will afford you more information with the continued exercises in the coming chapters.

# Welcome.

"The Holy Spirit, as part of a triune God, consecrates the sacred or holy in your body, mind and soul through your faith and relationship with Jesus and God."

The Word of God is the spiritual bridge between man and God. Many times, theologians are a little wordy and the knowledge of God is lost. I think Gordon Spykman captures the meaning of the Word of God when he says we need to see "the Word of God as the covenantal bond which establishes the relationship of promise and obligation between God and man, as the key to understanding revelation in its unity and diversity, and as the norm for all human response, including dogmatics. The Word of God is the final resting place in theology's restless search for the 'missing link'" (Reformational Theology. A New Paradigm for Doing Dogmatics,1992. P. 71-72).

As a Pastoral Counselor, I was focused on the cure of the soul which came through the healing ability of scripture. The cure and care of the Soul takes on a new dynamic for believers due to the function of the Holy Spirit. The Holy Spirit gives you the ability to be active in your healing through the fruit of the Spirit because of the Holy Spirit's ability to intercede on your behalf before God. As a believer, the healing power of God's Word is believed in and expected, while this healing is a mystery for non-Christians. Your healing journey needs to be sustained by the ultimate Soul food: the Fruit of the Spirit.

The Fruit of the Spirit needs to be the measuring stick of being conscious, and is the ultimate Soul food because it can nurture ( 1 Thessalonians 5;14,15), comfort ( Romans 15:13; 2 Corinthians 1:3,4;), intercede before God ( Romans 8;26,) instruct ( Luke 12:12) and a guide ( John 16;13) or can be a helper (John 14:16,) for your healing Journey . You are not alone on this journey. If you are held captive by shame and guilt, deceived by outdated defense mechanisms or overused indulgences, then you are not experiencing the fullness of the fruit of the Spirit. You want to be full of this fruit because it builds character, integrity, and self-control. This fruit will protect the character it builds by fortifying your personal boundaries and coping skills to handle life's problems. This fruit is the ultimate Soul food because it springs forth from the Spirit of God within you. God's heartbeat and strength are at work in you via His Spirit. God's Spirit and essence are one with you in a physical sense. You could say the DNA of God is now flowing through your veins.

Many Christians do not understand that their faith in Christ has brought God's essence into their hearts, minds, and Soul. This transformation is on a cellular level. The creator of the heaven and earth is now a part of your mental, emotional, and physiological makeup (2 Corinthians 5;17); at one with your being or Soul. Your psyche is now literally transformed spiritually. This is not a state of mind or a feel-good experience. The substance of God in the form of His Spirit is part of your spirit's DNA. God's Spirit and yours are one. This can be seen in an Apostle Paul's letter to the Romans.

In Romans, the apostle Paul wrote "and hope does not disappoint, because the love of God has been poured out within our hearts through the Holy Spirit who was given to us" (Romans 5:5 NASB). This "heart" was not your physical muscle that pumps your blood throughout your entire body. The "heart" is a part of your feeling and rational brain. Your "heart" is your innate primitive emotions to your rational awareness. It may be called the total embodiment of that which moves you. Brennan Manning refers to the Holy Spirit as being "the bond of tenderness" between the Father and Son" (Brennan Manning, The Wisdom of Tenderness, 2002, Page 23). Your "heart" is what moves your body and Soul. God's love and Spirit fills or transforms your Soul to be His sanctuary. Now the Holy Spirit and God's love pumps through you mentally, spiritually, and physically like it did with the apostle Paul.

You walk around with your attention on those things that feed your flesh and forget about the power you have inside you. Your attention is not on your spiritual DNA but indulgences that comfort your flesh. The tempest of your past feeds your today(s) and tomorrow(s). Your fleshly DNA moves you, while your spiritual self and God are only an afterthought. It is amazing how the emotional weather of others gets the attention of your mind's eye. You can even control your emotional weather although you choose to sit in your emotional rain and cold.

Before you can step out of the cold and rain that you are emotionally in, you need to know about the Fruit of the Spirit. The Fruit of the Spirit is moved by the Spirit of God within you. You could say that the Fruit of the Spirit grows on God's Vine (John 15:4, 5). You can eat of these fruits at any time no matter the emotional weather which surrounds you.

The fruits of the Spirit are "love, joy, peace, patience, kindness, goodness, faithfulness, gentleness, self-control; against such things there is no law" (Galatians 5:22-23 NASB). This fruit has power over the flesh and mind. If you are walking by the Spirit "you will not carry out the desire of the flesh" (Galatians 5:16 NASB). You can change your script by walking in the spirit. Walking in the Spirit is an intentional act which your nature and script will struggle with accepting.

The fruit of the Spirit is a gift to battle the tempest of the world. This gift of the Holy Spirit transforms your Soul or psyche by God's presence. God created a "living soul" which was filled with His "breath" in Genesis 2:7. Your soul will be transformed by the Holy Spirit through faith in God's Son. Your Soul will be filled with God's Spirits and the fruit of His Spirit. You are no longer the same person. You have been grafted together with God and this Union cannot be broken. Once you are grafted with God you will no longer bear the same fruit as you once bore (John 15:5). This transformation begins and ends with love.

It is important to understand God's love before speaking of the Soul. The first fruit of the Spirit is love. The essence of God and the action that arms the Holy Spirit is love. It is not an accident that love is listed as the first fruit. It goes back to the need to love your God with all your heart, mind, and soul, loving your neighbor as yourself (Luke 10:27). If your motion in life is driven by love, then you will have a great chance to experience the other fruit. This begins with the active awareness of God's love. Love is the new ***law*** of the New Testament. You are freed from the constraints of the law of the Old Testament through Christ. The Gospel or Good News is that Christ's life, death, and resurrection was based on love.

This Greek word for love is *agape*. The first of the nine fruit of the Spirit is a noun in Greek. A noun represents the embodiment of a person, place, or thing. This fruit of love is not a verb that portrays action. *Agape* is a noun that solidifies God pouring Himself into you and not just the act of loving. The love of the Spirit is an earnest way of being benevolent as God is benevolent. The Fruit of the Spirit which indwells you is *agape* love.

To put *agape* love into context we must refer to 1 Corinthians 13:4-7 that state "Love is patient, love is kind and is not jealous; love does not brag and is not arrogant, does not act unbecomingly; it does not seek its own, is not provoked, does not take into account a wrong suffered, does not rejoice in unrighteousness, but rejoices with the truth; bears all things, believes all things, hopes all things, endures all things" (NASB). "'It' is God's own love growing as a 'fruit' in the hearts of men, no one can claim it as a merit for self-salvation" (The interpreter's Bible, vol 10, 1953, p.565). All blessing, or knowledge is only white noise without love. Love is synonymous with God (1 John 4:7, 4:18).

*Love* embodies the rest of the nine fruits of the Spirit, beginning with joy. Joy is internal and becomes an external manifestation of the love of God. Joy in communion, service or trials are for the honor of God. This way of loving will have an action of joy and peace, yet joy and peace are also nouns. They are to be and not just an experience or an emotion. Joy is a calm way of being cheerful. The experience of joy for many would be labeled as peace.

*Peace* can be seen as the act of resting (Matthew 11:29; Hebrews 4:11) or serenity in God which is active. It is a knowing or being in God's rest even at time of tribulation. This peace stems from God's comfort and power that is active during storms. All creatures can experience peace but only Christians can experience this type of rest in God. This peace can be kept in your heart and mind (Phil. 4;7). In our culture we equate this peace with physically resting.

Resting physically in our culture does not happen much due to the activities or control of the external pressures of the moment. The word for peace in Greek can mean being quiet. Being quiet is also actively resting in God. In Psalms 46:10-11 it says "Be still and know that I am God: I will be exalted among the nations; I will be exalted in the earth. Jehovah of hosts is with us; The God of Jacob is our refuge" (ASV). Be quiet and know that God is with you in all life's tribulations is true peace. In our culture if you had peace many may label you as lonely or lazy. The act of being at peace is truly a fruit of the Spirit. "Now the God of peace be with you all. Amen" (Romans 15:33 ASV).

You might only have "peace" when you crawl in bed or are drinking your morning coffee. I spoke to a meth addict today and asked him when he had peace, when he was not high. He responded, "When I have a rock (methamphetamine) and I start loading my pipe. I'm in true peace." You may have the same "peace" crawling into bed as your body is letting down or the moment that you hold your first cup of coffee. This peace needs to be labeled as contentment. Every addict has a euphoria before they use yet peace is absent. Peace is an inside job. Peace is an extension of your relationship with God that transcends the present moment without interrupting it. The "God of peace" (1 Corinthians 14;33) has His sanctuary, a dwelling place, in you (2 Corinthians 6;16). You must dwell in your temple to experience the peace that passes understanding. Peace is not dependent on your external environment but a gift that can be opened no matter what your circumstances. It is the same with the next fruit of patience.

The next fruit of the Spirit is of *patience.* Patience is constantly encouraged by best friends, good parents, and loving grandparents. This fruit is also a virtue of the church. Patience is resting in God's timing and not your own. Patience is a type of forbearance which helps you avoid the desires to react. The Greek word can also mean long-suffering. Long-suffering pertains to the trials, tribulations, and injuries by others that you will receive living East of Eden. Many Christians will react unconsciously rather than looking through their spiritual eyes of long- suffering.

Your Heavenly Father has *long- suffering* and *patience* with you. You have experienced the painful isolation and feeling of being alone; your Heavenly Father is waiting for you. God has given you His Spirit of patience to endure suffering and fleshly desires. If you have ever loved someone so much that you would have given your life to stop their pain and anguish then you can understand this gift of patience or long- suffering that God has for you.

The next fruit of the Spirit mentioned is the gift of *kindness.* Kindness is being good and upright. This goodness is a Spirit filled goodness. When this same Greek word is used elsewhere in scripture it refers to the action of meeting others needs and has more of an action component rather than *feeling good*. It is more like doing good to those that need good. This kindness is radical in nature. It must stem from a nature greater than yourself. The Spirit in you is the prime mover in giving to others without a desire to get something in return.

This kindness is being in the moment while being moved by love to help another person. It is an active kindness that stretches every present moment and lives in a loving act to yourself and/or someone else. I see kids doing this so often with others. They are not caught in the urgency of the moment, while their innocence guards them against expectation. Expectations contaminate acts of kindness. Watching kids' kindness highlights the innocence of giving. Their giving is not self-seeking and is an action in this dance of intimacy.

I have my clients practice this dance of intimacy or expression of God for 20 minutes a day. Many tell me that 20 minutes of being actively kind to themselves was "hard" or "impossible." Actively loving themselves got lost due to the many activities that the present moment offered. One of my clients, a rebellious 16-year-old male, gave me a great gift. He gave me a measuring stick of kindness. He said, "I tried to be kind. Damn man, I knew it was to get some bucks from my dad, get mom to shut up or because I wanted someone to notice me. But I found out how to be kind for a long damn while." He moved back into that peaceful place while telling me about his experience. He said, "When I find that place where grace and love meet, then I can do it as long as I want to."

As he spoke, he was able to pull me into a place of peace with him. I love those moments when time has no beginning or end. He went on to tell me how he was "able to be kind." "I had to look at how God would be in relationship with others and me.... I found myself running to the car to help mom, mowing the yard for dad, and combing my sister's hair." He actively put on God's kindness which gave him the ability to be kind. I need to say, his thoughts or actions of putting on God's kindness activated, stimulated, or called forth more of the fruit of the Holy Spirit within him. In the next two months, he began to love himself with acts of kindness. His kindness grew for others as he began having a genuine kindness or healthy love from himself.

I could see how his growth in kindness was an intentional act of being faithful to God. He put on God and put away himself. This act had conscious intent and was an act of being faithful. He did not know that he was internalizing kindness for himself. This act of worship or obedience to God brought on more fruit of the Spirit. He was unaware of the internal movement of the Spirit of God. He opened the door to a power greater than himself that transformed him. It allowed me to see the power of God's transforming love, as he was faithful in his acts of kindnesses. This young rebel's actions changed his entire family. They began to encourage each other and to look through God's eyes. This young man modeled the next characteristic of the Spirit of God which was faithfulness.

*Faithfulness* is a fruit that does not deal with your belief or faith in God. Faith "is the assurance of things hoped for, the conviction of things not seen." (Hebrews 11:1 NASB). Your faith in God was a rational choice while your faithfulness is a fruit or byproduct of the Holy Spirit. This fruit of faithfulness stems from the Spirit of God in you. This type of "faith" is like a "calling" that calls forth obedience.

Have you experienced the Spirit calling you forth to be faithful? That "voice" or "knowing" is persuading you to not do this but instead do that. Faithfulness is a strange but clear conviction. You almost must intentionally push this conviction down to get what you want out of life. I have struggled with not listening to this persuasion while choosing to do what I wanted to do. The more I squelched the Holy Spirit's persuasion to be faithful, the more I became mindless in my own pursuits. I missed the fact that the future is in the hands of God and believed it was in my hands. I can understand this Madame Guyon quote which says, "Many people want to direct God, instead of resigning themselves to be directed by Him; to show Him a way, instead of passively following where He leads"(Page 353 Streams in the Desert by L. B. Cowman. He quotes Madame Guyon. Copyright 1996 by The Zondervan Corporation). I was usually reminded of my choices when I had to pay the consequences of not being faithful.

Christians need to be reminded that God's faithfulness is permanent (1 John 2:17). It is not based on your works (Ephesians 2:8-9). God did not need you to be perfect to ensure His love; it is unconditional. He only wants your heart. I had clients that got lost in the human condition or sin. They moved away from God due to their shame. God became smaller and smaller as they limited Him. They made God in their own images and projected their judgment and legalism on to God. This usually created more shame and guilt. This expressway of shame moved them further down life's highway and away from God.

The fruit of *faithfulness* is a mirror image of God Himself. God will be faithful to you and your sin will never stop Him from loving you. God is a gentle giant that wants your love. If you give Him your love the shoulds, oughts and whys in your mind will pass away. The calling to be faithful will be welcomed reminders of your Heavenly Father's love.

The next fruit of the Spirit is *gentleness.* The same word in Greek could be rendered as "meekness" (The Interpreter's Bible, vol. 10, 1953, p. 569). This Greek word is a form of humility. This is strength in Greek. It is a *gentle* strength. This deals more with your temperance which by the nature of the Spirit is gentle. A gentle temper almost sounds like an oxymoron. Matthew 5:5 says, "Blessed are the meek; for they shall inherit the earth." Being meek is a true inner strength that can be vulnerable while standing up for your beliefs or yourself.

This form of humility will empower you to listen to yourself. "Humility is the honest recognition of your own worth—your worth as God sees you. It is a delicate balance between recognizing your sin while knowing how much God loves you and values you" (Divine Moments for Men,2008, p.1:42-143). Can you imagine that God wants you to be gentle or good to yourself. This humility has no shame. God wants you to take the whip out of your hands. He does not want you to beat yourself up. You are a child of God and what loving parent wants to have their kids beating themselves up. God wants you to have healthy humility. The Holy Spirit has and will have a healthy self-respect for you.

The last of the fruit of the Spirit is *self-control.* "Self-control is one of the hardest character traits to maintain because it means denying what comes nature to your sinful nature and replacing it with a godly response" (Divine Moments for Men, 2008, p.251). There is a good reason that self-control is mentioned last. It is a mastery of self which comes from a self-restraint or control provided by the Spirit of God. This control is not human; it is from God. Each of the fruit of the Spirit is part of God's Nature. These gifts of God are yours with the Holy Spirit. The more you use the other gifts of the Spirit you will have a greater sense of self and self-control.

It is important to know the Spirit of God is a mirror image of God. When you want to know the character of God just look at the fruit of the Spirit. Does this sound like a judgmental God waiting to condemn you? He is empowering you by giving you His character. Now that is a loving Father.

God has given or equipped you with skills to face life. These gifts are healthy ways to protect and enrich yourself while providing you the ability to face the struggles of the world. These gifts of the Spirit were given after Christ's death. Deception and death were brought to mankind by Satan at The Fall. Satan never thought the Holy Spirit would be given by God to mankind at Christ's death. Satan had no awareness of this gift. Who would have thought that God would give His Spirit to all that believed in Him?

Adam and Eve were tempted by the fruit on the Tree of Knowledge of Good and Evil. This fruit of knowledge created an awareness of their fleshly desires. This knowledge separated them from God. God gave those who believe in him the fruit, not from a tree, but of His Spirit. This fruit bears life and not death. It is a free gift for those who accept Christ (Acts 2:38). This fruit is not the knowledge of good and evil; it brings forth the knowledge of God. (Ephesians 1:16-17). The fruit that separated man from God was replaced by the fruit of His Spirit. This fruit is a gift for believers in Christ. By Christ's blood offering all believers have the free gift of the Spirit of God.

Before Jesus' death all believers in Yahweh, Lord God, the great I Am who I Am had to have a blood offering or sacrifice to approach God. Satan in all his arrogance, knowing that Jesus was the Son of God, believed that he could take the life of God's Son. He believed he could keep God's Son in Hades or hell. What arrogance! Satan was and is under the illusion that he is

God (2 Corinthians 4:4). Satan never believed that Jesus of Nazareth who was the son of the Most High God would be able to be raised from the dead. He never saw God giving his own Spirit to anyone that believes in Jesus. Satan neither had nor will ever have any love for mankind. Satan's only interest was to hurt God and to prove to his dominion that he is God (Isaiah 14;12-15).

The fruit of the Spirit is a testament of God's love for you. They are literally given to you by God. You have the authority over Satan and the ability to conquer any and everything in life. All believers in Christ need to celebrate each of the fruit of the Holy Spirit; we need to look at these gifts through the filters of man. If you look through your eyes of faith, you will experience a spiritual reality of knowing nothing will separate you from God's love, grace, and power. If you do not know how to use or tap into these fruits you will be starving spiritually, and sin will beat you down.

You may have depression, anxiety or been victimized by abuse and forgotten your true ancestry of being a child of the Highest God. Remember the words of Brennan Manning: "Do you believe that God loves you, not the world, not the church, not the person next to you, but that God loves you, so much that He would rather die than be without you?" (*Brennan Manning talks, "Abba I Belong to You" given in 1984*).

It is so important that you rest your heart, mind and Soul in God's unconditional love while traveling on your healing journey. The hardships of life are reckless, at best. You will be tempted by lies, fears and darkness of your past on your healing journey. The powers and principalities of this world will want to stop you from knowing yourself and your Heavenly Father's love for you. Living East of Eden brings conflicts, poor teaching, and abuse. You will need to be intentional to experience the fruit of the Spirit because you may struggle with the flesh which can stop you from experiencing God's radiant love.

This gift of the Spirit of God was given to you to combat temptations and sin. If you have the invincible character of God to deal with sin, then what is the reason you do not use it? Temperance or self-control in our culture is associated with abstinence or your own strength, while the temperance of the early church was a strength associated with power over evil things (Romans 12:17-21) and a moderation in all things (Philippians 4;5). The Spirit of God will help you moderate all things. If you are struggling with any indulgence, then you are not alone.

The next time you think you cannot do something, call forth the Holy Spirit. The more you can tap into the Spirit of God and not your own strength, the more you will be able to experience or see the fruit of the Spirit. The Creator of all things has power over all things and sees all things can be experienced and used by you. You can use this fruit of the Holy Spirit to overcome sin, indulgences and heal your past abuse issues.

You probably have not tried to practice walking in the Spirit. If you are going to get good at anything you will need to practice, practice and practice. Have you ever been told or taught how to practice using, enlisting, or calling forth the Holy Spirit? There are many ways to sharpen these skills. If you don't practice working out you will not get stronger, if you don't study you will not get smarter and if you don't practice a skill then it will become weaker and less useful over time.

The old saying "If you don't use it, you will lose it," is true. This is scary if you think about what you have not practiced using God's Spirit. How do you gain strength in the Spirit? Do you get strength by knowing Gods Word, prayer or going to church? The answers will be yes to each of these questions. But these answers may not be enough to experience and use the power of God. It's like talking to your teacher, going to class, and reading the book and expecting an A. That expectation will not work because you have not studied. It is like you are going to the gym and doing the same workout every time. You will stay in the same shape, and not get stronger or be in a better place.

If you are a normal Christian, then you will go to church each week. You may take the next step and go to Sunday school or bible study. Some of you have studied or *looked over* the Bible study during the week. This type of spiritual workout is weak. You will grow and not lose your spiritual strength by this spiritual workout. How much would you grow if you were actively engaging to grow spiritually?

The spiritual exercise of going to church or Bible study is passive learning. The minister or Bible study teacher is doing the work. You may be taking notes but have not studied or practiced them during the week. Now, just think about if you had to study and stand up to preach the Sunday service. Would you train differently?

Do you want to experience God's love, peace, and strength? The love, peace and strength pass all understanding because it is of God. In our culture buying bigger and bigger stuff or medicating with drugs, alcohol, food, porn, gambling, or shopping to feel the same "peace" or get " strength" is most common. Looking through the Holy changes your perspective in life. How are you going to gain the ability to experience and live through the Holy Spirit?

First and foremost, you need to dwell in your own temple. In 1Corinthians 6:19 it says, "Or know ye not that your body is a temple of the Holy Spirit which is in you, which ye have from God? and ye are not your own "(ASV). You will need to dwell in your temple to experience the Holy Spirit and stop avoiding, medicating, or busying yourself. Stopping all external distractions will be difficult but not as hard as it will be to stop all your internal distractions. Taming your internal distractions can be like taming a bunch of monkeys while driving.

When you begin dwelling in your temple you will hear the Holy Spirit. You may not know this because of your old tapes or script. If you hear your historic critical parent that has all the shoulds, ought toos, supposed toos and whys of your past, just breathe out those thoughts because they are not of the Holy Spirit. If you hear your childlike emotional brain saying words like, "I can't, have to, makes me, always, never and all the time" then just breathe out those thoughts. These words or thoughts are not part of the character of God or the fruit of the Spirit.

When you are "dwelling" in your temple by sitting quietly and breathing out all your unwanted thoughts and feelings, your mind will become quieted. This is the reason you may want to only concentrate on your breathing.

Breathing in the fresh life-giving air and breathing out all your unwanted thoughts and feelings, as you exhale. This breathing will quiet your mind, so you will be able to hear the Holy Spirit. Dwelling in your temple will take practice. Listening to the Holy Spirit may even take more practice and time. You can cut this time down from years or months to weeks or days. You can do this by creating a visual picture of the Holy Spirit or God.

Creating a visual picture that personifies God's Spirit in you can be intimidating. We know from Genesis 1:27 which says, "And God created man in his own image, in the image of God created he him; male and female created he them"(ASV). The knowledge of being created in God's image can give you a visual picture of God. Personifying the attributes of the supernatural in natural form with human characteristics might sound sacrilegious or a violation of sacred things, yet, you are to have the mind of Christ (1 Corinthians 2: 14-16) and that is not sacrilegious. We also know that Christ was in human form (Acts 2:22) and Christ and the Spirit are one (John 14:26). The Holy Spirit "shall teach you all things and bring to your remembrance all that I said unto you" (John 14:26 ASV).

This personification of the Holy Spirit will improve your ability to have these "remembrances." If you put the qualities of the Spirit in the form of a risen Christ, then you will be able to call forth or listen to the will of God. Lastly, you will need to practice listening and following the leading of the personified images of the Spirit to sharpen these skills.

An example of listening to the Holy Spirit can be seen by anyone that has lost their sight. I had a supervisor that lost her ability to see, yet, I found out that she saw more than I was able to see with vision. She had honed in her other senses to compensate for being blind. She would listen to her client's body movements, tone, volume, and words to hear their true meaning. She could sense who was going to speak in the group, before anyone spoke. It was sad that she could not see but saw more than most people with sight could ever see. She used and sharpened her other senses to a razors edge. You too will heighten your own senses by not looking by sight but through faith.

Are you listening to the Spirit of God in you? You will need to trust your faithfulness to hear the persuasion of God. This persuasion will lead you to move on God's timing and not on your own time. You will begin to lean not on your own understanding but God's. You will experience a transformation from the inside out. You can be changed by intentionally listening to God; the Creator of heaven and earth which resides in you. Love will move into your Soul and life.

## My Story: Jon

Jon is a great example of a heathen becoming a man of God while being healed from his past abuse issues at the same time. Jon was a 52-year-old black male. He was struggling with his indulgence in pornography, infidelity and had "a little eating problem." Jon was "a spiritual man but not real religious." Jon came to counseling because “My wife left my ass last week."

Jon agreed to six sessions of pastoral counseling to, "Get her (his wife) off my back." He was bragging about being a 6-year-old and "being with a big beauty." Jon was a talker but was guarded with his feelings. Jon was guarded due to being sexually abused by a "13 or 14-year-old babysitter." Jon had a flamboyant personality that made people feel liked and respected. Jon never met a stranger and was glad to see you even if he had never met you. When Jon would walk out my office all the clients in the waiting room told him bye as if they had known him all their lives.

Jon wanted to know the "fastest way out" of counseling. Jon wanted to "get God back in my life." Jon wanted God back in his life because he was seeing a Pastoral Counselor. I gave Jon an assignment to give him answers on how to "get God back in his life." He was asked to explain his view of the Holy Spirit. He was to close his eyes and picture or give a physical figure to the Holy Spirit. Once Jon had a visual picture of the Holy Spirit, he was to get quiet. I told Jon, "that by giving physical features to the Holy Spirit you will be more likely to use the fruit of the Spirit and or hear God. Once you have this visual picture, you need to get quiet and close your eyes and spend time with this image of God in you." This was all the information that I gave Jon. As Jon left the session he said. "I will do that exercise."

The next session, Jon had a word picture of the Holy Spirit. Jon had the picture of "a big little overweight black man." He was dressed in a " sharp pin stripe suit and has deep eyes that looks right through me." Jon was able to talk of his "patent leather shoes," " his loud voice" and " his nice smile." Jon was asked to spend time talking to the Holy Spirit each time he was tempted to womanize, look at pornography or overeat. Jon was to listen to Him at night before he went to bed. Jon agreed to do both assignments.

Jon was a changed man when he came back the next week. Jon came in and the first thing he said was, "Thank you." Jon had "a real father now." Jon gave example after example of the Spirit "talking me through it" and "not doing anything, not one slip." Jon had hope and several of the Fruit of the Spirit. Jon had peace, joy, faithfulness, and self-control. Jon began reading books to deal with his indulgence of "porn" because that was his "biggest problem."

Jon read *Everyman's Battle* and *Sex Man and God* in one week. He craved anything and everything he could read. Jon said, " I read in my spare time and the preacher talked me through it." The "preacher" was the name he gave to the Holy Spirit. Jon was focused on and listening to himself and Holy Spirit instead of medicating and avoiding himself.

Jon came in for his fifth session and said, "the preacher said I need to talk about the babysitter thing." Jon talked about what he remembered about his "abuse." Jon talked about his abuse and had flashbacks during the session. He had increased sadness for "little Jon." Jon had anger at his "father" in the session because he remembered "telling him about it (the abuse)."

Jon had anger with his father because when he told his father about what the babysitter was doing, " He just laughed and kept saying, 'That's my boy.'" Jon knew the little boy was "scared" and "didn't like it." Jon was encouraged to speak to his "little boy" as he spoke to the preacher. Jon was able to talk to his inner child and " let him know that our father's behavior was not right. You know that made the preacher mad." Jon said the " preacher has him and He is talking to both of us." Jon became aware that he was looking at pornography, " hoping one day I wouldn't be scared to make love with Shandra (his wife)."

Jon agreed to continue counseling until, "you or the preacher tells me to stop." Jon was encouraged to talk to Shandra about his reasons for using porn and his fear. Jon had fears that Shandra would think he was "gay or something." Jon said he would "pray" about it. I asked him to talk to the preacher about talking to her.

Jon came in the next session and said, "I spoke with Shandra and she started crying and gave me a hug." Jon went on to say that she wanted him to come home. I asked Jon the reason he did not move home and he said, "I'm not ready." Jon struggled for three weeks until he voiced his fear of going back with Shandra: "I'm scared I won't please her in bed."

He agreed to talk to the preacher about his fear. He came into his next session with a smile and reported that he moved home with Shandra. Jon said, "I talked to the preacher and found out that Shandra just wanted me to love her and that I will be more than enough in bed." When I asked about how he did in the bedroom, Jon smiled, "It was the first time I ever made love with a woman. I'm glad it was with her." What Jon meant about the "first time" was in his authentic self.

Jon used the Fruit of the Spirit by creating a figure to embody them. The preacher was a gift that helped him use the Fruit of the Spirit and experience a healthy father figure. Jon found healing from his addictions and worked through his abuse issues. Jon found his authentic self and was able to experience love for the first time.

My clients' biggest fears with personalizing the Holy Spirit are that: "You can't trust it." "That is sacrilegious." or "How do you know it is what God would say or do?" If you have these fears or questions then you can check your answers with scripture, your church doctrine, or your pastor. Personalizing the Holy Spirit or Jesus brings forth truth. The Spirit of God will convict you if you get the wrong information. In my 25 years of being a Pastoral Counselor, the problem for my clients had not been with personalizing God or the Holy Spirit. They had problems with their scripts, automatic negative thoughts, intrusive thoughts and/ or distortions.

You may struggle with the fear of visualizing the Holy Spirit. Let us look at the pictures of Christ that are on walls and in many Bibles. These pictures of Christ are someone's picture of him. These pictures or drawings of Jesus Christ were not taken or drawn over two thousand years ago. How did we get this picture of a Caucasian with long hair and a clean clear complexion? The picture that symbolizes Jesus Christ resembles a gentile more than a Jewish man. Do not get me wrong, I love that picture of Jesus because I grew up seeing Jesus as white, tall and a handsome male. I am not going to be upset when I see a short, slightly heavy-set male that has a dark complexion and short hair in heaven.

When I get to heaven it will not matter if Jesus is short or tall in stature, has light or dark skin, with long or short hair. I anticipate seeing Jesus as a man that has loved me before I was born; loved me so much, that he gave his life for me. I believe he will come up to me and give me a hug and call me by name. I can envision him having scars on his forehead from the crown of thorns that he wore; the scars on his hands and feet from the nails that were driven in him on the cross and the puncture wound in his side that was given to him by the centurion soldier at the cross. Yes, he will have a glorified body, but I believe these scars will be there on him. They will be there until Christ has " bound him (Satan) for a thousand years; and he threw him into the abyss, and shut it and sealed it over him, so that he would not deceive the nations any longer," (Revelation 20; 1). then the scars will pass away.

Your theology and picture of your Heavenly Father, Jesus or the Holy Spirit may be different than mine. My concern is for you to picture your Heavenly Father, Jesus, or the Holy Spirit in you, for you and with you. Some of my clients hear critical messages and old tapes from their past. These tapes are legalistic, heavy handed and judgmental. This critical spirit is not of God. So, please do not project it on him or allow your old tapes to stop your spiritual experience. If you hear judgement and critical old rules from your internal critic, remind them that "Legalism in any form is not Christianity" (The Crisis of Fear, Thornton & Borchert, 1988, p.134). If you give your old tapes and script power, they may keep you away from experiencing God.

It is sad that you may walk by sight and miss the God image in you. God created Mankind in His image and you can experience this same God in an image that represents Him. This internal representative of God will embody the fruit of the Spirit and His knowledge. My hope is that your picture or theology will be of a God that loves you unconditionally, forgives you totally and will never leave you nor forsake you. You will experience the true Triune God if you are seeking Him spiritually.

Seeking God is a spiritual workout. These exercises consist of worshiping God through praying, studying God's Word and having fellowship with other believers. Your discernment and knowledge of God will strengthen with these spiritual workouts. This Soul food will come with a healthy spiritual workout while building in God's protection and empowerment in you. You will trust your spiritual experiences and be empowered by the Holy Spirit in you. You do not need to spiritually workout alone.

Remember, you need to have at least two or more of your friends to support you on this journey. Your journey will require Soul food, workouts, and fellowship. Please do not minimize the need for fellowship in your spiritual growth because, "Iron sharpens iron"(Proverbs 27:17). The main thing is "'one man sharpens another.' This Hebrew word *"iysh" meaning* man" (Bible Dictionary, William Smith, LLD,1948 p.377) can mean brother, fellow struggler or friend in the same struggle. This word has the connotation of a face to face conversation with a like-minded person. This is important because you need someone, like-minded, close to you. My clients usually run from like-minded friends because they have increased fear of being judged by those that know them. I hope you will face your fear and ask those closest to you to have your back during your healing journey.

The power of the Spirit goes past the fruit of the Spirit to intercede for you with God. Romans 8:26 says, " In the same way the Spirit also helps our weakness; for we do not know how to pray as we should, but the Spirit Himself intercedes for us with groaning too deep for words" (Romans 8:26 NASB). The intercession of the Spirit is giving utterance to your "weakness." The same weaknesses or illness that you may have hidden from yourself and friends for years. The Holy Spirit is bringing your illness before God in ways that are "too deep for words." This is truly an act of love.

It is important for you to know that the Spirit has your back and is actively loving you in your illnesses or weaknesses. The Holy Spirit will help you confront and unearth the root of your problems or insecurities which abide in your soul. This same spirit will never abandon you nor stop interceding before the King on your behalf. Your past or present shame and/or guilt, indulgences, or sins, will not break this intercession. Many Christians will not bring their sin before God due to fear of being rejected, judged, and condemned by Him. You may have memories of friends, family and church members judging you or being self-righteous. You are still giving them power if you are seeing these same qualities in God. Do not allow other past opinions to stop your fellowship with God and others today.

God knows all your dirty laundry because He is all Knowing. The Holy Spirit will intercede on your behalf before God. God is just waiting for you to come when you miss His mark so He can forgive and love you. When you are experiencing your authentic feelings, you are looking through the windows of your Soul. You may be looking through the mirror of your soul: a distorted lens that reflects your past dysfunction onto your present reality.

As you look through the mirror of your Soul you may hear the negative words, become aware of fragmented images of your past abuse or wounds of your indulgences which hurts your mind, and Spirit. Just remember the King of Kings, Lord of Lords and Prince of Peace has sent His own Spirit to intercede for you. The Holy Spirit that dwells, standup, and intercedes for you "with groaning too deep for words." Now if that does not give you hope or chills, nothing will. You need to apply this knowledge if your pain is deep, belief is weak, or you are lost in an indulgence. You need to remember your God's character which can be seen by the fruit of His Spirit. These fruits are ***love, joy, peace, patience, kindness, goodness, faithfulness, gentleness, and self-control.*** Are you experiencing the fruit of the Spirit in your life? Yes. No. Are you willing to personify i.e. give personal attributes to the Holy Spirit in you? Yes. No.

This personification of the Holy Spirit can be your image of God or Jesus. Take time to dwell in your temple and look to see or hear the Holy Spirit in you. You can ask the question: What would God say about seeing His image in me?

Write down what you are hearing from the Holy Spirit:

Then trust your discernment. You will experience the Holy in you. God's Word needs to be "hidden on your heart" (psalm 119;11) and I had clients do just that by having a God journal. They wrote their heart's knowledge of and from God daily. The God journal transformed their lives.

You will build a strong spiritual life if you do not allow your sinful nature to get in your way. Your God came to redeem you by sending his Son, Jesus, to die for your sins. You are allowing your sins to keep you from Him. This really does not make much sense does it? When Jesus was alive on this earth, he was known for being "a friend of sinners "(Luke 7:34). If Jesus were here today, He would be your friend. A friend that would love you despite your actions. He would not use illicit drugs with you but would pick you up when you could not walk. Jesus would be a friend that never belittles, ridiculous or breaks your secrets. Jesus would be a friend that you could trust to die for you if it came down to it.

You will be able to get a picture of Jesus and his Father's characters by looking at each of the fruit(s) of the Spirit. In Galatians 5:22,23, The word fruit is singular and comes from the Greek word "*Karpos.*" *Karpos,* fruit, "is singular" (Word Pictures in New Testament, 1931, p.313) and would be thought to mean that all nine of the characteristics comes in one fruit. I take it to mean this "fruit" is the Holy Spirit that has all these qualities of God that are in you. Yes, the Holy Spirit controls these attributes, and they are produced as you become more Christlike. I cannot separate the outward Christlike behavior from the inward movement of the Holy Spirit. I believe they go hand in hand.

You will need to be intentional about experiencing the Holy Spirit. The Holy Spirit fills your Holy of Holies or Soul. Many Christians question their salvation because they are not experiencing the fruit of the Spirit or the movement of the Holy Spirit within them. The indwelling of the Holy Spirit is outside your consciousness yet can be conscious.

There are several ways to access the Holy Spirit. They are:

- intentionally practicing the fruit of the Spirit
- a spiritual experience with God i.e. being slain in the Spirit or speaking in tongues
- practicing religious rituals such as praying, reading scriptures, singing, and fasting etc....

Or

- personalizing the Holy Spirit by intentionally walking in your Holy of Holies to have a conscious awareness of the Holy Spirit

***Allow yourself to Stop,***
***Look***
***Listen***
***To yourself***
***Experiencing the Holy***
***Spirit in you.***

Allow yourself to sit quietly and focus on your breathing. Breathing in the fresh relaxing air and exhaling all your stress and tension as you exhale. Do this breathing pattern three more times. If you have any mental or emotional distractions allow yourself to empty them as you exhale. Close your eyes to not be distracted. Allow each breath to move you closer to a calm and peaceful place to be with God's Spirit. Once you reach a calm mental place be aware of the color, sounds and the things which bring peace and beauty to your soul. Breathing in the peace while calling forth the Holy Spirit.

Be patient and breathe, allowing yourself to be open to the form which the Holy Spirit will take for you. Once you have this mental picture of the Holy Spirit then experience Him in you.

Stop and just spend time with this God image in you. Stop and experience this image in silence. Be aware of what this image is wearing, doing, and saying. Just experience this image of God in you. You are experiencing the Holy. Experience the Holy for a time then slowly use your breathing to move back to the room you are in now. If you want to have more guidance you can go to YouTube, then type in "Crazy Or Not Here I Come" to the Soul - experiencing the Holy Spirit in you.

Once you have finished the above experience, give yourself time to journal. Write down what you experienced. Be specific about the details of the image that you saw and experienced. You can ask this image of God questions or share your thoughts and feelings with Him.

## The Soul - Home of the Holy Spirit

The Holy Spirit indwells your holy of holies or Soul, but what is the Soul? You are on a healing journey to your Soul and need to experience the bond of tenderness with your Heavenly Father. I am privileged to be able to speak of the bond of tenderness that feeds your Soul. I am also intimidated by this privilege. I am fully aware that there is a personal soul and a spiritual Soul. You can say the room is the same but filled by the natural or the supernatural.

God has a sense of humor. When I was in seminary, I laughed at the panel of experts that were explaining their views of the Soul. The two topics I would never choose to write about after leaving graduate school were the "soul" and "regression work." Now, I am writing on both. Yes, God is smiling upon me today. The adage "Never say Never" has truth to it. Over the years I have been asked several questions about the soul like:

What is the soul?
Where is it?
Is it real?
Is it my spirit?
Can I lose it?
Does everyone have a soul?
Can your soul be evil?
Did God make the soul?
Did God make evil and good souls?
Is the soul and God the same thing?
Can I eat soul food or listen to soul music to strengthen my soul?

I will answer these questions by giving information on the Soul and giving a biblical definition of the Soul. Giving definition to the soul is like giving definition to God. It is necessary but impossible.

Here are two short definitions of the soul: The first is by a psychiatrist and author of "The Road Less Traveled," Dr Scott Peck who said, "The soul is God- created, god-nurtured, unique, develop-able, immortal human spirit" (Scott peck, Denial of the soul, 1993, p. 132). While the second is by a theologian and author, Bremen Manning, of "The Ragamuffin Gospel" and "Abba's Child" who said, "the essential energy of the soul is not an ecstatic trance, high emotion, or sanguine stance towards life: It is a fierce longing for God, an unyielding resolve to live in and out of the truth of our belovedness"( Abba's Child p. 152.). Belovedness refers to God's love for you as your Abba or daddy. I will not give a definition to what cannot be defined. Most people would associate the word soul as a spiritual word. Most people would associate God to the word soul. Some would say the concept of God is implied in the concept of the soul.

I had atheist clients that did not believe that they had a soul because they did not believe in God. I had atheists and agnostics who believed they had a soul but did not attribute it to God. They may define the soul as being the deepest and most complete aspect of who they were as a person. They would say their souls were their deepest sense of self that transcends knowing but could be known. They may say that the soul is mortal and has a nature greater than themselves.

My explanation of the soul will be linked to my theological perspective. My theological perspective is based on a biblical view or the Word of God. This will color my perspective of the soul. I will attempt to answer all the above questions about the soul based on my understanding which will be inadequate. I am not being hard on myself because the experience of any mystery cannot be fully explained.

You will have your own definition of the soul. As you get closer to your authentic self, your definition of the soul may change due to your experience. Your soul will change but will be colored by your thoughts, feelings, and experiences. Over the years, my definition of the soul has changed based on my knowledge or experience of myself and God.

I can say that I went to seminary to learn about God and the soul. I admit, after four years of studying, I had knowledge of both. I had greater knowledge of God and the soul while having less understanding of either of them. My years as a Pastoral Counselor sharpen my understanding of the psyche, the Greek word for soul. This understanding gave depth and breathe to my care of the souls of my clients.

The Greek word "psy-khe" refers to "the soul [ which] is the life principle"(The Letter to the Hebrews, William Barclay, 2nd Ed 1957, p.35).

This life principle is "the living being, or the self as the subject of appetite and emotions, occasionally of volition" (The Interpreter's Dictionary of the Bible,R-Z, Vol. 4, 1962 p.428). In psychology, the soul is your conscious and unconscious mind or sense of self. The soul is the center of your rational choices, emotional desires, and afflictions. Your soul extends from your personality to your sense of self or your " being." Psy-khe is used 102 times in the New Testament.

The psyche is a dynamic term in the biblical text. The Greek word for Soul is sometimes translated as person (1 Peter 3:20), life (Matthew 6:25), heart (Ephesians 6;56) and the mind (Act 14:2). These traits of soul would signify the psychological term for personality. If you are going to understand the true dynamics of the soul, it depends on the life force or spirit that moves it. One needs to look at the word for spirit to understand this dynamic.

The Hebrew word for spirit was n *é'phesh* which "is broadly translated as 'breath,' 'wind,' and in the psychological and theological sense 'Spirit'" (The Interpreters Dictionary of the Bible, A-D, Vol.1,1962 p.465). God's Breath gave all mankind life. *Ne'phesh*, breath, was used 754 times in the Old Testament. In Genesis 2:7 man became a *néphesh* "living soul" or living breath of God representing "' a complete person'"(The Interpreters Bible, Vol.1,1952, p.494). I need to refer to Genesis 1:27 that says, "God created man in His own image, in the image and likeness of God He created him; male and female He created them" (AMP). This image or likeness of God is the body for the Breath of God. Your breath or spirit is from God. God's breath gave life or spirit to the image of God which mankind was created (Genesis 2:7).

In Genesis 2:7 " the LORD God formed man of dust from the ground and breathed into his nostrils the breath of life; and man became a living being" (Genesis 2:7 NASB). This breath or spirit of God created life and "man became a living being." This breath created a living being that had rational thought and a heart (mind) which the New Testament equate with the psyché. The Fall separated man from God's Spirit. Mankind's freewill broke the relationship of God's Spirit and the created image of Himself. This relic of God left an imprint on mankind's psyché (Romans 12:3). Mankind will strive to fill this void left by the God's Spirit with the spirit of the flesh.

Your spirit of the flesh is natural and fills your soul, yet this spirit is self-serving, left to its own volition. The spirit and soul are two different entities. The soul was not created by you; it was not made with human hands. Your soul was created by God and for God. Your soul is like a sanctuary made by God for the purpose of being filled with God's Spirit. Everyone has a soul and a spirit, yet it is of the flesh. You and I can fill this sanctuary with the spirit of the worlds (1 John 5:19) or God's Spirit. Your spirit, life-force is of the world and part of your soul. Your soul and spirit are two different entities that can only be separated by God's Word and God (Hebrews 4:12). Your spirit, or life force, is of the flesh and your soul is invariably "self-loving." Many will believe as Scott Peck "specifically designated that soul to be spirit" (Denial of the Soul, 1997, p.156).

The soul follows the guidance of the spirit which governs it. Your psyche or soul can be tied to your natural spirit which is of the flesh or world (Gal. 6;18; 1Cor.2:11;1 Tim. 4:1; Rev 16:13,14) or the Spirit of God which is a supernatural one (1 Thessalonians 5;23). Freewill makes it possible to choose good or evil to fill your soul. God will honor your choice. You have several spirits to fill your soul's sanctuary; your freewill will make the choice.

The spirit of the world, or God, operates within your consciousness. The spirit is somewhat free from the influences of your soul. Your soul's choice of spirit will be influenced or colored by that choice. Yes, you can be a Christian and still move by the spirit of the flesh or the word. The mind will move with the spirit which is moving it, or it is pursuing. This is the reason you are transformed by the renewal of your mind, (Roman 12:2) and you will need to have "the same mindset as Christ" (Philippians 2:5). Changing spiritually is a process of taking off the old spirit and putting on the new one (Ephesians 4:24). Your soul is dynamic, yet the spirit gives it life or death. Your soul is eternal and cannot be slain yet can choose to figuratively die through sin (Ezekiel 18;4; Romans 6;23), or die to sin ( Luke 9;23-23; Galatians 5;24; Romans 8; 12-13). Your Soul can live through faith (1 Peter 1:39) and joining the royal priesthood (1 Peter 2:9).

Your soul can be separated from the body at death (2 Corinthians 5;8; Matthew 10;28). The spirit can be separated from the soul (Matthew 10;28) and separated from God in life (Ephesians 2:8-10) and in death (Roman 6;23;

John 3:16; Matthew 25:41). Your soul's desires or choice of spirits will be honored by God. Your choice of God's Spirit is a matter of faith.

God will honor your choices even when it hurts Him. The image you were created in calls out to its maker. I believe the Imago Dei, the image of God in you (Genesis 1:26, 9;6; Psalms 17;15), gives you the ability to want more than the human life force and calls out for the Spirit of God's character. You were created in a 3D image of God; this is more than a reflection. This image is a physical and spiritual "likeness" of God (James 3,9). Adam originally was filled by the Spirit of God, before the Fall, and this knowing and experience of God resides in all mankind.

Christians can feed their Soul with "Soul food" from the Holy Spirit or with the spirit of the world. Christians have a conscious choice to follow the impulses, instincts or repressed desires of the flesh or Will oneself to follow God. Some would argue that repressed desires create the greatest damage or sin for Christians. "' Medically, the worst form of sin, as Dr. Brown reminds us, is not the sin that has overthrown us, nor the sin that has been conquered, but the sin which we have simply allowed to live within us unfought and unfaced and now lives a vigorous life as repressed. When a repression of this sort has been squarely faced and acknowledged before God there is a sense of freedom and liberty" (G. J. Jordon, A Short Psychology of Religion,1928, p.75-76).

You will need to consciously put on and actively enlist the Spirit or you will be seduced or tempted by the Father of lies which is of the world ( 1Peter 5;9; James 1;13-18). Anytime you are focused on the holy through meditation, prayer, fellowship, or bible study it will feed your Soul. Uplifting and calming music can feed your soul. When I experience natural beauty, I feel close to God and my soul is filled. I believe atheists and agnostics can fill their soul on beautiful music and natural beauty. Usually anything that edifies or builds up the self will feed the soul. You will find that positive words and acts of kindness for yourself and others will feed your soul. Why do these things feed your soul?

It may be for the same reason that people use adjectives that describe what filling their soul feels like: light, majesty, mystery, open, peaceful, joyous, enlightening, comforting, healing, spirit, truth, fresh, knowing, innocents, clean, pure, not human, holy, whole and calm. Now think about your God: does He have these attributes? What are the reasons Christians and non-Christians use these adjectives for what fills their souls? It is because the Soul is neither human nor natural. Your Soul is transcendent, holy, and immortal and made in the image of God.

Your soul and spirit maintain a delicate balance when you are mentally and spiritually healthy. Being spiritually healthy can be a matter of faith or alignment with the sacred or holy in yourself. There may be some readers that do not have a personal relationship with God. Can you experience the Imago Dei, image of God, in your holy of holies? Or Does your soul need to be sanctified by God to be spiritually healthy? You can experience your soul and have spiritual health and not have faith in God. I have met a lot of people that were spiritually and mentally healthy and did not have the Spirit of God filling their souls. They feed their soul with adjectives that were mentioned above and were content or happy.

Many contemplative thinkers and mystics will use a wide variety of non-religious practices to feed their souls. These practices can be music, dance, prayer, meditation, painting, journaling, and reading biblical wisdom literature to name a few ways they feed their souls. There are many books that are fascinating on how to free up your conscious thought and to increase your enlightenment, yet many who read these same books believe this enlightenment will fill their Soul. This is not true.

Yes, there are many contemplative Christian writers opening new ways to look at God's Word. It is important to know, as a reader, the author's faith, heart, and mind concerning God. It is important to know that several things can feed your soul but only acceptance of God's Son will fill your Soul (John 14:6). It can be filled only with the Holy Spirit. Your acceptance of God's Son through faith leads to sanctification of your Soul by God. Being sanctified is "to render or declare holy, to consecrate, to separate from things profane" (Archibald Thomas Robertson, Word Pictures in the New Testament, Vol4, Epistles of Paul, 1931, p.38). God has sanctified you, set you apart, for the use of the holy. Being sanctified is the process of being made holy or pure.

You cannot fill your Soul any other way. Yes, many contemplatives, mystics and spiritualists would see this theology as bigotry, arrogance, or ignorance. Biblically, no amount of contemplation, higher consciousness or being spiritual will make you holy or lead to salvation. In 1 Thessalonians 5;23 it says "Now may the God of peace Himself sanctify you entirely; and may your spirit and soul and body be preserved completely, without blame at the coming of our Lord Jesus Christ" (NASB). The word "now" is speaking to those that had accepted Jesus' message. Jesus' message was "I am the way and the truth and the life. No one comes to the Father except through me" (John 14;6 NIV).

It is important to know that God, "Himself sanctifies you entirely." Your entire spirit, Soul and body is sanctified or made holy through His son Jesus Christ. This is the biblical testimony of how your spirit is set apart from the psyche or soul.

It is important to be spiritually healthy. You need to be spiritually healthy when you are dealing with mental illness, relational conflict, or internal and external indulgences. The goal is activating the Holy Spirit or putting on the mind of Christ. You will need to find the balance between your mind, body, and Soul. When one of these is out of balance the other ones can bring you back in line or balance. It is easier to be brought into balance when your mind, body and Soul are sanctified.

As a Pastoral Counselor, the psyche needs to be heard and processed in line with the Holy. The cure of the Soul is a spiritual journey. When I had my license as a Marriage and Family Therapist it was taboo to deal with the Soul. Not considering, the Soul misses the mark of true healing. This healing journey to the Soul is a psycho-spiritual journey to cure or care for the psyche.

Psycho-spiritual healing comes through using the Holy Spirit. You will be drawn to your old learning which came through the flesh, while being tempted to step into the spirit of the world. Listening to your inner child deals with the wounds of the flesh and using the Holy Spirit's Soul Food will nurture the wounds of the flesh.

I believe Jesus wants to remember the scars of his pain and suffering.

These scars also carried the pain and anguish you and I have gone through at Satan's hand. These scars will vanish when the warfare is over. The victory came on a blood-stained cross, but the battle continues until Christ returns to earth to have the final battle. The warfare now is over destroying that which God has loved so much: His children. As a child of God, you will be sanctified, restored, or made whole when you are with your Heavenly Father. Jesus is the exception because he wants to remember until the final battle is over.

Pastoral Counselors are trained in both disciplines and have mastered the integration of the two disciplines. I need to clarify that psycho-spiritual "counseling" is not only "biblical counseling" but integrates the psychological, mental, and emotional, aspects of the soul. Pure biblical counsel usually comes from a pastor or priest. I have seen a lot of my clients hurt by this form of help. I find a lot of people trained in theology have little training in the knowledge of the psyche or the cure of the Soul. Giving biblical answers without dealing with the mental and emotional wounds is dangerous.

How would you feel if you were depressed and given biblical verses and asked to pray for spiritual healing and did not get well? You may feel more depressed. This form of help will usually create more spiritual shame or anger with God which will increase your depression. You would probably have more anxiety than you had before the biblical council.

You can look out the windows of the soul by dealing with your psychological wounds and increasing conscious awareness. You can look out the windows of your Soul by activating the Holy Spirit to clean your psychological wounds and have the mind of Christ while being conscious. Your healing journey to find your authentic self will be one of courage, transparency and dedication which includes the Holy.

## Remember:

You may have depression, anxiety or been victimized by abuse and forgotten your true ancestry of being a child of the most High God. Remember the words of Brennan manning," Do you believe that God loves you, not the world, not the church, not the person next to you, but that God loves you, so much that He would rather die than be without you? "(. *Brennan Manning talks, "Abba I Belong to You" given in 1984*).

# CHAPTER NINE

## A SELF PORTRAIT OF AN ADDICT

"There hath no temptation taken you but such as man can bear: but God is faithful, who will not suffer you to be tempted above that ye are able; but will with the temptation make also the way of escape, that ye may be able to endure it. Wherefore, my beloved, flee from idolatry."

1 Corinthians 10:13-14 ASV

**KEY POINTS:**

- Your indulgences (i.e., areas of your life where you engage in harmful imbalance) stem from repressed memories and unwanted emotional experiences.
- Confronting present emotions and previous repressed emotions will empower your recovery.
- Self-control is a sovereign gift from God to you.

**Reflections:**

- The goal is to recover the "self" from self-pity, self-loathing and/or self-doubt.
- Are you struggling with a "hidden" indulgence that is keeping you captive?
- Are you willing to take the first step in recovery and admit you have a problem?

## Self Portrait of An Addict

The heart of addiction is emptiness, while its mind is one of lust. The stomach of addiction is of flesh and blood, one that craves the object of its desire. The spirit of addiction is that of a child crying for its idols. Its persona, or face, is full, expressive, and likely joyous. Its words are cutting, slanted to deceive others and itself. This deception allows a self-portrait to be a part of everything and nothing at the same time. Meaning and purpose comes from the idol it serves. Service to its idol fills its stomach full of emptiness and its mind full of lust, draining itself of life and its soul of God.

## Welcome.

I am not judging anyone addicted or indulging in their idols because I would be judging myself. I have lost moderation by being codependent. I have allowed the emptiness and lust of my father's reflection to poison my being and soul. I have experienced the desire to fill his cup with noble deeds to the point of losing myself. I have allowed indulgent people to take my blessings, heart and mind to their idols and ending up empty myself.

As a recovering codependent or co-addict, I know the emotional state of the one that is indulgent because it was projected onto me. My father got lost in alcohol like I got lost in pleasing him; both paths lead to insanity. I allowed other people's idols to control my feelings and thoughts, and as a result my soul was contaminated.

Living with "a portrait of an addict" in your life will likely lead to a loss of yourself. You will lose yourself to the negative messages or behavior of the addiction, which are the seeds of self-despair, self-doubt, and self-loathing. Many will avoid the addiction and its reflection by overindulging in food, alcohol, work, etc. Living with a portrait of an addict has the same effect as living with a perpetrator of the heart. The wounds are those that affect your mind and soul while leaving a void of unmet needs and a damaged inner landscape, which often serves to perpetuate further addictions.

Let us explore the difference between indulgences and addictions. Some would call indulgences addictions. In our society, addiction is a disease that is not curable. Indulgences would be synonymous with addiction if addictions were curable. Indulgences are a choice and can be focused on a behavior, a substance, or emotion that alters your mood and creates a mental and/or physical dependency. You may have an indulgence and not be aware it is controlling your life. Repressed memories are covered or medicated by indulgences that hide your true self-image. You cannot experience your authentic God given image while chasing indulgences to alter your reality.

An indulgence is when you indulge to excess or show a lack of restraint. The antidote to this problem is moderation. What fuels indulgences are avoidance of your past emotional experiences, rejection, conflict, or failure. You are human and will experience pain or suffering. Experiencing your suffering will give your life, while grounding you. You will lose realty and yourself by defending yourself against what is real and escaping through indulging. Defense mechanisms do not allow you to experience reality, which stop moderation and awareness.

Indulgences stem from unmet emotional needs. The indulgence is a distraction to avoid or numb your emotional pain or anxiety. Self-medicating with an internal or external indulgence brings temporary relief and long-term problems. "Trauma and addiction go hand in hand. The traumatized person who experiences deep and intolerable emotional and psychological pain, or suffers from such states of physiological arousal as rapid breathing, racing heart rate, or anxiety, may discover the dangerous lesson that a little bit of alcohol, some heroin, cocaine, a joint, sugar, or sex brings quick and reliable relief. Initially, pain goes away, and a sense of equilibrium is restored... Eventually, however, the brain and body become addicted, and larger and larger amounts of the addictive substance are needed to produce the same effect. Then feeling great is no longer enough because the body and mind have been damaged by years of addiction, and the addict uses just to feel normal. What starts out as an attempt to manage pain evolves into a new source of it" (Trauma and addiction, Tian Dayton, 2000, p. Xvii). This evolution of pain and addiction comes through living with a portrait of an addict or dissociated aspects of trauma. Neither one is mutually exclusive. So, what about internal indulgences?

Internal indulgences are bred in the same petri dish as external indulgences. One of them traumatizes others and the other traumatizes you. Karla McLaren gives two responses to trauma that reflects this phenomenon.

In her book, "The Language of Emotion" she "observed two basic ways that people respond to their disassociating traumas: either they learn to traumatize themselves, or they learn to traumatize others. When survivors were responding to unrelieved trauma by traumatizing themselves, they usually repress it and re-create its atmosphere in their inner lives. The trauma and its aftermath settle into their inner landscape and create feelings of powerlessness, dread, and hopelessness" (2010, p.95). Dissociated trauma is fertile ground for all indulgences.

"The second response is to turn around and become a traumatizer of others — to express traumatizing behaviors upon others to relieve the disturbing effects of the trauma [or external indulgences]. Survivors who traumatize others experience feelings of powerlessness, dread, and hopelessness — just as the self– traumatizers do — but these survivors don't clamp down on their pain or contain it; rather, they visit it upon others in an attempt to understand, deaden, or master it" (2010, p.95). The first response will likely result in internal indulgence that later moves to external ones and the second response to trauma will likely result in use of external indulgence that later moves to internal ones.

You may not think that internal indulgences will destroy you or affect your external indulgence. External indulgences that are not moderated will destroy you externally first and later internally. Internal indulgences usually show greater damages internally before you see the damages externally. You may not be able to list many internal or external indulgences. You, like others, may not be aware that you are going to extremes with your indulgence(s).

## Exercise: Identifying Your Indulgence Tendencies

*This is not a regression exercise. There are no special instructions included. Answer simply and directly in your journal.*

Here is a brief list of internal and external indulgences. Circle the ones that apply to you.

**Internal Indulgences:**

- self-despair

- self-doubt
- hopelessness
- sloth
- loneliness
- greed
- envy
- jealousy
- procrastination
- lust
- self-loathing
- self-pity
- melancholy
- anxiety
- anger
- self-critical
- self-debasement
- boredom
- cruelty to self (self-mutilation)
- self-deceit

**External indulgences:**

- alcohol
- drugs (prescription and illegal)
- food (overrating, bulimia, or anorexia)
- pornography
- work
- infidelity
- tobacco (smoking or smokeless)
- television
- shopping
- working out
- religion
- laziness- being aimless
- gambling
- other, __________

Your awareness of your own indulgence pattern is important. Your external indulgences have more of a mood-altering effect that puts a substance in control of your state of mind, affecting your mood. If your mind and body is physiological and emotionally dependent on an external indulgence, you will need to deal with your dependency issues before you experience the child within you. If your indulgences are not contained, they will affect the child within you. If you have an internal indulgence, then you are less physiologically dependent, yet your mood has a higher possibility of being altered than external indulgence and likely dependent on your early learning or dissociative aspects of your trauma.

Now if you are honest with yourself, you have over indulged to gratify yourself. You just have not made it a habit. You might have indulged for a few days, months, or years. Normally, people are not likely to deal with their overuse until they have problems that arise from their addictions. You may not acknowledge that you have a problem with overindulging because of defense mechanisms.

Indulgences grow in silence, undetectable until they take over your time, attention, and energy. Indulgences are undetectable at first because they stem from healthy gratification when used with self-control, but without moderation can gradually become more perverted. Your first use of any mood-altering substance of behavior will feel great. After years of compulsive behavior, you may find that what once brought you comfort is now decaying your soul. The greater you decay, the greater your use of a defense mechanisms like minimizing, rationalizing, and denying covering your present decay. These indulgences become idols, which separate you from your authentic self and God.

Let us look at the top three external and internal indulgences I see clinically. These are the primary three areas of addiction our society struggles with today. We will look at the external indulgences first because most people are not aware of internal ones.

### 1. External Indulgence: Overeating

The top external indulgence is overeating, which has become an epidemic in our society. You must eat to provide your body's biological need, but the problem is not eating, it is "over" eating. Over-indulging begins so innocently that we all have done it. Beginning with first, an extra piece of cake, a little more of that dressing, eating that extra bag of chips, to ordering a " biggy" fries when a small will do. The first time anyone overeats, it is likely innocent enough and even encouraged by those that love you.

How did a biological need, socially accepted practice, and reward for good behavior by every loving grandmother become an indulgence, problem, addiction, or sin? It is a thin line that is hard to distinguish. It is hard to know because you are not aware of the line you are crossing. People do not consider why they are eating more. The lack of personal awareness makes a socially accepted behavior unacceptable or physically unhealthy. You are not aware of the emotional cost because of the "good feeling," "high," or "comfort" it provides. Lastly, those who are enabling you to indulge usually are doing so out of love and will likely criticize you later.

I know hearing that your close relatives deceived you about your looking good in those pants or that you gained more weight can be hard to hear. Think back; in most cases, no one mentioned your problem until it was already out of hand. When listening to your family members who are judging or critiquing you now, you may find comfort in knowing that they were the same ones who enabled you to overindulge. My clients' enablers gave super treats, overlooking the compulsive eating to feel better about themselves or to overcompensate for the time, energy, or attention they were giving something else. Yes, they were easing their own guilt at your expense. If you are dealing with the judgment of your enablers or their concern with your overeating, then knowing they enabled you will help you with your shame and guilt. Most enablers use the same defense mechanisms as the compulsive overeater.

It is socially acceptable to minimize, rationalize or justify one's weight in our society. You have heard, "No, you're not gaining weight." "That looks good on you" to "fat is beautiful." The lines get blurry because of minimizing how much you eat, rationalizing the reasons you eat, and denying your overeating. "That piece wasn't that big", (minimizing) "I deserve this because I worked hard" (rationalizes) "I was hungry" (denies), "I didn't eat all of it" uses all three. These lies go on at home and in the church.

If you have ever been overweight, you will remember these moments:

- when you had to suck in your stomach to pull your pants up or to button them together
- taken off that skirt because it would not fit over your thighs or
- looking in the mirror and recognizing that you were "fat"
- eating another piece of cake when you knew you were "full"

The reality that you were out of control may have not registered because of your use of stronger defense mechanisms like suppressing and repressing these inner knowings. The pain of being out of control slips into unconscious fragments that begin to control your life.

Your brief awareness of losing control will be quickly suppressed and once again will be out of your awareness. Your self- confidence and awareness slowly vanishes. The window of your soul fades away as consciousness is lost and you start moving with the images in the mirror, losing a sense of self. The ability to be aware of your overeating comes by sitting in a moment of clarity to deal with the root cause of your indulgence. These conscious moments will arise while reading this book.

As you read about external and internal indulgences you may consciously struggle with your awareness or loss of control. Your lack of moderation has moved beyond a desire to be authentic, instead seeking a space where you no longer must feel or think. The self-perpetuating cycle of external indulgences begins and ends with you. The influence and use of an indulgence are based on your desire and volition. As the cycle evolves, you continue deteriorating and the indulgence use increases, yet the prime initiative and mover of this cycle is you. For without you, or a self, the indulgence has no power. Your sense of volition will wain as the self deteriorates and the use of indulgence increases. This cycle ends with the indulgence being given total control: enough power to kill the self.

## 6 Phases of Cycle of Indulgence Usage

Here are the six phases of the self-perpetuated cycle of indulgence usage:

1st - experience of the authentic self

2nd- experience of unwanted emotions
3rd- indulgence in mood altering activity or substance
4th- increased use of defense mechanisms to subvert a sense of control loss
5th- increased losses due to indulgence
6th- increased use of indulgence

This cycle will continue to the point of death of the self or until a new choice is made by you.

When your indulgences move past moderation, your defense mechanisms will become primarily unconscious. This cycle will intensify as your sense of self decreases and your use of indulgences increases to the point that the indulgence has been given total control. You can stop the cycle at any time because it is self-perpetuating. You have control.

The most effective way to exert control over your indulgence is to acknowledge the first step of the 12-step model. Even years of denial, minimizing, or rationalizing your indulgences can be ended with an admission (an exercise of volition) that you are "powerless over" food, alcohol, pornography etc. This recovery of self can move through a 12-step program and or Christian model called FACE. Each model believes that a power greater than yourself can restore sanity or self. Later in this chapter the model of Face will be explained in more detail. You will be given concrete spiritual ways to stop the cycle by "F"leeing the temptation, "A"cknowledges God's truth, "C"onfessing ( if you already indulgenced) or take the impulse "C"aptive if you are feeling tempted, and finally "E"nlisting the help of the Holy Spirit.

You need to be alert for ways you empowered your indulgence to move past moderation. Being alert is difficult due to the self-perpetuated cycle. This cycle begins with numbing of your unwanted emotions and by indulging in mood altering behavior which leads to engaging in the defense mechanism to hide your indulgence. When a defensive mechanism is needed to "protect" you from your overuse of an internal or external indulgence, there will be an increase in the indulgence. Your indulgence is moving from a source of pleasure to method to deny the loss that stems from the indulgence itself.

The emotionally numbing nature of indulgences and the losses due to indulging intensify the cycle. Let us look again at the vicious cycle of overeating which increased your defense mechanisms and moved you to increase your indulgence in food.

Your compulsive overeating has moved past moderation and is now taking away from your life. As you become aware, being overweight has stopped you from social, recreational, and physical activities once considered "normal." This awareness of your losses will increase your experience of the emotional cost of overeating which increases the use of food to medicate your unwanted emotions, which completes the cycle back to addiction.

## 2. External Indulgence: Alcohol Abuse

The second greatest external indulgence also begins as innocently as overeating. It is excessive use of alcohol. Alcohol use may begin with a drink with friends, a celebration with family, or a cocktail at dinner. Over time, alcohol consumption may move to three and four drinks at similar events. Then you use without the need for an event to alter your mind while numbing yourself to unwanted emotions. The cycle does not change from one indulgence to the other. You have heard "have another one," "let me get another one for you" to "have one with me."

You will use the same defense mechanisms to overshadow your awareness of over-indulging. You will have moments you remember being "buzzed" at a party, slurring your words, or not remembering previous events. The alcohol is not a problem because of (minimizing), "I didn't drink that much", (rationalizing), "everybody else did" and (intellectualizing) "I still go to work every day." Then like any "good" indulgence you do not register the cost of your health or relationships.

Then comes the awareness that your drinking is no longer social; you are drinking alone. You are not involved in social activities that once brought you joy. The greater your social and personal losses, the more likely you will feel self-loathing, despair, or shame. Now your indulgence becomes a way to medicate the losses that stem from indulging. It is a downward spiral from here.

## 3. External Indulgence: Sexual Compulsiveness

The third greatest external indulgence follows the same pattern but is less socially acceptable than alcoholism. It is indulging sexually to alter your mood. We have all watched a show with sexuality, seen pictures of nudity, or had sexual fantasies. It is normal to have seen nudity or had sexual fantasies. Remember in middle school or high school you spoke to your friends about your sexual desires or experiences. This innocence may have become a dangerous dance of intimacy. The dance of intimacy becomes more intense by looking at partly nude, totally nude, or sexually explicit pictures. Again, you can minimize "I only did it once", rationalize "we all were playing", to denying "I never looked at that porn site."

You find with time that you looked at porn sites more often. You were not aware that looking at or thinking about porn was taking greater time out of your day. You missed more and more social events or relational activities because you were looking at porn or having sexual chats on-line... You had brief moments of sanity which made you aware of these losses. The internal indulgences of self-loathing, self-pity, shame, and guilt arose. Sexual indulgences are much more difficult to see compared to overeating and alcoholism. The behavior that once was laughed about with friends is now being used to medicate your self-loathing and shame. The cycle continues a downward spiral from here. Sexual indulgences usually become more frequent in time, moving towards infidelity, debt, and possible jail time.

You may argue that these three are not the "top three" or personally arrange in a different order. The order can be argued, but the cycle and costs remain the same. Awareness of the problems comes when the indulgences create enough losses to the body, mind, and soul. The self portrait of an addict exists, but the fragments of yourself that survive will endeavor to create life. The best medicine for healing is abstinence with all indulgences except overeating and workaholism. Once you abstain from the external indulgence you can then deal with the internal ones.

The top three internal indulgences I see clinically are: self-doubt, self-loathing, and self-pity. They stem from projected images of others which have distorted your self-esteem and poisoned healthy love for yourself. We have all had healthy internal criticisms. For example: "I could have done that better," "I hope I didn't say something wrong" or "I blew it". Many such comments help us adjust socially or to improve.

Over time, however, you begin to hear and add to your internal critical messages with words from past external critics. You start saying: "I'm not good enough" "I will always be a failure" and "I might as well kill myself." These critical messages deteriorate your self-esteem and self-worth; they trigger your childlike brain to recall similar memories that will link your old emotional memories and their distorted logic with new ones. Then the critical self and overbearing "parental" messages are heard consciously. These messages are colored by your present and past emotions.

Your inner child and his/her logic begins coloring your adult thoughts concerning your present behavior. It is a closed system that feeds on its own poison. Even when you hear positive comments about yourself, your inner child will confirm the old negative messages he/she heard or believed about themselves. You are unable to recognize the positive things you have done and only hear that you are not ok with you and others are not ok with you.

Your past critics are now mirrored in your own internal criticism. You are now looking at a mirror of your soul and not through the window of your soul. These internal indulgences are manifested by further use of external indulgences or manifested in other internal indulgences. Once you move past moderation, the losses are apparent and will be met by stronger defense mechanisms which hide/ overshadow your authentic self.

The cycle is predictable. You will indulge in self-doubt, self-loathing or self-pity then cover your losses with an overused defense mechanism. Then you use external indulgences like sleeping, eating, drinking or work to medicate your emotions from your losses which increases your internal indulgences. You then deteriorate enough from victimizing yourself which leads you to victimize others. You mirror or project the dissociated aspects of your trauma onto others. You become the portrait of an addict or perpetrator for someone else.

You learn to project your past fear of criticism onto others, believing they are judging or criticizing you. Your inner child's past abusers or projections of being judged are what your "conscious" mind "sees." Your inner child's image in the mirror reflects a projected image of your historical critics on your present relationships or personalizes all negativity of others to confirm the images your inner child experienced growing up. Life becomes a self-fulfilling prophecy.

This projection and/or personalizing only propels the downward spiral. This downward spiral may be medicated with an external indulgence, leading to further emotional problems and physical illnesses. It is sad yet likely you will extend these thoughts to God. Fear of God's judgment, criticism or rejection develops, making you feel unworthy.

Confronting present emotions and previously repressed emotions empower you with the ability to stop internal and external indulgences. You will be able to look through the window of your soul which allows you to see the real you. Yesterday's fragments will help define you today. You will need to be aware of any images that reflect internal indulgences.

Here are brief descriptions of internal indulgences, beginning with self-doubt.

## A. Internal Indulgence: Self-Doubt

Unmoderated self-doubt is a dangerous internal indulgence. It can be seen as the opposite of faith. It corrodes self-confidence, trust, and willpower. You "*doubt*" what you believe about yourself, others, and God, which inhibits your behavior because you do not trust yourself. Self-doubt is the stepbrother to shame and leads to emotional bankruptcy and stagnation. You may feel sad, scared, and lonely if you struggle with self-doubt. Likely no one will know you doubt yourself, because people with self-doubt work hard to look good on the outside. They have great advice for others, "but it won't work for me" attitude.

You likely had authoritarian parents which usually demanded obedience, inflexibility and gave you little individual freedom. Your desire to please them likely stopped you from rebelling as a teenager. You learned to listen to the authorities in your life which increased your insecurities. The more you tried to please or be perfect the more you experienced shame. The sadness of not being good enough and the fear of not being perfect grew through the eyes of shame. Self- doubt or self-despair were not moderated and became an indulgence.

You lose God's best for yourself while missing His mark when using internal indulgences. It is amazing how you are enslaved by the things you tried to escape when you avoided suffering. The place you run to becomes the place you are enslaved by later. Indulgences, especially internal ones, are like the Israelites going to Egypt to escape a 30-year famine to only become slaves for 430 years. You may struggle with internal indulgences and have normal defense mechanisms to keep them from your awareness. The good news is that you will have moments of lucidity. These moments of clarity will be experienced as suffering. Though painful, they are times to escape your historic dysfunctional thinking patterns.

## B. Internal Indulgence: Self-Loathing

The next internal indulgence is self-loathing. You, like the self-doubters, likely had authoritarian parents. Judgement and punishment were the tools of your parent(s) "discipline." You heard constant criticism of your thoughts and feelings while receiving punishment for non-perfect behavior. You internalized your parent(s) anger and judgment and directed it towards yourself today.

Self-loathing is the opposite of pride. It is a true hatred of yourself and is immobilizing due to the fear of getting critiqued or judged by others. The negative tapes, in your mind, run these messages; "Everything I do is wrong," "I hate myself," or "I can't stand everyone judging me." As a self-loather, you will beat yourself up mentally and emotionally and think others believe the same things about you. You constantly look, wait, or expect others to criticize you or criticize what you have done. When you are not finding enough judgment from others you will reflect past judgment onto yourself.

You likely belittle yourself even when you achieve your goals. You build walls of self-judgment. You are your worst critic. Your self-concept is based on shame, not being good enough, yet your measuring stick is perfection. I see self-loathing as a slow burning self-hatred. It decays your self-esteem down from the inside out.

You were likely the scapegoat of the family. All the family problems were blamed on you while carrying their sins. The sad thing is, the more talented you were as a child, the more criticism you received from dysfunctional care givers. Loathers isolate due to projecting their self-judgment onto others. They honestly believe others are judging them and if they get positive strokes they will quickly be discounted.

As a self-loather, you have a true disdain for yourself. Self-criticism becomes your nature while your anger is fueled by unrealized or unrealistic expectations of yourself. You will likely move into a reactive position, which gives others power due to your constant need to be liked and accepted. The heart of the matter is an internal pain or sadness which you covered up by a desire to be strong, be perfect, or please others.

## C. Internal Indulgence: Self-Pity

The next internal indulgence is the opposite of self-loathing; it is self-pity. If you are suffering from self-pity you likely grew up with a permissive parent(s) that were inconsistent with accountability and/or boundaries. They met your needs by nurturing you without providing accountability for your poor choices. Self-pity comes from the pain of being "not good enough" and then encouraged by getting your needs met by being a victim.

If you have self-pity, then you were over focused on external expectations. You over focused on "trying hard." Trying hard, while not doing anything, is a way of not taking responsibility for your own needs and wants. Things will "never" change and you will "always" be "not good enough." You will not only suffer from pain from others not meeting your needs but the pain of regret for not meeting your own needs. Self-pity will be a victim at all costs.

"Victims" of self-pity become victimized by themselves. Self-pity over focuses on self and could be the underbelly of pride. Self-pity boasts in suffering while pride boasts in success. Self-pity will decay self-esteem, desires, and decrease integrity. You use blame and guilt to control others to get your needs met. Lastly, you will struggle with terminal uniqueness in the form of being insignificant. If you are isolated in self-pity you will experience loneliness which will move into hopelessness.

You are not aware that you are self-absorbed with your own troubles because you think others are the perpetrators. You expect to be victimized and make sure this prophecy will happen. "If only" consumes your thoughts while your heart's sadness is blamed on others. It is difficult to stop self-pity because the power for change is given to others which fuels your powerlessness, hopelessness, and mental isolation.

You will remember past pain when breaking indulgences. At the heart of your unhealthy indulgences are old and outdated messages and memories. Here, at the place of the first remembrance of a critic in your life, is where you break free from your old messages and where you will experience hope and strength to overcome your internal indulgences. There is, and always will be, an authentic God given self in you, that will lead you to overcome your historic learned beliefs about yourself. Finding the small remnants of your authentic self and the relic of God in you becomes transforming.

Transformation of your mind to reach beyond its ordinary limits is possible, but you must use your faith to know all things are possible for those that love the Lord. It is not of yourself but of God in you. This takes faith that you can do all things in Him who strengthens you. A beautiful story in 2 kings 4:1-6 speaks to increased need and not enough "oil."

In 2 Kings the prophet Elisha finds a woman with serious need and truly little means. 2 Kings 4:1-6 states:

"Now a certain woman of the wives of the sons of the prophets cried out to Elisha, 'Your servant my husband is dead, and you know that your servant feared the LORD; and the creditor has come to take my two children to be his slaves.' Elisha said to her, 'What shall I do for you? Tell me, what do you have in the house?' And she said, 'Your maidservant has nothing in the house except a jar of oil.' Then he said, 'Go, borrow vessels at large for yourself from all your neighbors, even empty vessels; do not get a few. And you shall go in and shut the door behind you and your sons, and pour out into all these vessels, and you shall set aside what is full.' So, she went from him and shut the door behind her and her sons; they were bringing the vessels to her and she poured. When the vessels were full, she said to her son, 'Bring me another vessel.' And he said to her, 'There is not one vessel more.' And the oil stopped" (2 Kings 4:1-6 NASB.).

Many would ascribe this story to be directed at financial need, yet she was struggling with more than a financial deficit. She had just lost her husband and had a creditor come to take her two children. She had unfulfilled emotional needs and heartbreak. Was she indulging in self-doubt, loathing or pity? I do not know, yet I could believe she moved through these emotional experiences. She said, "your maidservant has 'nothing'." The prophet did not look at her need or plight. He looked at her resources. She had "a jar of oil." Elisha had her go get more empty vessels, close the door behind her and pour from her jar of oil.

Now if you had very little oil, or self, and I ask you to pour what little self you had into other "empty vessels," to close your door on old thought behind you and pour what little oil, or self, from your jar you had - would that make sense to you? It would be easy to miss the small jar if you are using internal indulgences, yet if you can become aware of the small part of yourself that is not in self-doubt, loathing or pity then you can heal with only that small jar assisting you at the start.

Many may argue that self-despair is one of the top three internal indulgences. Despair can be a part of depression, anxiety, or addictions that can become an internal desire not to exist. This form of despair takes away from the value of yourself and God. Despair creates an internal tension between the self and God, despair erecting a boundary between the infinite and the finite. Despair is more than being unhappy or depressed; it is a state of existence.

Despair and the other internal indulgences can become a state of mind, affecting your core beliefs and sense of self. Despair sits in the spot that is for God Himself. The core of whom and what you are is under attack. Soren

Kierkegaard, a Danish theologian, recognized this when he wrote "The Sickness into Death" in the early 1849. The "sickness" was referring to despair, yet this can be applicable to any internal indulgence. Despair does not affect a person; it affects a self. Kierkegaard saw the self as a part of the soul. The self is afflicted in despair not afflicted by despair.

Kierkegaard believed despair was one of the greatest sins because it affected the infinite or Holy Other. We all have moments of despair and can move through those moments. Your despair can poison the Self or Soul, which affects not only you, but your relationship with God. The more you experience your suffering which caused your internal indulgences without avoiding the image which created it, you can be healthy or free by confronting what was told or projected on you. The more you are aware of the fragment that created them, the greater your opportunity is to conquer them.

Past hurtful emotional experiences are the root of internal indulgences. Your early emotional state is directly correlated to the amount and duration of negative messages you experienced as a child. Then your unconscious mind will reflect those old beliefs onto you and project them on others. Your inner child's beliefs will be acted out and affirmed by its childlike emotional brain. Internal indulgences began earlier in your life than external indulgences and are being fed by your inner child's categorical thinking. Regression work allows you to re-write your storyline that contains your early belief. By reconceptualizing and putting your past into perspective from your viewpoint today, you are changing your future. Your healing is based upon the work you put into it. Each exercise will deepen your awareness of your learned distortions that stems from your early training. Your inner child's core belief must be revisited with truth to change these internal states of existence.

Your early emotional experiences can be mild to severe. You may be aware that you have traits of one or more of these internal states. If you have these traits, then it is important for you to deal with your thoughts and feelings concerning the indulgence. They take your esteem, worth and value while straining the best of relationships. These internal indulgences will be dealt with by using the prism of your adult mind to reflect your inner child's learnings.

An internal indulgence begins with a natural emotion and expands on it until all moderation is lost. Say you have increased guilt and overindulge in blame or self-criticism; it can become self-loathing. Sadness or fear indulged in shame may become self-despair, and shame and anger expands fear to become self-pity. Your emotions need to be voiced and felt to be healthy. If you internalize them, they can become toxic. You may have learned to push them out of your conscious awareness by putting on a mask of trying harder, being stronger, or being perfect to combat internal states of existents.

The more you suppress your feelings the more they affect you. This will lead you to gradually find a way to medicate your mood while suppressing your feelings. Once this toxin develops, your medicating will no longer work or bring you a desired high, you will find yourself further away from whom God. Finding your way back to your God given state while walking in the darkness can seem impossible. You struggle with the illusion of what you used to be and the delusion that God cannot help you. This belief only strengthens your doubt, pity, loathing or despair.

While reading about the internal indulgences you may have become aware of one or more affecting you. You will need to be intentional about changing your indulgences because you are at a disadvantage while they are active in your life. You may have a desire to stop the indulgence but emotionally, mentally, and physically, you are dependent on the chemical released during your internal or external indulging and the emotional responses before, during, and after their use. Neurologically your "emotions produce peptides or molecules of emotion (MOE's) which dock in receptors on the cells. The same thing that happens with repeated use of heroin occurs with repeated use of the same emotion. Your body's opiate receptors begin craving that peptide. Your body becomes addicted to that emotion" (What the Bleep Do We Know, William Arntz, Betsy Chasse & Mark Vicente, 2005, p.170).

By changing your MOEs you change your internal indulgences. That is easier said than done. It is difficult to stop feeding your brain the familiar emotion because you "feel that way" and your brain "craves" it. Your emotions begin to color your thinking to get the familiar MOEs. Once your thinking is colored or distorted by your inner child's logic, he/she will project its view on to others which increases the delivery of peptides or MOEs to the cell's receptors. This is the reason an internal emotional indulgence is hard to break because it distorts your view of self, others, and God. You may not have an internal indulgence but have emotions that color your view of self or God.

## My Story: Ruby

Ruby was a beautiful and smart young woman when we met. She called for help after being beat down by a narcissist for years. She reached out at the leading of her mother and sister. The first time I spoke with Ruby I diagnosed her as "a hot mess." I remember this session like it was yesterday.

I saw a woman that had been beaten from years of severe emotional and verbal abuse. I could not see the lawyer, the organizer of a nonprofit, or the scholar because Ruby had swallowed others' poison for years. She was unaware of toxicity in her marriage and other close relationships. She was double minded due to a history of gaslighting. The seeds of psychological manipulation were poisoning her mind and Soul. Ruby struggled to stay in her right mind due to the years of being blamed and judged for things her husband was doing himself. She blamed her abuse of alcohol for her present despair. She had no awareness she married the perpetrator of early abuse that took place in her childhood. She was being triggered by repressed sexual abuse memories, yet was unable to look out the window of her Soul because her forgotten past was the only mirror she could see.

When I first spoke with Ruby, I could see the hurt 8-year-old girl. She was frail, sad and had severe anxiety. I could hear her inner child's cries, yet Ruby had decreased awareness of her inner child's trauma. Ruby was attempting to be an adult mom to her own young children. Even when separated from her husband, his psychological manipulation and emotional abuse continued. With little sense of self, she believed her present perpetrator when he fed her lies about herself. Self-doubt was her chief internal indulgence, and it had a powerful grip over her mind and heart.

As a child, Ruby learned to adapt by "being perfect" and "pleasing" others. She learned to be what others wanted her to be. This early pleasing was a shield of safety which later empowered her perpetrators to hurt her. After working with her, I knew the adult Ruby needed significant support.

She had a treatment plan for her alcohol indulgence, made shifts in boundaries to contain her husband's abuse, and began journaling to listen to herself. After 6 months, Ruby's alcohol use was contained, yet her boundaries were still violated by her husband with constant messages of her being "an alcoholic", "impaired" or an "unsafe" mother. This emotional abuse was met with sexual advances.

Through our work together, Ruby's boundaries became stronger with time. She gained healthier coping skills, while the child within her became louder, wanting to be seen and heard. Ruby worked to deny her past emotions, minimize her intrusive thoughts, and rationalize her memories. Ruby gained a greater sense of self and freedom to be herself, and this was the window to the child within her.

After she finally reached the decision to divorce her toxic husband, Ruby was finally ready to start processing her childhood sexual abuse, and as a result began to deteriorate again. Ruby began having body memories with intrusive memories of her past abuse, while also sleep walking at night due to her restlessness, fear, and stress. She worked hard at suppressing her conscious memories of her abuse over the years, but they were finally pushing to the surface of her awareness. The body memories continued as the fragmented images flashed in her mind. Ruby began the hero's journey.

Ruby went to see the child within her. The child, hiding in the bathroom, told of her sexual abuse, and put a face on her perpetrator. Ruby was relieved the perpetrator was not her father, yet he was a family member. Again, denial raged against the face of her perpetrator in the mirror. Yet, Ruby's love for her inner child grew greater than her denial. Ruby began listening to and nurturing the child within her. Both looked out the window of their soul, breaking her adaption of pleasing others and her internal indulgence of self-doubt stagnated their growth.

Today, Ruby listens to herself and the child within her. When her internal indulgence of self-doubt appears, it is no longer met with alcohol or defense mechanisms. Ruby quickly reaches out to her friends and support system to pull the weeds of self-doubt and instead plants a flower of truth. Ruby now stands free of abusive memories and can live in the here and now. She still hears the same abusive message from her now ex-husband, yet she can see his subtle message as attempts to control and is free of the abuse his words hold.

Ruby has taken the hero's journey and recovered her inner child while breaking free of past perpetrators. She is growing as a woman and a healer. Her external indulgences and past perpetrators are no longer in charge of her life.

Internal indulgences are deep wounds affecting a self; these are soul wounds. These wounds get infected and affect your personality or self-identity. These internal indulgences will deaden your heart and become toxic to your soul. This inward crossing of your inner child's suffering or logic and your present adult self will be able heal your soul wound. Your soul wound fueled your external indulgence(s), empowered your depression, anxiety and/or shame and will become a self-fulfilling prophecy in your future. If you pull this weed, your life will bloom.

## Self Portrait of God

There is only one parable that gives a self-portrait of God while dealing with all the above reasons for not experiencing or staying in a relationship with God. It is the best-known parable in the bible. This parable has been used in movies, music, and paintings. This parable was delivered by Jesus to the religious leaders of the day and to the people struggling with their feelings of being unworthy, broken, and sad for missing God's mark. Jesus used the second half of this parable to confront the religious leaders on their pride, yet the parable is known for depicting God's unconditional love, unmerited forgiveness, and mercy for his children, especially the ones hurting emotionally and relationally.

The parable speaks to those that took God figuratively out of their temple and placed themselves on God's throne or those that knew their darkest hour was not at midnight or dawn. It is speaking to the Christian and non-Christians that are living outside a relationship with God. It speaks to those Christians that had a relationship with God and choose to turn away by indulging in the desires of the flesh; getting lost in their internal or external indulgences. The parable speaks to those that are at the heart of their darkness and have truly hit bottom because they used their gifts to increase their "life" outside of Gods will.

This parable deals with the human condition of growth, which comes from an almost primitive basis to take God seriously. You, like many others, may be taking the journey to the Soul at your weakest point. At a point that your emotions are raw, and your relationship feels almost non- existent. The decay of your heart and Soul are unbearable and the silence of being alone is so loud. It is between living and not living. When death seems like a soothing relief, this is the parable of the prodigal son.

This parable in Luke 15:11-24 says:

"And He said, 'A man had two sons. The young of them said to his father, 'Father, give me the share of the estate that falls to me.' He divided his wealth between them. And not many days later, the younger son gathered everything together and went on a journey into a distant country, and there he squandered his estate with loose living. Now when he had spent everything, a severe famine occurred in that country, and he began to be impoverished. He went and hired himself out to one of the citizens of that country, and he sent him into his fields to feed swine. And he would have gladly filled his stomach with the pods that the swine were eating, and no one was giving anything to him. But when he came to his senses, he said, 'How many of my father's hired men have more than enough bread, but I am dying here with hunger! I will get up and go to my father, and will say to him, 'Father, I have sinned against heaven, and in your sight; I am no longer worthy to be called your son; make me as one of your hired men.' So, he got up and came to his father. But while he was still a long way off, his father saw him And the son said to him, 'Father, I have sinned against heaven and in your sight; I am no longer worthy to be called your son.' But the father said to his slaves, 'Quickly bring out the best robe and put it on him, and put on his hand and sandals on his feet; and bring the fattened calf, kill it, and let us eat and celebrate; for this son of mine was dead and has come to life again; he was lost and has been found.' And they began to celebrate" (Luke 15:11-24 NASB).

The parable of the prodigal son is a simple story that is used by Jesus to illustrate a spiritual lesson. Jesus wanted his audience to know about his Father's unconditional love shown through the father of the prodigal son.

The prodigal paints an image of those that are far away from God. The prodigal went to a " distant land." He. "squandered his estate with loose living." The prodigal son used his inheritance on " loose living" or " wild living." He was drinking, partying and probably sleeping with prostitutes. He "squandered" his wealth. He found his
self in a " famine."

Have you noticed that living " loose" usually leads to an emotional, mental, relational, and spiritual famine? The more one uses indulgences to fill themselves, they will fine that healthy fruit do not grow. The more alcohol, drug or pornography used and abused will lead to a famine. The prodigal son became hired help to feed and take care of swine. Now it is important to know that the prodigal son was of Jewish descent. The Jews viewed swine as unclean. They would not eat, touch, or be around them (Lev. 11;8). The prodigal son not only feeds, but most likely sleeps with the swine or pigs. Yet this parable says that he would have "gladly filled his stomach with the pods that the swine were eating." This would have been an abomination to the Jews. The prodigal son hit bottom and decided to go back home to attempt to work for his father.

In a spiritual light, the prodigal son repented as he turned away from fleshy desires. Repentance, not resistance is a turning from self-will and self-indulgence; it is a turning toward God and a glad submission [obligation moved by love] to his rule of love"(The Broadman Bible Commentary, vol. 9, 1970, p.126).

He had healthy humility or shame, as can be seen by him saying "I'm 'no longer worthy to be called your son.'" This shame is neither of God nor by his father. The prodigal son's shame was from the "father of lies" the adversary of God, which is Satan. The prodigal's father "saw him." Most of us would have seen his tattered and dirty clothes, bare feet, or starving body. We might classify him as a bum or alcoholic, yet his father saw his son.

The prodigal's father "felt compassion for him, embraced him and kissed him." This is a picture of God's love when you turn away from your rebellion and indulgences and towards him. The father put shoes on his feet, clothes on his back, and killed the fatted calf. He restored him to his rightful place in his family. This is not the usual picture the church paints when you have missed the mark or are struggling with a different lifestyle. The father goes one step further. He places a ring on his figure.

A ring was significant in Christs' day. The ring had the seal of the family on it.

If you wore the ring of the King, you could speak on behalf of the King. You could buy and sell for the King and sign it with the seal of the ring. The contract was as binding as though the King did it himself. The prodigal son was put back in his rightful place in the family. The father told the eldest son, that represented the church, "to celebrate and rejoice, for this brother of yours was dead and has begun to live and was lost and has been found.'" (Luke 15:32 NASB).

You may be like the prodigal son and made wrong choices as you grew up. As you looked at how you handled your rebellion you may be aware of healthy humility from your visit " to a distant land" or your " wild living." You may be actively experiencing a famine in your life due to your use of indulgence. You need to know that your Heavenly Father will run to meet you and celebrate that you have returned to Him. You will be able to look through spiritual eyes as you proceed on your journey. You will be able to put the fragmented pieces of your life into perspective to look again from your Soul's window.

Speaking from a Christian perspective, the Holy Spirit of God fills your mind, body, and Soul. You are not the same; you will bear different fruit and be one with God forever. This holy union with the ultimate cannot be described with words. There is a renewal of your mind (I Corinthians 2:16), in dwelling of the Holy Spirit (1Corinthians 3;16) and you become a new creature. (2 Corinthians 5:17). If you have experience and accepted Jesus Christ as your savior, then you have experienced renewal everyday (2 Corinthians 4:16). The key is knowing God; using this experience of God to create or edify your life. In a spiritual sense, you are redeemed by God. What was once lost is now found.

Redeemed by God means you are vindicated or justified through the blood of Christ. Jesus was the sacrificial lamb sent by God. Jesus was sent to pay the price that you could not pay (1 Peter 2:24). When you hear from pastors, scripture, or others about not being worthy, this refers to being with God without Christ's blood offering. Without Christ, you are worthy and loved as a human being but are not worthy to stand before God with sin. He will not be close or tainted by that which is unclean because He is Holy (Revelation 15:4). You can only be clean spiritually through Jesus' blood (John 14:6). By accepting that Jesus Christ died for your sins you are spiritually clean (Hebrews 9;14) and able to stand before God.

It is extremely important for you to know and understand that you are worthy and OK on this earthly plane. You are not OK or worthy to stand before God on the spiritual or vertical plane because of sin. The vertical plane or axis hinges on the ultimate, non- human arena, while the horizontal plane or axis hinges on the earthly or human axis. You cannot speak of standing before God in the vertical plane without being holy. The only way to put on the holy is through Jesus. You may be offended that you cannot be OK now to stand before God without Christ. Your ignorance of the Holy or vertical axis will lead to anger and possible shame. You may understand the difference between heavenly and earthly things and the vertical and horizontal axis and still believe you are worthy to stand before the creator of the universe. This is not ignorance but arrogance.

If you accept that you are worthy as a human but need to be worthy spiritually to stand before God, then you can accept, by faith, that Christ died on the cross for your sins (Romans 4:25) in order for you to stand before God. If you accept God on God's terms, then you are a new creation. Your Soul becomes one with God (1 Corinthians 6;17). You are a new creation, free of shame. Shame is not of God; it is the antithesis of God.

If you, as a believer in Jesus Christ, still have decreased trust, increased shame, constant guilt and are full of indulgences, then you need to rest in God's grace. God's grace covers all your sins (Romans 5;15,20-21; 6;1). You live now in faith, being "justified (acquitted, declared righteous, and given a right standing with God) through faith, let us [grasp the fact that we] have [the peace of reconciliation to hold and to enjoy] peace with God through our Lord Jesus Christ (the Messiah, the Anointed One). Through Him also we have [our] access (entrance, introduction) by faith into this grace (state of

God's favor) in which we [firmly and safely] stand. And let us rejoice and exult in our hope of experiencing and enjoying the glory of God. Moreover [let us also be full of joy now!] let us exult and triumph in our troubles and rejoice in our sufferings, knowing that pressure and affliction and hardship produce patient and unswerving endurance. And endurance (fortitude) develops maturity of character (approved faith and tried integrity). And character [of this sort] produces [the habit of] joyful and confident hope of eternal salvation. Such hope never disappoints or deludes or shames us, for God's love has been poured out in our hearts through the Holy Spirit Who has been given to us. (Romans 5:1-5 AMP)

You are a new creature or person in Christ. and are accepted by God through grace (2 Corinthians 5;17). Your experience or belief that you are not worthy is looking through fleshly eyes and not spiritual ones. If you look through the eyes of the holy you will experience God's grace (unmerited favor). God's favor and unconditional love is unmerited, Grace cannot be earned (Romans 11:5ff; Ephesians 2:5). Brennan Manning in The Ragamuffin Gospel speaks of Gods acceptance of you. Brennan says:

"And Grace calls out, you are not just a disillusioned old man who may die soon, a middle- aged woman stuck in a job and desperately wanting to get out, a young person feeling the fire in the belly begin to grow cold. You may be insecure, inadequate, mistaken, or potbellied. Death, panic, depression, and disillusionment may be near you. But you are not just that. You are accepted. Never confuse your perception of yourself with 'the mystery that you really are accepted by God"' (2005, p.28). You, like the prodigal son, are loved by your Heavenly Father. Your Heavenly Father hurts that you have been hurt (Isaiah 63:9) by others and yourself. Your acceptance of God's Grace will feed your Soul. You will be able to bring your fragmented pieces, (i.e. Captain Hook, Never Neverland, indulgences, and rebellion) together on this journey if your temple is filled with the Holy Spirit of God.

Many Christians do not use God's Word or the power of the Holy Spirit to heal emotional wounds or conquer indulgences because they are not aware of the How Tos. You need to "study to show thyself approved unto God, a workman that needeth not to be ashamed, rightly dividing the word of truth"(2 Timothy 2:15 KJV). In 2 Timothy 3:15,16 says "Every scripture inspired of God is also profitable for teaching, for reproof, for correction, for instruction which is in righteousness" (2 Timothy 3:16 ASV). It's hard to "put on the mind of Christ" without studying God's Word. The more you hide God's Word in your heart (Psalm119;11) the more you will grow spiritually. You will need to flee temptation (2 Timothy 2:22) and by using your spiritual knowledge (proverbs 3:5-6) which will help you take your thoughts, feelings and behavior captive( 2 Corinthians 10;5). These three steps will help you enlist or engage the Holy Spirit (John 16:13) consciously. Growing spiritual strength is not a passive experience.

God says, "lean not on your own understanding" (Proverbs 3:5-6) because it is based on your old tapes, storylines, and the emotional logic of your inner child. It is difficult to not lean on your own understanding because your emotional brain will respond in 50 milliseconds when your rational one will take 500-600 milliseconds. Your child-like brain moves 10 times quicker that your rational brain. If you react from old dysfunctional behavior or relapse into an addiction, then you need to FACE God knowing you are covered in Christ and grace. Your adult mind needs to think spiritually to be guided "into all truth" (John 16:13) which will stop your historic shame, pain, or fear. Knowing how your brain works may stop your internal critic's judgment as well.

Once you Face God you can apply His truth to your present situation. Knowing you cannot be separated from God's Love (Romans 8 37-39). This truth can bring comfort to your depression, peace to your anxiety and humility to your shame. If Christ is for you who can be against you. You are more than conquerors in all things. Resting in this knowledge is a sacred space that brings peace, hope and joy. Knowing you can do all thing through Christ who strengthens you. (Philippians 4;13) This" knowing" can lead you past your afflictions. You can change your script of depression, anxiety, and panic attacks. You can change your internal and external indulgences through being vulnerable and Facing God.

You need to be vulnerable and FACE God's plan for healing. FACE is an acronym for spiritual healing and growth. F- FLEE A- Acknowledge God's truth C- Confess or take Captive and E-Enlist the Holy Spirit. You will learn how to consciously enlist, engage, or call upon the Holy Spirit in the chapter called Soul Food.

You will need to Flee old information or temptation and Acknowledge God's truth. God's truths on grace, hope, love etc... will help you take Captive your old thoughts, feelings, or behaviors. This gives you time to hear the Holy Spirit in you. By following God's plan, you will generate new emotional responses and behaviors. This process Enlist the help of the Holy Spirit within you without being covered by the fragments of your old critical beliefs or indulgences. If you are tempted with an external indulgence then Flee the temptation, Acknowledge God's truth, take Captive your thought and feelings and Enlist His Spirit. IF you fall back into your rebellion or indulgences then you will need to FACE them. You will Flee the temptation, acknowledge your weaknesses and God's Strengths, confess your sin and Enlist the Holy Spirit's help with the identified problem. This ability to FACE yourself and your choices will lead you to your authentic self while putting on the mind of Christ.

The formula for spiritual healing must be intentionally applied to your emotional wounds. Your inner child will not apply these spiritual steps of healing because he or she had teaching of the world (Colossians 2:8, I Corinthians 1:21, Ephesians 2:2ff)) You were of the flesh and not of the Spirit growing up, therefore you learned the things of the flesh which is not of God (I Corinthians 2:14). These spiritual steps to healing and growth enable you to confront your old emotions and their logic by building healthy self-esteem and growing spiritually through the Spirit of God.

## Remember

Confronting present emotions and previously repressed emotions empower you with the ability to stop internal and external indulgences. You will be able to look through the window of your soul which allows you to see the real you. Yesterday's fragments will help define you today. You will need to be aware of any images that reflect internal indulgences.

# CHAPTER TEN

## RED'S STORY

"The light shines in the darkness. But the darkness has not overcome the light" (John 1:5 NIRV).

**KEY POINTS:**

- We all make early life decisions that change our lives
- Life crises, when faced, have the greatest potential to bring life
- True answers arrive through listening to your innermost Self

**Reflections:**

- Are you willing to bring light into your darkness?
- Be aware of your memories as you read Red's story.
- Does your inner child have a teddy bear to love?

Red's hero's journey from beginning to end. Red's story is a great example of doing inner child work by being internally and interactively mindful.

Red's story, like your inner child is sacred. Red was not aware of the first line, paragraph, or chapter of his book. Red was not interested in changing his earlier chapters, because he got lost in his chapter one. Red was more interested in how he wanted to write the ending of his story. He had prejudged his early chapters based on his trials as an adolescent. He made powerful decisions as a teen that not only colored the later chapters, but his earlier ones. His present life crisis was colored by his beliefs as a 15-year-old boy. It is amazing how one experience in the life of an adolescent or young adult can color not only the earlier chapters, but also the ones that follow them. Red's journey to the Soul came out of a life crisis. Red did not have the luxury of reading his first chapter or the ones that followed it. He did not have time to build a support system due to the nature of his crisis.

Red's hero's journey was unique. No quest follows a familiar path. Red's journey models the entire content of this book; for this reason, his process of healing will be discussed in detail.

## My Story: Red

I got a new intake that stated his full name was "Red." Red filled a few blanks on the four-page intake. He signed all the forms as "Red." I walked out in the waiting room and saw this 6' 6" male that weighed about 280 pounds standing by the door. This man was big. He had black leather motorcycle pants with black heavy boots. His black leather had layers of dirt, road grim and what appeared to be fresh bloodstains on them. He stood there in a leather vest with no shirt. He had black tattoo sleeves from his wrist to the top of his shoulders. He had a red beard that was probably eight inches long. It was as wide as it was long. Red's beard was dark red and had not been combed for months. Red's face was red. His hair was past his shoulders and had not seen a comb in a long time.

I greeted Red and asked him to come back to my office. Red came in, sat on the couch and put his boots on the table. I still to this day have never seen boots that big. I would guess they were a size 16. They were laced up and had three clasps. These boots demanded attention: they had what appeared to be smudged blood on them. Red sat on the couch, looking down at me, and said, "Do you have a problem?" I knew he was asking about his boots on my marble table. I replied, "I thought you came here because you had one." Red sat there. (*after a long pause*) He smile and said, "I guess you are right. (*Long pause*) I believe you are the last man I'm going to speak to."

I did not know if Red was homicidal or suicidal. I asked him how he was going to kill himself. He told me, "I'm going under the bridge to shoot myself." Red was lethal. He had intent, a plan and means to kill himself. Red had a 45 on his Harley in my parking lot. I asked Red what he wanted from me. Red said, "You are my priest today." I told Red that I was neither a Catholic nor a priest, but that I could be his minister or pastoral counselor. Red leaned back on the couch and told me his story. It was as if he had known me for years. It went like this to the best of my recollection.

"I was 15 when I left my nice, clean Methodist home. I did not say bye to my dramatic mom or my bible-thumping dad. I walked off from football practice field and said, F__k this shit. I am going to the Dakota's. I never returned to that school or home ever again. I got picked up hitch hiking by what became my old lady. She picked me up on her bike and said she 'would take me down the road a bit.' She later changed her mind; we went to the Bad Lands. She was the first and last woman I will ever love. Before she got sick, we spent 12 years on the road. Once she died, I took her ashes and her bike back to the Badlands. She wanted to be there. It has been a ride man. It has been the shit and then some. I hated losing her (*Red's voice was cracking and he wiped away a tear*), but she was a mess (*he began to smile*). Well life goes on. You know that; it's been a rough ride the last eight years."

Red got quiet and sat for about three minutes in silence. Red was actively being internally mindful. He was being internally mindful without knowing it. Eileen Caddy in *God Spoke to Me* said, "The greatest thing you can do for any soul is to turn them within and enable them to find their true Self, to enable them to find me within the death of their being. Let each soul seek within and there fine the solution to every problem, the answer to every quarry"(p. 118). He was hearing the heartbeat of his Soul. He was dwelling in his temple for the first time in years. I was not in the room, the world stopped being, and he was dwelling in a special place. It was as he ran into himself after eight years of riding, this was a Holy moment in which he could experience the reflections of his Soul.

Reflection comes and goes like dreams because most people will quickly cover them with defense mechanisms. Red was normal; he followed his emotional experience with minimizing, rationalizing and denial. Red continued: " Well that is not important now. You know that life comes and goes. Shit happens."

Counselor: Red, what were you thinking or going through in those three to five minutes?

Red replies: Nothing. I think that I need to get on with it.

Counselor: With what?

Red: Well I came in here to get shit off my chest before I go.

Counselor: Go where

Red: That's a damn good question. (Silence) Heaven hell, the abyss, or the great open road. (Pause as to have me answer) Well I think it will be a ride anyway.

Counselor: You could say that.

Red: Shit man. I heard the stories of the Bible and had those crammed down my throat all my life. I have experienced Hell on earth and spent time in the abyss. Life is a bitch and then you die, mother f__ker. Do not set there and judge me you pompous ass.

*(Red is projecting his father's images on me; some would call this transference. Red is now actively acting out his early beliefs without awareness. This behavior has been acted out for years but never unearthed or processed.) (Long Pause)* You are just going to sit there and judge me. Mother F__ker. (*Pause*)

Counselor: I have experienced the abyss and hell on earth myself. It is a bitch.

(*Red sat there not knowing what to do. I took him right back to the place the power struggle or projection began. I gave a response that was not made by his father. My response was real and was based on this reality.*)

Red: I have experienced shit that would make your hair on your head curl. (*Red begins to smile. The reason is, I am bald)* Well, shit man, that is a bitch *(Referring to my lack of hair.*) I have killed men, seen, and done shit that would turn your f__king stomach. I have been beat almost to death and left to die. Hell, on earth.

Counselor: What is it like to be on the edge of the abyss?

Red: The abyss is a dark place. I want to step in (*pause*) because it is hell here. (*Silence*)

Counselor: Red, the abyss is real. Are hell and Heaven as real to you?

Red: I believed that my life has been spent in one type of hell or another-- all my life. I hope I experience heaven one day.

Counselor: So, you are a man of faith?

Red: I accepted Christ as a child, but I do not think that shit works.
(*I knew from the content of this first session the text of the script he was following to experience hopelessness. It is important, purpose of this book, to label parts of* Red's *script.*)

Red's scripted beliefs were:
- all or nothing
- he has no hope
- he looks through negative lens
- He does not trust himself or others
- He saw that he was not ok, and the world was not ok
- He was ultimately alone
- He would be better off dead

This script was based on an adolescent chapter when he:
- left home and would never go back
- left everything behind
- ran away alone
- stopped trusting others
- wanted to die

Spiritual beliefs of his script were:
- God does not care
- faith does not work
- hell is on earth

- heaven is not real
- life comes and goes: a nihilistic view
- God is not all loving and does not care for him
- God's presence is questioned.

(*The session continues until the last five minutes when Red speaks about his plans and how he will step into the abyss.*)

Counselor: Red, are you sure you want to step into the abyss?

Red: Yes sir. (*spoken with respect*)

Counselor: (*I was speaking with the adult and not the adaptive child response i. e. the scripted response from childhood.*)

Counselor: I am glad you came in and spoke with me today Red.

Red: I knew I was to speak to someone, but I did not know why. I feel better. (*Red feeling better is not a good sign because now he has energy to step into the abyss.*)

Counselor: Red, if for some reason you choose not to step into the abyss, will you come back and do the work it takes to live life fully?

Red: I am and have lived hard; I am full of life.

Counselor: You are full of a lot of things, (*Red laughs because he had periodically throughout the session told me that I was "full of shit like everyone else"*), but I'm saying that he lived life fully and not being 'full' or 'fed up' with life. There is a reason you came into my office today. I do not want to argue about that reason. I believe the reason is greater than both of us. I know if you do the work you can stop living in hell and stop running from shit.

Red: I do not run from anything.

Counselor: Red you ran away from home, your parents, coaches, school, state, and God.

Red: But (*I interrupted before Red could finish in order to avoid a power struggle*)

Counselor: Red I respect you; I stop you because you were going to defend yourself and there is no need to do that today. I am not going to give up my view and I respect yours. I am asking you to give me your word that you will come back to work through shit to live life. Do you want to schedule another appointment today?

Red: No sir. I don't think I will need to do that.

Red got up and shook my hand in a firm grip. His hand was strong as a vice; my hand molded to fit his palm. I was glad he stopped squeezing or I would have cried. He looked at me and said, "Thank you." He paid me the full fee and walked out. I really did not know if I would ever see Red again. My discernment was covered with the knowledge of his intent to step into the abyss. I had a deep sadness the rest of the day. Thursday that same week, two days after I saw Red, I heard a loud Harley outside my window. I knew I had an opening the next session; and I hoped that Red had taken it. I walked out of my session with anticipation of seeing Red. He was not out in the waiting room. I went to the front office and checked in my box to see if someone, especially Red, had taken the hour. The hour was still open; there was not note of him scheduling and appointment in my box. I walked around the corner to go to the restroom and a familiar face stepped out. It was Red.

Red: You got any time available this week or today. (I felt like giving him a big hug, but he was still Red)

Counselor: Well come on back. I have the next session open. (*He followed me back to my office and sat down on the couch. I sat down.*) Well, how are you?

Red: (*He did not say anything. He reached in his vest and pulled out a 45 bullet. He tossed the bullet to me. I caught the bullet and looked it over. It had a small indention in the primer, which the firing pin had left on it. This bullet had been fired and did not go off.*)

Counselor: Well that is something. I know what I would call it. How about you?

Red: I would call it a bad bullet.

Counselor: Yea that is a million to one chance, if not more considering it was your ride to the abyss. I would call it a miracle by God. I will not belabor the point, but I know I am happy to see you.

Red: I wish I could say the same. Coming here was one of the hardest things I ever had to do.

Counselor: You did not run this time. That is impressive.

Red: Well, I knew I could not live with myself if I did not come in here. I turned around twice to get back here.

Counselor: Well I am glad you came back. I know this will be the best thing you have ever done for yourself, if you do the work.

Red: I am here. Just tell me what to do and I will do it. The only thing I will not do is give up my bike or wear a suit. (*Smiling*)

Counselor: We're not going to get crazy or anything. You will just have to make the journey to the "Badlands" of your Soul.

Red: You are shitting me. Aren't you?

Counselor: I have not yet and do not plan to. I am going to encourage you to go back and see the little boy you left behind. The part of you that you do not know is calling the shots.

Red: I believe you have lost me. I do not understand the going back part. I have not been home in years, and I do not know about the inner child shit.

Counselor: Well you will sit there with your eyes closed and go back in your mind's eye to see the part of you that was sad, scared, or mad. You are probably like most people and had a safe place. A safe place that you could go if you were hurt by others. Do you know where your safe place was growing up?

Red: I would have to say my fort.

Counselor: Where was that fort?

Red- It was down the rode past the bend and at the creek. I road my bike there then pulled it in the woods. It was a way back from the dirt road.

Counselor: Could you find it again?

Red: Of course, but I bet things have changed now.

Counselor: They may have. The question is will you go back.

Red: Well I guess so. Are you sure about this shit?

Counselor: Red I am not sure about much, but I am sure about this path. I will let you be the judge once you go back.

The session continued for about 10 minutes before he agreed to go back to the fort. Red closed his eyes and began to relax. I did a relaxation technique and Red began to relax deeply. Red was asked to picture himself at the bend. He was to hear and see the creek. He was to walk down the path to the fort and look for the part of him that he needed to see. I saw Red's face turn a shade towards sad. I asked him to tell the little guy that he was safe and that he was him all grown up. He was to tell him that he was safe and that he could trust Red. I encouraged Red to spend some time with him and to listen. He was to trust his own responses. Red had tears running down his face. I encouraged him to take his time and be there with and for the little guy. After about 10 minutes, I encouraged him to say goodbye for this time. If he were going to return later, he needed to tell this part of himself he would come back to visit. I asked Red to bring all the thoughts, feelings and experiences back to the room, by opening his eyes. Red took about five minutes to open his eyes. This was a long time.

Here is how I remember the rest of that session:

Counselor: What did you see or experience Red?

Red: (*he had difficulty speaking and cleared his throat twice*) Well I saw a little boy. I guess about nine or so. He was getting wood ready to make a fire. He did not pay me any attention. I told him who I was and that I would keep him safe. He did not look at me

for a while.

Counselor: Well did you see his face, or did he say anything?

Red: I saw his face. It was blurry for a while. (*Long pause*) He asked me what those marks where on my arms. I told him they were tattoos. He did not like them.

Counselor: Red, you looked sad and had tears. What were you going through with him?

Red: I just remember how lonely I was all the time. Everybody thought I had everything. A big house, perfect family, church going and a great athlete. I could not please my parents; nothing was good enough. It sucked growing up.

Counselor: You were sad about not being good enough?

Red: Shit, I do not know.

Counselor: Did the little guy say anything to you?

Red: Well, I think he was pissed at me or something.

Counselor: I do not get it.

Red: He said, 'You left me too.' Then he went and got more wood. I told him

I would take him for a ride on my bike. He just sat by the fire. I do not know where the fire came from, but it had flames.

Counselor: Red did you tell him you would be back?

Red: Yes, but I do not think he believed me.

Counselor: Well he probably did not believe you. You do not trust anyone, and he does not either. I hope you will honor your word. He cannot give you trust; it is earned. I know he matters to you because you were sad. I know you can give him a lot, but he will give you more than you could ever give him. You can change his life and he can give your life. Now it is up to you. It is not about your parents, coaches, or teachers. You have the ultimate control.

Red left the session in silence. He was in deep thought. He had been mindful and had seen the part of himself that he needed to see. He was not reacting anymore. He had power to change his own destiny. Red rescheduled for the following Monday. I really hoped he would keep his appointment.

Sometimes, the journey to the Soul creates great ambivalence, which is met with the desires to fight or flight. He used both. I knew he had a chance to medicate with pot or alcohol because I could smell both on him in the first and second session. Lastly, he could use his defense mechanisms, which would be suppressing, minimizing, or rationalizing his experience.

The following Monday, Red was on time. I met him in the waiting room; there was something different about him. He was dressed in his same leathers, but they were clean. He did not smell like pot or alcohol. There was something different about his presence. He looked softer. He was sitting down in a chair and not standing as he had usually done. Once in session, he again put his feet crossed on my table. He said, "I went back and talked to the child every day. He acknowledged that he had not smoked pot in the last 24 hours. For Red not to smoke pot in 24 hours was huge because he had not spent a day without smoking pot since junior high, per his report. When I asked what he did with his inner child he sat back and said, “We sat around the fire and talked. I don't remember being happy at home, but I think he's happy at the fort." We spent the entire session talking about his three visits to his inner child.

Red was concerned that his inner child would not trust him, did not like him much and would work at avoiding him. Red was running into mirror images of himself. He had been doing all those things for the last 25 years. The big difference between the two of them was that the child had happiness, faith in God and a love of others. Red wanted these forgotten things, but he would need to face himself. He found it hard to distrust and runaway from himself. Red always had a reason to not trust, leave, use drugs, and fight but he did not want to now. He was in a proverbial pickle.

Counselor: "Where does the little guy get his hope and happiness from?

Red: Why do you ask?

Counselor: Because these things are missing in your life. You are amazed that he is just like you (but he has not lost his hope or happiness. I believe it is important that he has a relationship with God and doesn't see everyone as 'f__king hypocrites.' His faith is important; the reason he doesn't trust you is as important. You want to fix him without listening or asking questions. Sometimes you have to give up control to get it. You are doing the work, but you need to open your heart and mind while trusting his answers. There is a reason you are the way you are now. So listen; you will have knowledge of yourself.

You have pushed down your core beliefs, medicated and used your defense mechanisms to cover them up. This work is a journey to the heart of your beliefs that you have written on your soul. Some of your script was distorted because you did not have the knowledge or ability to make a well-informed decision. You have covered up the true matters of your heart with defense mechanisms. You do not need these defense mechanisms to cope anymore, but you do not know it.

Red: (*looked at me for what seemed to be five minutes*) I believe what I believe, God Damnit. I am not going to listen to you call me crazy. This stuff is crazy.

Counselor: You can find your own answers. I am giving you a way to do that, Red. You are getting angry and wanting to run again. I do not care what you choose to believe, but you left him once before and are wanting to do it again. That is up to you. This is work. If you want to do the same old thing, you will get the same old result. I will honor what you and the little guy believe about life. Analysis is just a window to the soul, inner truth, and an art healing.

You have a Soul problem. You need answers. I am giving you a way to find your answers.

Red: I want you to write down what you have told me in the last 20 minutes. I will read it and think it all over."

Red left the session with the premises of this book. I had never had a client ask me to write down 20 minutes of what was said in session. I wrote out approximately what was stated above and added a written assignment. The written assignment consisted of 10 questions: Red was to write with his dominant hand and then answer with his non- dominant one. He was to do this right after he spent time with the child within him. He scheduled his next appointment that same week. Again, I did not know if Red was going to show up or run away. Old patterns are hard to break. It is nice to have your own truth and answers, but it takes work.

Red's next session began with him handing me a sheet of paper. This paper was torn off a note pad. It was folded up in a neat little square with the ends tucked into the square. It was folded like the notes passed around in junior high or high school. I would never think a big man in black leathers with tattoo sleeves would ever fold or know how to fold a note like this one. Before I opened the note, I knew this note was meaningful and part of Red's Holy of Hollies. I opened the note as I would open a sacred document. Red sat with his feet on the floor, while sitting up with a slight lean towards me.

I had the piece of paper open; it had seven of the ten questions on it. Each question was written out and the answers appeared as if they were written by his non- dominant hand. The answers were difficult to read. I still have tears running down my face remembering this moment. I read the questions and answers silently. I asked Red if he would mind if we discussed these questions one at a time.

These are the question and answers:

1) Do you trust me? No. You are a big bully. You scare me. I want to, but you do not listen to me. You tell me what to do.

2) Do you believe that I will protect you? No. You left me, and you are mean. You left and forgot me and bear. I had friends and you hurt

them. You are always mad.

3) What do you want from me?
   I want you to love me, hear me, let me have friends and talk to God. You are not listening to me again. You do not care.

Red speaking to his inner child, "I care for you and love you with all my heart. I did not know I could not hear you, that I hurt your friends, or that you wanted to talk to God. This is hard for me. I have been on the road and it has been a hard road. I am listening, please give me a chance. You are pushing me away and hurting me like I did to you and your friends. Will you give me a chance?"

Child: I am talking to you.
Red: Thank you

4) Will you come with me? No. You will not take care of me. You never have and never will. You left me.

Red: You are right. I will eat, sleep and live everyday with you in mind. I will ask you every morning and check with you every night. Do you believe me?

Child: I want to.

5) What hurt you so bad? You. You. You.

Red: I am sorry, and I am sorry. I did not know.

6) What do you want? You will not do it.

Red: Yes, I will. I will show you, but I do not know what you want.
Child: I want bear, friends and to play again.

7) Do you believe in God? You know the answer.

Red: Yes. You believe in God. Is that right?
Child: Do you?
Red: Yes, I do. Do you believe me?

Child: Will you go to church or read the bible to me?
Red: I do not know. I got tired of dad preaching to me and hearing about God all the time. I will think about it.
Child: Dad is not God. I like God and he saved our life.
Red: I do not know that was a long time ago. Do you understand?
Child: He stopped the bullet, didn't he?
Red: How did you know that?
Child: I know a lot. You tried to kill me. God told me that he would stop you.
Red: I do not know about that. What do you mean?
Child: You prayed for it to stop.
Red: You are right. I forgot. OK, I will pray with you, but I do not know about the church thing. Are you ok with that?
Child: Will you read it to me?
Red: Yes, I will. Do you believe me?
Child: Yes."

After we processed his letter, I handed it back to him. He folded the letter back up and stuck it back in his inside vest pocket. He quickly placed his hands over his face.

Red:" I blew it. I got pissed and ran off. It has been a hard ride. I thought I had the answers. I woke up in someone else's life when the bullet failed. I am talking to the child I never knew I had and would not have believed it anyway. I have been living and I lost myself. I am somewhat confused right now. I got to get on the road. It's the anniversary of my old lady's death. I go back every year.

Counselor: Are you going to tell her about the little guy and see what she thinks about him? (*Red told me that he tells her about his life every time he goes back to visit her.*) He will keep you grounded and sane.

Red: I will. I told him that I would every day. I do not know what she will think about all of this."

Red scheduled his last session the next day. I had faith Red would make his next appointment. I must say, I did not know what to expect. Red changed his life in six sessions. This change had to come by him hitting rock bottom. I hated that he did not have a couple of months to integrate his new understanding of himself. Red's final session started different. Red was sitting in the waiting room. A small little girl was wanting to play with him as he sat quietly. Her mother kept moving her away from Red. She wanted her to talk to the man that was dressed in a suit and well kept. The little girl was drawn to Red. She kept moving back to him. He played with her and then her mother would quickly move her back towards the nice, dressed man.

The nice-looking man was a perpetrator. The little girl knew intrinsically that Red was safe. I would bet Red had not played with a child in years. Just to think he almost stepped into the abyss a little over two weeks earlier. Red stopped playing with the little girl and asked me to come outside to see something.

I went outside and walked over to a sweet looking Harley. It was red with an attractive angel on the gas tank. The angel was partly nude, and a small golden bear was on the front of the bike. The bear was tied down on the long handlebars. I went over and spoke with bear. The bike was impressive, especially with the angel on his tank. This was bear's "madden voyage." Bear was on the front; then he would have a permanent seat on the back. We walked into session and Red told me why he got bear.

Red: "I surprised the little guy with bear this morning. I got bear to remind me of what I promised him. Bear will remind me every day that I need to listen to him.

Counselor: I am impressed with you, choosing to do the work and listen to your inner child. I am wondering what that bear means to you?

Red: I looked for bear at Toys R Us. Once I saw the bear, I knew he was the one. I had a warm feeling and positive memories of my mom and dad. It brought tears to my eyes.

Counselor: Sounds like you are feeling some of your authentic emotions again. You have been callused for over 20 years, or at least eight. You are on the right track. I believe you have great things in store for you. I know that you will begin to live life. You will even be a spiritual man.

Red: I do not know if I would go that far.

Counselor: Well, I would. You coming here and the bullet not firing was not an accident. You were willing to take your life and God gave it back to you. That is no accident. You took the journey to your Soul and came back in two weeks with your Authentic Self. That is impressive. Do you have any questions because I know this is your last session?

Red: I do not know how all this works, but I feel different. Will these feelings stop?

Counselor: No. It will not wear off. You will need to listen to your inner child and yourself. If you have any doubts about what you need to do or have a feeling for no reason, then take time to listen to the child within you. If you do not, then you will go back to your old behaviors, thoughts, and feelings. You can check your reality and choices with him. Red, usually the inner child needs the adult's wisdom, but in your case, you need the child's wisdom. The more you do this work, you will build new neuropathways and find that the child will grow up. You will become one. If you do not spend time with him then you will likely go back to what you have known.

Red thanked me and got up to leave the session. Before he left, he gave me a hug. I would never have thought that Red would ever have given me a hug. He gave me a hug like he shook my hand. It was fitting that our time together ended with a bear hug. He did cure his Soul, which anyone can do. His despair was acted out to the point that he was willing to take his own life. Red had a second chance and used it. I did not know if I would ever see him again.

About five years later, I heard a loud motorcycle outside my window. It was Red. I met him outside by his bike. Bear was still with him, riding on the back; he looked a little weathered. Red told me he was doing well and that he was keeping his promise to his inner child.

Many self-help books deal with the signs and symptoms of an illness but not the reasons for it. The ability to re-write or change your earlier chapters not only re-wires your brain but will also change your life. Red's own enemy was self-despair, which played out in the form of anger. Red's early chapters saved his life, even though Red's adult had them colored by the beliefs and decisions of an adolescent. His inner child was not going by the same beliefs as Red. Many times, the cure for the soul comes from the adult to the Child Within, but in this case, the earlier chapters brought truth and healing.

You may be going through something different due to having different childhood experiences. Red's later chapters were illusions against the dark arts of the world. Red confronted his adolescent beliefs with the truth and innocence of his early learning. His childhood experiences were covered by an adolescent's avoidance or use of defense mechanisms that kept him trapped for years. Red listened to the child within himself and experienced God.

You may be going through something different due to having a different wound. The illusion of a defense against the darkness is only that: an illusion that imprints and remains on your mind and soul. You will find that avoidance or use of defense mechanisms will keep you trapped by your past perpetrators and blocked from you true self and God. This is the reason that listening to your historical beliefs while speaking truth will draw you in to your own mind, body, and soul. You will find truth and freedom through this inward crossing for yourself and God in you.

By journaling and doing the NDH exercise, you have been speaking truth into your past experiences in and personal, physical, and individual ways. Now, you are going to be mindful looking through your mind's eye. Through your mind's eye, you will visualize the part of you that experiences sufferings. You are detaching from your past sufferings to experience truth. This healthy detachment allows you to use the prism of your mind to reconceptualize your past. By refracting your avoided history through your mind's eye, you will experience your past's true colors. This truth will give you the ability to change what you are projecting onto others.

## Remember:

Avoidance or use of defense mechanisms will keep you trapped by your past perpetrators and blocked from your true self and God.

# CHAPTER ELEVEN

## THE HERO'S JOURNEY

"For everything there is a season, and a time for every purpose under heaven:"

Ecclesiastes 3:1

**KEY POINTS:**

- Christians guard their hearts and mind from external temptations, yet not from their early learning.
- Physiologically, emotionally, mentally, and spiritually you can reconceptualize your trauma and change your brain and life.
- Early traumatic memories and beliefs influence your decisions today.

**Reflections:**

- Do you wear a mask to cover your indulgences or wounds?
- Are you a good guide for the child within you?
- Will you be the first adult to stand by him/her daily?

# Welcome.

In Battlefield of the Mind (1995), Joyce Meyers confronts the mind's battle with evil when she writes, "Wrong thoughts are the root of our problems and that we can change our life by changing our thinking. God's word teaches us that our minds must be renewed, so we learn to think like God thinks" (p. x). While it is important to know we can change our lives by changing our thinking, we must acknowledge the difficulty of changing our thinking because of familiar mental loops we all fall into. The opportunity to rewire our thoughts and the importance of this practice is studied by the fields of Cognitive Behavioral Therapy (CBT) and Dialectical Behavioral Therapy (DBT).

As the Hero of your journey, you too will need to take "every thought captive" (2 Corinthians 10:4-5, trans). The battlefield of the mind is your past learning. Many Christians are trained to guard their minds from external temptations but forget to examine distortions in their early learning. Christians are vulnerable to remaining in negative early mental loops because they rest in the salvation experience. Many believe once they accept Christ as their personal savior, they are mentally clean from all unrighteousness and do not need to work at changing their thinking.

Clinically, many of my Christian clients are not aware of problems with their scripted beliefs that may fuel painful and hypocritical actions. Christians are aware of the present temptations of the world but not the scripts that lead to indulging in these temptations.

I have a new respect for Romans 12:2, which says, "Be transformed by the renewing of your mind" (ASV). Renewing your mind is an active process of putting off beliefs that are not of God, which is easier said than done. It is difficult to take off your old learning because it is hereditary and deeply ingrained. You have a, "Certain short-term genetic predisposition -- not just for height, weight, and color of our hair and eyes, but for behaviors and attitudes. We carry with us some of the emotional baggage or blessings of our ancestors" (Dispenza, 2007, p.18). The same traits that hindered your parents are passed down generationally.

These certain short-term genetic predispositions were spoken about in Exodus 20:5 which says, "You shall not worship them or serve them [ false gods or idols]; for I, the LORD your God, I am a jealous God, visiting the iniquity of the fathers on the children, on the third and the fourth generations of those who hate Me" (Exodus 20:5 NASB; Deuteronomy 5:9). The sins of the father were passed down through four generations. It is important to know that Jeremiah 31:29- 34 does not hold youth accountable for parental sin. Jeremiah 31:30 speaks of the New Covenant, which says, "But everyone will die for his own iniquity; each man who eats the sour grapes, his teeth will be set on edge" (Jeremiah 31:30 NASB). This verse does not say the sins of the father would not be passed down generationally; it only states that people would not be held accountable for these genetic predispositions. "We can either pass our pain down through the generations or pass our healing down. The choice is yours" (Dayton, 2000, p.309).

It is important to understand your scripted beliefs. Just because you are a Christian, sanctified by God, and filled with the Holy Spirit does not mean you do not need to deal with early learning that was informed by distortions of the world. As humans, we all have "stinking thinking" that fuels dysfunctional behavior. Your old thinking can create depression, Posttraumatic Stress Disorder (PTSD), anxiety, and eating disorders, while leading you to overuse internal and external indulgences. Proverbs 23:7 says, "For as he thinketh within himself, so he is" (NASB).

You will need to be intentional to change your thinking, and thus change your brain.

Later in this chapter, you will have the opportunity to transform your mind by moving "within" yourself through exercises. At this point, you have received many of the tools to experience the child within you. Now, you are aware of your early storyline, experiences in Never Neverland, Captain Hook, and aware of your inner child's thoughts, feelings, and a located safe place for your inner child to exist. In this chapter, you will have the opportunity to get close to your inner child's past experiences while building more clarity for your child within. You will be able to bring your adult truths or God's truths to your inner child.

Your struggle with life is a thinking problem, not a God problem. Christians need to know how to change their thinking. The local church may teach parishioners how to live, but it does not educate them on how to clean out their souls from "within." Christians need to understand how to change their emotional brains that were hard wired by the world. Ephesians 2:3 says, "Among them we too all formerly lived in the lusts of our flesh, indulging the desires of the flesh and of the mind, and were by nature children of wrath, even as the rest" (NASB).

The above passage deals with our hard-wired beliefs that were built on indulgences "of the flesh and of the mind." As children, we grew up in the "flesh" and are, "by nature (hardwired) children of wrath." Our heritage is the lust of the flesh and built on the knowledge of the world. We walked according to the course of this world, according to the prince of the powers of the air, of the spirit that now worketh in the sons of disobedience" (Ephesians 2:2, ASV). The emotional brain learned from the teaching of the "prince of the air," referring to Satan. Our earthly inheritance is built on the "prince of the world" which is not God, yet is a part of the mind.

Today's research shows that the interaction between parents and children also forms the hardwiring of a child's brain. "Everything that occurs in a child's social world affects neurochemical and neurobiological structures. Nature and nurture do not compete, but work hand in hand, two systems constantly influencing and shaping each other" (Dayton, 2000, p.89). Contemporary research shows that learned behavior is also hard-wired and this hardwiring can be changed by constantly renewing your mind.

We can consciously renew the conscious mind by using God's Word even though our historical make up and learning was not of God. Our past learning may lead to unhappiness and an unfulfilled life. Personal history is wired into the brain, while temptation of the flesh will continue from "the spirit" of the father of lies (John 8:44). Christians have a two-fold problem. First, bringing our historic learning into the present moment. Second, dealing with the dilemma of temptation in life.

Many of my Christian clients struggle with internal and external indulgences, mental illnesses, and relational issues that are of this world and not of God. They do not understand the reasons for their struggles because they are "Christians." They desperately want peace and happiness, but are unaware that, "The mind is the battlefield" (Meyers, 2011, p.79). Relief, redirection, and reconceptualizing take place once they gain an awareness that many of their problems are not the result of poor faith. Once aware of the battlefield, they direct the fight to their historical beliefs and begin winning the war. They began the heroic quest to conquer the mind.

If the mind is the battlefield, then it will take a hero's journey. The hero's journey towards "healing, involves re-telling and reconstructing the story of the trauma in the harbor of that safety, allowing the emotional circuitry to acquire a new, more realistic understanding of and response to the traumatic memory and its triggers. As a patient recalls the horrific details of the trauma, the memory starts to be transformed both in its emotional meaning and in its effect on the emotional brain" Emotional Intelligence (Goleman, 1995, p.211).

Physiologically, emotionally, mentally, and spiritually you can reconceptualize the traumas for your inner child. Reconceptualizing the issues of your inner child's mind will allow you to begin the healing journey. Spiritually, God has given you His Spirit to help you search the old while putting on the new adult mind. The Holy Spirit, "Searches everything, even the depths of God" ...and "no one comprehends the thoughts of God except the Spirit of God" (1 Corinthians 2:10-11).

As a clinician, I see the cost of evil with my clients daily. Many have built their historical beliefs on lies. The evil one wants to kill and "devour" you (1Peter 5:8). He kills and devours you through sin. In Galatians 5:19-21, Paul writes, "The works of the flesh are manifest, which are these: fornication, uncleanness, lasciviousness, idolatry, sorcery, enmities, strife, jealousies, wraths, factions, divisions, parties, envying, drunkenness, reveling, and such like; ..." (ASV). The work of the flesh has a cost to your mental and emotional health. The emotional cost might be self-loathing, self-despair, self-hatred, self-pity, self-doubt, shame, fear, or sadness. These internal feelings will decrease your self-esteem, internal safety, and trust of others.

Someone needs to tell the little girl who was fondled by her cousins, penetrated by her uncle, and was not believed by her parents that this was sin and not of God. Someone needs to tell the little boy beaten by his father, touched sexually by his mother, and suffers with homosexual thoughts and depression that his experience was not of God. The sin of others damaged the psyches of these children and are part of the battlefield of their own minds.

Your inner child needs the attention of your adult mind to be free. The little boy or girl in you needs safety, love, and support from you. A part of this journey is attending to the wounded child who dwells within you. As you continue to reach out to your inner child, you will experience more truth and healing. You will be able to deal with the internal and external indulgences that hide your psyche's wounds. Dealing with your wounds will lead to your inner child. Both of you will be liberated from past learning and no longer be enslaved by the past.

Dawn Scott Jones in her book, When a Woman You Love Was Abused writes, "Delving deep inside to explore the inner child is both difficult and rewarding for the survivor. Most survivors [ of sexual abuse] feel that discovering the child within gives that child a voice and listening to her cries are an important part of healing. Many survivors have reclaimed parts of their playful and childlike personalities after being introduced to their inner child and allowing her [him] to release the painful memories she's [he's] held" (2012, p.91). I would highly recommend this book to husbands who love a woman who has been abused, and for women working through sexual abuse issues.

As a child, there was little protection from the sins of the world. Charles Whitfield writes, "...most families across the world are dysfunctional in that they don't provide and support the healthy needs of their children. What results is an interruption in the otherwise normal and healthy neurological and psychological growth and development of the child from birth to adulthood. To survive, the traumatized child's Real Self (True Self or Child Within) goes into hiding deep within the unconscious part of its psyche. What emerges is a false self which... Is unable to succeed because it is a simply a defense mechanism against pain and not real" (Whitfield, 1989, p. xvi).

This false self may develop depression, anxiety, or even psychosis to adapt to the surrounding environment. The mind reflects its old emotional learning, which increases self-pity, self-despair, and self-loathing. Such reflections tear at the fabric of your spirit and soul. It is difficult to tell those in emotional anguish to stop self-mutilating themselves when they do not know how to stop reliving the pain of early childhood abuse. Telling them to experience their authentic feelings and love the child within sounds absurd. Yet, these people are unaware they are looking through the child's eyes, feeling old emotions and experiencing thoughts of previous abuse. Stepping away from self-harm while stepping toward the pain and fear enables them to lessen the emotional and mental pain of the past.

The mind needs to be on guard from the past's poison. It is important to guard your mind with "all vigilance." The Psalmist writes, "Keep and guard your heart with all vigilance and above all that you guard, for out of it flow the springs of life" (Proverbs 4:23, AMP). "The heart is not primarily the symbol of emotions, though emotions are not excluded, but of thought, of the mind and will of the inner person. The heart must be guarded closely because it is the central source and controlling factor in life" (The Broadman Bible Commentary, Vol 5, editor Clifton J. Allen, 1971, p.23).

More than anything, your "heart" needs to be guarded. Proverbs 4:23 not only grants permission to listen to your thoughts and feelings but speaks to the necessity of guarding your heart while protecting it from inappropriate thoughts. Literally, your mind can lead or influence your life. Many Christians have distorted beliefs or views about listening to their thoughts and feelings. God encourages you to guard your thoughts with his truth (1 Peter 5:8). It is hard to guard what you are avoiding or consciously pressing down. You need to listen to more of your early scripts by experiencing your inner child in the following regression exercise and journaling. The second regression exercise will increase your self-awareness while developing a deeper relationship with your inner child.

God encourages us to clean the "inside of the cup" in Matthew 23:25-28. This passage deals with hypocrites that "appeared beautiful" on the outside but were full of "indulgences" on the inside. Most pastors speak of not being hypocrites and tell you to apply God's Word, yet they are missing the power of cleaning out your old thoughts and feelings. Jesus is speaking to the religious leaders, scribes, and Pharisees, of the early church, telling them not to be hypocrites. It needs to be noted that the use of hypocrites is in the form of an active verb. Hypocrite in the verb form means "to separate slowly or slightly subjects to gradual inquiry" (Robertson, Vol. 1, 1930, p.181). If they were inquiring about their hearts, they would not pretend to wear a mask of being spiritual or Godly.

What needed to be separated "slowly" and with "gradual inquiry" was the hearts and souls of their false selves. They were not to be full of "dead men's bones" (Matthew 23:27) and "iniquity" (vs. 28). Their hearts and minds needed to be reviewed and cleansed to match their behavior of being pure and holy externally. The Pharisees and scribes were "self-indulgent" in the things of the flesh.

Life would be so much easier if you did not carry all your historical learning with you. Your past scripts limit your rational decision-making. If you did not project your history on to the present, you could rest or have peace at the same time. You could overcome present temptations. The past would not keep you captive. What incarcerates you is your inner child thoughts and feelings, and a distorted image of God. The main thing you need to know is that your inner child learns by self-confirming old teaching taught by a world that has missed God's mark.

God calls us to look forward and not to allow the past to have control. Jesus said, "No one, having put his hand to the plow, and looking back, is fit for the kingdom of God" (Luke 9:62, NSAB). God was our creator and has a working knowledge of how our brains work. Learning to be conscious in our authentic God given self is the key to being spiritually content. While there are numerous books describing how to live Christ-like, most do not deal with cleaning your emotional, mental, and spiritual lenses. If you do not clean the lens of your Soul, you will not see clearly. Cleaning your lenses is difficult, "Because our True Self [the Child Within] is so hidden, and because our false self is so prominent, awakening may not come easily" (Whitfield, 1987, p. 63).

This awakening will bring you the hidden gifts of your inner child. The child within, "…is expressive, assertive, and creative. It can be childlike in the highest, most mature, and evolved sense of the word" (Whitfield, 1987, p. 63). You may attribute your historic thoughts and feelings to your inner child, which may increase avoidance or compulsive behaviors. You can experience God's best by providing safety and security to your inner child. The child within you holds God's gifts of innocence, spontaneity, and creativity. These God given traits are covered by pain and suffering.

You are on a Hero's journey to your soul, and it is not easy. You, like all heroes, must face this journey alone. No one can take the steps for you. While support is comforting, some battles are fought alone. Choosing to travel a road many have ignored may be because of the fear and pain along the way. Taking the initial steps inward is challenging. Consider all the hero stories that you have watched or read. Is the hero excited to go? Does the Hero go against great odds, undergo hardship, and overcome difficulties? Usually, heroes or heroines confront the temptation not to go and find themselves alone or abandoned. All heroes face internal and external struggles, yet they always completed great conquests on their journey toward transformation. Think of your heroes growing up. The ones that you wanted to be, real or imagined.

### Exercise: Examining Your First Heroes

*This is not a regression exercise. There are no special instructions included. Answer simply and directly in your journal.*

1. Who were my heroes or heroines?
2. Were they alone?
3. Did they have support? Yes. No.
4. Were they excited about their journey? Yes. No.
5. Did they have trials or tribulations? Yes. No.
6. What were their trials?
7. Were they tempted, or asked not to go? Yes. No.
8. Did they get abandoned or lost on their journey? Yes. No.
9. Did they have to fight the "bad guys" or villains? Yes. No.
10. Did they win the battle? Yes. No.
11. Did they have to leave home or go to a foreign land? Yes. No.
12. Were their travels difficult? Yes. No.
13. Was the journey worth it? Yes. No.
14. Were they transformed? Yes. No.

Most of the above questions can be answered by a resounding "yes."

Everyone dreams of being heroic. We all crave the transformation of a heroic quest, but do not want to take the path of tears and struggle along the way. Jesus Christ had the same struggles on his heroic quest. Why should your journey be any different? Just look at the story of Jesus.

Jesus came from simple beginnings, born in a manger (Luke 2:1-20, trans) with poor parents. He grew up just like all the other kids. He was thirty years old before he started his Hero's journey (Luke 3:23, trans). When Jesus started his journey, his life changed internally and externally. Jesus knew he had to become a blood sacrifice to win the battle (Psalms 22:16-18). He knew he would have to descend into the depths of hell to win the war (Hosea13:14; Ecclesiastics 24:45; Zachariah 9:11, trans).

The hero's journey is to your "badlands," to reclaim your child, which holds your "lost memories" daily. Many of my clients manage to rescue their inner child and take that child "home." Occasionally, they get busy with life and begin experiencing old behaviors and symptoms again. They needed to continue nurturing the child within them until the child was part of them. Most usually stopped the journey because they began feeling better and not due to fear.

My clients' journeys are difficult because their primitive brains generally attempt to self-protect by confirming bold imagined threats. The childlike mind projects past fears onto the adult. Your journey to the "badlands" will be different because a solid relationship with your inner child has already been built through earlier chapters. Safety has been secured and the medicine of truth has been adapted to your inner child's wounds by doing the previous exercises.

Your regression work is not just cognitive and emotional; it is also figurative. My clients who use regression to reclaim the inner child from old childhood experiences find that the child within would return to the old place where they were originally found out of a triggered sense of fear. Clinically, I did not know my clients would figuratively regress, i. e., the inner child, which embodies their past experiences, would literally return to the old experience. I was aware that the emotional brain would look back to see forward. Understanding the inner working of the brain explains how the mind embodies past learning, yet the power of the mind to go figuratively back to past trauma speaks of the power of early learning on the psyche. My clients that did not stay in a relationship with the child within them had to reclaim their inner child again from the past.

On the other hand, my clients who spent time reconceptualizing their past thoughts and doing the exercises did not regress figuratively (i. e., the child part did not go back physically to where they were originally found). The adult part of you needs to be active in bringing your present thoughts and feelings to the child part of you. The child's old and outdated beliefs and feelings are being changed by your present knowledge. If you are not listening or speaking to your inner child, he or she will bring back your old, distorted beliefs and feelings.

To put inner-child work into perspective, you can see the child within through your mind's eye. This child part of you has little knowledge of your life now. The child is literally trapped in the past. He or she is still in the small town, small house or room with the old familiar thoughts and feelings. These old familiar thoughts and feelings are not forgotten but played out through you. You can change the child's mind about the world and change your life. The greater your trials, tribulations, or traumas were in your childhood, the greater the growth will be for you and the child within you.

Your fear of suffering from old wounds has poisoned your mind and soul. Begin spitting out the poison today. Again, you might not know how to reclaim yourself from your historic abuse or trauma. Just take a moment and ask yourself:

When was I innocent? Write down your age. _________.

When was I not scared of suffering? Write down your age. _________. Or

When did I lose my innocence? Write down your age_______.

You may know these answers from your previous inner child work, or you may still not know the answer to these questions. When I was first asked these questions, I did not have answers. I must admit that I was not happy about not knowing the answers, especially when my peers had their answers. I had to think about my innocence from a rational place.

The following assessment will aid you in discerning how to experience your authentic self and come to know your core answers. Take time to do the Inner Child assessment below.

## Exercise: Profile of Your Inner Child

*This is not a regression exercise. There are no special instructions included. Answer simply and directly in your journal.*

## I. Profile Questions

Were you abused? Yes No

What type of abuse? Circle on of the following:

- verbal
- emotional
- physical
- sexual
- neglect
- mental
- other __________.

Answer the following questions concerning your abuse.

1) How old were you when the abuse began? ________.
2) How old were you when the abuse stopped? ________.
3) a-Do you remember your life before the abuse? If so, what age were you? _______.

   b-What were you feeling before you were abused? _______.
4) Did the abuse change you? Yes. No.
5) When you are not doing anything, what are your feelings?
6) What would you feel when you are thinking about the abuse?
7) If you had the chance to go back and tell yourself something about the abuse, what would you say?
8) What age would this part of you be?
9) What do you think God would say to you ABOUT your abuse?

10) If God were going to talk to a part of you about the abuse, how old would he/she be ______?

11) If God had the chance to go back and tell YOU something ABOUT your abuse, what would He say?

12) What would:

A) God's graces say to you about your struggle with this abuse?

B) God's unconditional love say to you about your struggle with this abuse?

## II. Profile Assessment

What was the age of your answer to question # 8? ______.

Does your answer to question 8 correspond to question 1, 2, or 3? (Circle the number)

If you answer of question 8 does not match 1, 2 or 3, then which one is it closer too? _______.

Is this number close to your answer in question 10? Usually question 8 is the age of your inner child. Everyone is different. You will have some direction by the above answers.

Now write down the emotion or emotions in question 5 ________ and in question 6 _________.

Are these emotions the same? Yes. No.

Is the emotion in question 6 greater than question 5? Yes. No.

These are the emotions that are being medicated or avoided.

## III. Abuse Assessment

Question. 1. Identifies the abuse.

Question. 2. Identifies the timeline and safety. This is usually the age of your inner child. This age usually corresponds with the answer to questions 8 and 10.

| | |
|---|---|
| Question 3a. | If "No" then your memories are likely those that stem from abuse. |
| Question 3b. | This was/is your authentic God given feeling that was covered by your abuse. |
| Question 4. | Checks awareness and mindset |
| Question. 5. | Is your medicated emotions |
| Question. 6 | Is a more intense emotion than answer 5 |
| Question 7 | Needs to correspond with God's answer in question 9 |
| Question 8. | Is your intuitive knowledge of the age of your inner child |
| Question 9 | Puts your abuse into perspective |
| Question 10. | Is a clarification of your inner child's age. You will need to compare this age to the close one of your answers to question 8 or possible questions 1 or 2. |
| Question 11 | Deals with God's concern for you while separating you from your abuse issues |

Question 12a and b are how you need to attend to your inner child. You will need to give grace and love to this part of you.

This assessment will identify your inner child's age, thoughts, and feelings. You need to love the child within through God's grace and love. Trust in your intuition and the assessment to know where to go to find your inner child and assess your experiences and ages to know where your inner child is safe.

Your journey to finding your authentic self is almost complete. Your hero's journey has looked into the mirror of your soul and seen the relics of your authentic self. Later in this chapter, you will have the opportunity to continue breaking old, mirrored images projected by others and experience your inner child. You will find your inner child, rewriting the storyline for your life. Suffering of your past will give meaning to your future as you continue to travel towards your inner child, becoming the author of your script. You will continue the journey to experience the child within you to bring love and truth to him/ her.

Tian Dayton refers to this process of healing as "memory editing." Memory editing pulls up the stored emotional experience of long-term memory by giving a voice to repressed emotions then edits them with our conscious mind. She sees learning as "a process of tearing down and building up brain cells. Memory is stored in clusters. When, *through our desires to remember*, we bring one of these clusters forward —as we watch the memory unfold within the screen of our mine -- we are tearing down and building up brain cells. When we review the memory, we see it differently. We may discard old meaning that we had attached to events and introduce new meaning from now being able to see it in a new light. Then, when we restore the memory —that is, when it returns to a last conscious state — it is stored differently in a new cell assembly. It is, in fact, with new insight and new understanding" (Trauma and Addiction, 2000, pp.113-14).

## My Story: Mattie

Let us put transformation and healing into practical words. Here is Mattie's story: Mattie remembered the repressed fragmented images of once-forgotten memories. These fragmented images occurred when her inner child was emotionally and sexually abused by her dad. Through her mind's eye, Mattie was aware of the fragmented experiences and saw the child within her alone, hiding in her bedroom. Mattie was aware that the child within her had fears of being abused every night. She can see her panic, shame, and sadness. Mattie knows that the little girl believes all men will abuse her because dad was a man. As she sat on the bed with the child within her, she experienced the memory of thinking "it's my fault." Mattie remembered the experience and she thought that the abuse would not have happened, if "I didn't sit on his lap." As Mattie sits on the bed with her inner child, she is aware of her belief that "God is punishing me."

This remembrance has brought unconscious learning to Mattie's conscious mind. She wonders if this is the reason she has anxiety and does not trust men or God. Now she can find out the truth by listening to her inner child's hurts and fears. Mattie can edit her memory with truth or go by the old message or belief created by the trauma. When she changed her child-like thinking, she changed the beliefs and the emotions they once held. She changed her child's point of view by actively confronting her beliefs that men are not safe, she deserved it, and/or God was punishing her. Mattie can bring her present personal and spiritual truths, gathered outside of her scripted beliefs or old tapes, to her inner child.

In Mattie's mind's eye, she saw herself holding the child within her, listening to her inner child's beliefs and telling her the truth. Mattie gave her inner child life examples to match her truths. She can feel her inner child's panic decrease and rest in her arms. Her inner child is no longer alone. A sense of safety and peace came over her. Mattie told the little girl to have courage and determination, which brought empowerment and change into her life. Mattie spoke to her inner child about her present safety and reminded her that she no longer lives with her dad. The child within her becomes aware of her truth and breathes a sigh of relief; a smile comes upon her face. Mattie noticed that she felt different. Mattie experienced a strange type of peace that came over her body where the anxiety used to reside.

As the days passed, Mattie began sleeping throughout the night as her interest in wine decreased in the evenings. The crippling anxiety she experienced for years is all but gone. No longer projecting the past on the present, she began to enjoy herself and believe that she was attractive. This new knowledge and insight began to stop her historic pattern of isolation while bringing a new confidence.

As she continued to talk to her inner child about God, Mattie could review her old decisions, while understanding the reason for her earlier beliefs. She could reject or accept her old beliefs based on her present truth. She began sharing her experience and knowledge of God with her inner child. This internal dialogue allows the child within her to know that God is not punishing her. For the first time, her inner child gets to experience the God that the adult Mattie knows. Mattie was aware of emotional changes but did not consciously understand how she had affected her unconscious memories. This process of mentally editing or being interactively mindful changed her past script, which got acted out in her conscious life.

By being interactively mindful like Mattie, you will provide adult responses to your past feelings and your inner child's emotional logic, hearing your old, distorted beliefs and negative thoughts of your script while changing them. You have already spoken with the child within you by journaling and writing with your Non-Dominant Hand. Now you get to experience your inner child visually, viscerally, and emotionally. You have read some of your early script; now, you get to visually meet the part of you that lived it, by traveling through time and visually experience the child within you. Step into your Holy of Holies, this is hallowed ground. Experiencing this hallowed ground will allow you to transform your life.

This entire book is about how to experience your true God given self while breaking all the old reflections on the mirror of your Soul: these past experiences define you. As you experience the window of your Soul through your mind's eye, you find and will experience your inner child. Your inner child needs a true guide to show him/her the way. You will be this guide for your inner child. You will be the light which leads him/her out of darkness. You know his/her safe place, feelings, and old beliefs. This knowledge, with your present wisdom, will give you the power to change your storyline. You will be able to give the child within you understanding and freedom from his/her history of neglect, dysfunction, and abuse.

You have the medicine for all old wounds, received directions for any wrong turn taken, and knowledge to change any old message believed by your inner child. Can you imagine having peace from the inside out? Your early chapters have the greatest effect on your life, even if you had a "normal" family. Most people that live East of Eden had to deal with some form of trauma or abuse that affected their psyche.

Just imagine if you knew then what you know now. Would you have taken a different path or had different thoughts and feelings? You will have a chance to change your yesterdays and tomorrows, today. You will be given an opportunity, later in the chapter, to visit the child within and directly change your childhood beliefs and the feelings you experienced while changing your life.

You will be responding to your past distorted beliefs by experiencing the true colors of your past. Your present truth will change your past beliefs which evolve today, while changing your brain neurologically. Sometimes listening and watching your past experiences are enough to change your script and life. If your experience is from an emotionally charged or chronic event, you will need to step back into a relationship with your inner child. An emotionally charged event could be a one-time experience like a car accident, loss of a loved one, or life-threatening illness, to being raped, beaten, and mentally or verbally abused. Chronic or habitual experiences are emotionally charged events that happen over a period. This period could have been weeks, months, or years. These chronic experiences or traumas carry more emotional "baggage" or an imprint on your mind and soul. Remember, the earlier the experience is in your childhood, the more powerful the imprint is on your mind and spirit.

If you experienced trauma early in your childhood, then you may have more intrusive thoughts and feelings. These thoughts and feelings have played out repeatedly as a child, which affects your experience of yourself and the world around you. You are unaware of how these early experiences have directed your steps. These early emotional decisions will be carried out several hundred, if not thousands, of times while a later decision will be carried out less over your life span. Your script directs your life's steps as DNA directed your genetic makeup. Early traumatic memories and beliefs influence your decisions today. I am asking you to listen and interact mindfully. You will have the strength and awareness of your losing yourself today to its teaching.

## Internal and Interactive Mindfulness

What is being internally mindful? Being mindful is being present in the moment while being conscious of your present thoughts, feelings, and body sensations in that moment. Being mindful internally is difficult. Being mindful and conscious of your past experiences or learning goes against all your defense mechanisms. Due to your unconscious defense mechanisms, you will need to detach from your early learning to experience them clearly. Detaching from the inner child to see him/her sounds counter intuitive; however, detachment from your inner child's learning gives you an opportunity to be aware of them. This would be considered healthy detachment with your child within.

Healthy detachment is a neutral response. Detachment or dissociation is usually experienced during times of abuse or great stress. Detachment during abuse helps you prolong your sanity while being abused. Detachment can be used as a defense mechanism i.e., you detach from your emotional state or authentic emotions. You can use detachment for healing. The art of healing is to find that neutral place to observe and be aware of your inner child. You are not responding or reacting to him/her. You will be detached while being mindful/aware of your past "unwanted" thoughts and feelings. You will not be moved by them as you once were by the experience. You may even "see" the experience that hurt or scared the child within you. Internal mindfulness is becoming an observer to your inner child's old thoughts, feelings, and experiences. You are not to judge but watch and listen with empathy.

You may think having empathy will stop true detachment and color your view of being with your inner child. I believe empathy will add to your ability to be mindful and will not interfere with healthy detachment. Empathy will draw you back into your historic thoughts and feeling while building healthy detachment. Empathy allows you to be drawn to the child within you, which intensifies your mindfulness of him/her.

This same empathy can give you accurate ways to attend to yourself. It is worth the risk of possibly reliving the feelings of your trauma, not the experience of the trauma. If you re-experience your authentic feeling of the original experience, then you will be able to bring your present truth to the part of you that experienced it. Your detachment from the early experience and empathy for the child within you gives you the ability to reframe or reconceptualize the experience. By reconceptualizing the experience from your adult perspective, you break your earlier held beliefs and their emotional ties to the trauma.

This new perspective will decrease your need to avoid or use defense mechanisms concerning your present reality while decreasing present intrusive thoughts, flashbacks, and abreaction. Abreactions are living or experiencing a past event so vividly that you feel as though it is really happening in the present moment. Many clinicians will use "reliving an event" rather than calling this experience an abreaction. Many of my clients are scared to do inner child work because of the possibility that they will have abreactions.

In my clinical experience, my clients were less likely to look through the eyes of their experience if they were being mindful. My clients that didn't do regressive work were more likely to experience their past abuse by living it out, projecting it on others, having intrusive thoughts, dysfunctional behavior patterns, night terrors, bad dreams and increase use of internal and external indulgences. Being internally mindful empowers you and will help you confront your emotional wounds.

Interactive mindfulness is where you observe with an empathetic eye, your inner child. The next step toward changing and healing is interactive mindfulness. Interactive mindfulness is where you can respond to your inner child's old beliefs with your present knowledge while gathering understanding and wisdom. Speaking with your inner child allows your adult brain's truths to be applied to your inner child. This new information will help your inner child break free from moving with sensory data and his/her old emotional logic. The knowledge from your frontal lobe will help your inner child break free of his/her old negative messages and outdated thinking from times past.

Being internally mindful of the child within you will help you detach from your old feelings and beliefs. You may not know what it is like to not experience shame, guilt, pain, loneliness, fear, anxiety, anger, or hopelessness. You may not remember a time you have not experienced depression or anxiety. You may not believe that you can break the strong holds that are destroying your life. You may have forgotten that you are valuable, worthy, and lovable. Interactive mindfulness will empower you to change your past, present, and future story. You will experience triumph in past defeats, victory over past emotional losses and peace with past suffering.

**An example of being internal and interactive mindfulness:**

Let us say, your belief is "I'm not good enough," and you experience fear in social situations. The first thing you need to do is remember one of the first times you felt scared. Your remembrances will take you to the time you heard or believed you were not good enough. Once you remember this time, then close your eyes and allow yourself to see the time and place you first experienced fear. Then give close attention to the reason you thought you were "not good enough." You are already being internally mindful once you have these three elements of the experience in mind. You will deepen this experience by closing your eyes and experience your memory through your mind's eye.

You can see yourself in class with other kids laughing. You remember the teacher questioning you about your reading and can see the little boy or girl sitting there in fear. You can observe with empathy your inner child being laughed at for what he/she misread aloud. You watch until you have an accurate understanding of the experience, thoughts, and feelings of your inner child. Then open your eyes and take time to contemplate what you experienced.

Give yourself time to process your inner child's thoughts and feelings in this remembrance. You will become aware of the belief you carried from the experience. Once you are aware of your old beliefs, then check to see if the feeling matched the experience. It could be a racket feeling. Once you know your inner child's thoughts and feelings, check them with your truth today. This truth is what you would tell your inner child. Now you are prepared to be interactively mindful.

Interactive mindfulness begins by closing your eyes while using your mind's eye to revisit the classroom. In your mind's eye, you can see your inner child sitting at the desk being scared to read or hurt because of being laughed at by others. Once in the classroom you can stand by your inner child's desk and speak to him/her. You can tell your inner child your truth and let him or her know that he/she is okay. You need to take time to listen to your inner child's belief about what you have said to him/her. You can allow this interaction to go on if you want to.

You will be able to be internally and interactively mindful with your inner child that was laughed at, ridiculed, or bullied. If your inner child was beaten or sexually abused, your remembrance needs to take place in the child's safe place. You can let your inner child know he/she is not alone, the truth, and assure him/her of safety. Can you imagine your inner child's experience when he/she is being held and loved by you? Knowing your truth, that you can read and graduate high school, will break the message of not being good enough and your fear will dissipate.

By speaking with your inner child, you will be able to respond to your inner child's emotional logic with your adult reasoning. You will be able to change his/her early learning and the emotions that were attached to his/her beliefs. You have already interacted with the child within you by reviewing your early beliefs and writing with your NDH. Now you get to experience your inner child visually, viscerally, and emotionally. You have read some of your early script. Now you get to meet the part of you that lived it. You will travel through time and experience the child within you. You will step into your

Holy of Holies. This is hallowed ground. Experiencing this hallowed ground will allow you to change your life.

As you unearth and experience your inner child, you will look through different lenses: at yourself, the world, and God. You can neither be whole without the child nor can he/she be whole without you; this will help you get closer to your God given self. Your God given self will be conscious most of the time and not living unconsciously. Your child-like self wants to capture the moment and be with the leaves that fall, while touching the ones on the tree, experiencing the wind on her/his face and the dirt between her/his toes while feeling the excitement and anticipation of the moment.

Proverbs 27:17 states: "As iron sharpens iron, so people can improve each other" (Proverbs 27:17 NCV). Now this is true with internal and interactive mindfulness. This work is between you and you. As you do the work, you are sharpening several other tools. You are breaking free of dysfunctional behavior, building self-esteem, gaining, and using wisdom, re-writing your script, and learning to be mindful. The tools that are getting sharpened will help build healthy coping skills, boundaries, and relationships in the future. The work will allow you to experience the wounded part of yourself and bring healing to her/ him or the part that is not aware of the abuse. This "part of you" needs your guidance and wisdom. You need his or her hidden innocence, curiosity, and spontaneity.

Many of my clients get disillusioned by the name "inner child" when they are working with a part of themselves older than 12 years old. The age of the part of you is not as important as what this part of you is going through at the time. Many readers will know when their life changing experience occurred, and it might not have been as a child.

You will know the place and time your life changed yet may be unaware of how it is affecting you today. The ability to experience freedom from past captivity is up to you. The journey to the Soul is not age specific. The child within you might be a 26-year-old that had a life changing experience which still colors your life.

For this reason, internal and interactive mindfulness draws you into your own mind, body, and soul. You will find truth and freedom that comes through an internal search for meaning. Meaning derived from your truth and not from others. In the pending exercise, you will get the chance to understand how your past suffering has affected you while transforming your mind.

You have done the Inner Child Assessment and the NDH exercise in earlier chapters. I hope that at this point you can identify your inner child's age, experience, thoughts, and feelings. You need to look through the fruit of the Spirit as you speak with the child within you. Looking through your spiritual lenses will help you stay out of your script and tune out your old tapes. You need to trust your intuition and the assessment to know where to go to find your inner child. You need to assess your experiences and ages to know when your inner child is safe.

For example, if your trauma happened at age 11, you may go back through your mind's eye and see an innocent 10-year-old or even younger. You may regress to the age when the abuse stopped. You want to regress to one of these preferred ages. If you know where the child's safe place was growing up, then you will not need to worry about regressing to the period of active abuse.

Remember, you are not going back to relive any abuse. You are going back to be with the part of you that you need to see. It does not matter if you go back to the time before or after the experience, accident, or trauma. You just want to be intentional to go to the child's safe place. When you experience your inner child, he/she may be scared, sad or alone; you need to be with and love him/her.

Through your mind's eye, you will be able to experience your inner child with internal mindfulness and have internal dialogue with interactive mindfulness. In this case when you go back and find the 11-year-old in his/her safe place. You will need to let him/her know:

- that you are him/her all grown up.

- that you made it through the trauma, accident, or abuse.

- that you are safe.

- that your home is safe.

- that you will protect him/her.

- that the perpetrator is not at your home.

## Exercise: Interactive Mindfulness

*This is a Regression Exercise. In this and all other regression exercises, intentionality. If you are not intentional, your past scripted belief will color your present reality. Intentional, focused, and slow-moving reflection will make your unconscious conscious, while giving you more control, awareness, and esteem.*

Sit in a quiet place and become quiet. Allow yourself to breathe in ... the fresh... relaxing air.... Releasing ... the stress ... tension in your body... as you exhale.... Breathe in ... holding ... holding ... releasing your breath ... by exhaling. Exhaling ... all the stress ... tension... of the day.... Allow yourself to breathe in deeply.... Breathing out all the remaining stress and tension ...Finding peace...with each breath.

As you relax ... you will remember ... thoughts ... feelings ... and experiencing memories ... of the part you need to see.

Give yourself time.... Time to remember ... your safe place. Seeing the part of you before the trauma, accident, or abuse (those with and external indulgence will look before "the indulgence, addiction or negative thinking."). Seeing ... the part of you... that you need to see.

Breathing in ... relax... with each breathe. Breath out ... moving back ... seeing ... being... in a safe place ... long ago. Going back ... with each breathe you take.... Relaxing ... with each breathe you exhale. Finding ... seeing ... experiencing ... the part of you ... that you need to see.

Once you are with her/ him give yourself time... time to see ... what this part is wearing ... going through ... allowing yourself to be seen. At this same time allow yourself to respond with empathy...Reaching out with words ... telling ... express your heart ... as you exhale.... Sharing safety ... as you inhale each breath bring more ... more ... peace.... Allowing yourself to empower him/ her to have a voice.... Finding that breathing is effortless.

You find that time no longer exists.... Listening ... hearing ... and being ... with the child within you.... Speaking from your heart with truth, while listening to the child within you.

Again, if this part does not verbally speak to you, listen for the answer you had at the time. You are bridging the gap that time once filled. Spend time ... in the moment...Do not judge the child or yourself.... Giving yourself permission ... to reach out physically ... to this part of yourself. Trust your intuition ... Being... with him/ her ... as he/she is with you. Take time ... to hear ... and be with this part of you. Knowing... That you are more important than time. (Stay if needed)

Before you leave ... take time to say good-bye.... Giving him/ her time.... Time... to do the same.... Knowing you will be back ... trusting he/she will rest... in your words.

As you turn to leave.... Breathe in ... fresh ... relaxing air. Breathing out ... all the stress ... tension ... as you exhale.... Finding that you can bring all your thoughts ... feelings ... and experiences ... back to the room.... By opening your eyes.

Once you finished the exercise, allow yourself to journal. Listen to your truth and feelings concerning your experience.

In time and after a couple of these experiences you may want to remove or reclaim your inner child from there and then and bring him/her to the here and now. The most important piece in reclaiming your inner child is getting his/her permission. Your inner child needs to be willing to go with you. The child's decision is based on the relationship you have with him/her and your present safety. Your inner child must be willing to go. If the child within you wants to leave the past, then take his/her hand and walk to the entrance of the safe place. Once at the entrance of your safe place, then in your mind's eye, step out of the safe place into your house.

Once you have your inner child in your safe place take time to orient him/ her to your house, family, and life now. It is important to walk your inner child around your house, while letting him/ her know you live. Your inner child needs to know that your house is safe and how long the dysfunction or abuse has been stopped. The child within you may have no knowledge of life after the dissociative experience. You are giving information that the child part of you needs to know to create safety and peace.

Clinically, I have found that if my clients had little awareness of their abuse, then the child within them had little awareness of their life after the abuse. The amnesic barrier that came from the dissociation experience worked both ways. If you have awareness of your abuse, the child still may have little awareness of his/her life after the abuse.

## Review: Interactive Mindfulness

- What do I do if my inner child will not leave his/her safe place?

*You leave your inner child in his/her safe place. First, you will need to build a relationship with him/her. This may take time to build a healthy relationship with the child within you. That means giving your inner child a voice and doing what others may not have done: listen to him/her. Use the time to teach your inner child about your present thoughts and feelings which slowly brings him/her into your world.*

- What if I do not see the child's face?

*This is an indication that the child has lost his/her self-image. You will need to bring definition and truth to the child's unvoiced emotion within you. You will need to listen with an empathic ear and speak truth to the child within you. Do not be discouraged if the child within you struggles with accepting your truth. Your truth is a gift for your inner child. Soon, your inner child will have a face and a voice. If your inner child's face is "fuzzy," it is likely you heard that you were not important or even that you needed not to exist.*

- What if the child is happy and free?

*The child within you is free of any wounds, suffering or abuse issues. This usually means you carried the past thoughts and feelings of your suffering or there is another dissociated part of yourself. What I call the free child is what Carl Jung called "the 'Divine Child' and Emmet Fox called it the 'Wonder Child'" (Healing the Child Within, Charles L Whitfield, 1989, p.1). Your free child is your authentic self, which you will need to listen to. This free child will can help you confront you present distorted thoughts and feelings.*

- What if I cannot find the child within me?

*This usually indicates two problems. First, you are not in a safe place in your present life i. e you are indulging, in an abusive relationship, or carry a lot of the old messages of your critic or perpetrators. Secondly, you may have ambivalence about doing this work because of fear. You will first need to face your fear to change your scripts in your life.*

- What if I see the child within me being abused by my old perpetrators?

*As the adult, you can step into the abuse to stop the abuser. You survived the abuse, but your inner child does not know this fact. This will rarely happen if you have done the earlier work.*

*Or you can slow your breathing and move back to the place where you started, intentionally finding out your child's safe place. You had a place that the perpetrator never knew and could not touch you. This is the place you need to meet your inner child. This safe place will be free of your perpetrator.*

You can go to YouTube and search for: Crazy or Not Here I Come, and do the Interactive Mindfulness Exercise by Walter Swinhoe.

## Conclusion.

Here is a poem written a day after my 34-year-old client experienced her 8-year-old inner child. Her 8-year-old self chose to stay behind a rock and write in her journal. My adult client was angry with her inner child due to her inner child's innocence and peace. She wrote this poem the next day:

"I saw her clear as day

She had mousy brown disheveled hair

Her skin was slightly oily, and her legs were hairy

Her nails were dirty

She had no makeup on

Her clothes did not match, and she did not seem to care

She did not know she was a little chunky

She had never contemplated her complexion

And she had never tasted alcohol

Her mother was still alive

And she did not know who she was:

Myself, as a child.

Before I made myself an enemy

I made eye contact with her

I felt a rod go through my mouth and into my heart

It exited down through my stomach

That I loathe in the mirror every day

I stared at her

Jealous and angry

More than anything, protective.

I had to protect her from who I had become

And I was curious

Why she did not hate herself

The way I had hated her?

The way I grew up to hate myself?

Here is my apology to that little girl:

Sweet, kind, sensitive child, I am 34 years old

I am so sorry I treated you so badly.

I am so sorry I showered you with insults and picked and pulled you apart

I am sorry I contemplated everything that made you who you are

As if it were a flaw

And I am sorry I ignored every gift you had

And chose to focus on every imperfection that was not even real

You were so precious!

I would never do what I did to you

to my own child

Why did I do it to you?

Can you forgive me?

Do you understand how beautiful you are?

Can you see your sincerity?

How deeply you feel is a gift, please do not make yourself callous

Please do not take the easy way out.

Please never stop creating stories

Never stop dreaming

Please, I beg you, stay you.

Life will get hard

Kids will be cruel

You will begin to hate your body

You will begin to question yourself

Please, do not lose your sweet, creative, and gentle heart.

I am so sorry at 34 I left you at 8 years old to grow up alone

In the coldness and cruelty of this world

I am sorry I left you to make my own body an enemy

To make my own heart and enemy

To make myself an enemy.

You knew me better than I know myself

You loved me

And I left you.

Sweet child, stay with me forever

Remind me daily of who I am

The gifts that I bear

Remind me that 3 pounds means nothing

And that my weight does not define my soul

Remind me of who I am

And how I started

And why I am

Please

Little girl

Be stronger

Than I am

And come back to me"

I hope you will continue your journey to the Soul as my client did through this poem.

## Remember:

The child within you may have no knowledge of life after the dissociated experience. You are giving information that the child within you needs to create safety, peace, and life.

# CHAPTER TWELVE

## LET US GET OFF THIS MOUNTAIN

"And hope does not put us to shame, because God's love has been poured into our hearts through the Holy Spirit who has been given to us." Romans 5:5, ESV

**KEY POINTS:**

- Self-control is a sovereign gift from God to you.

**Reflections:**

- The goal is to recover the "self" from self-pity, self-loathing and/or self-doubt.

## Welcome.

"Taking an interest in one's own soul requires a certain amount of space for reflection and appreciation. Ordinarily we are so identified with movements of the psyche that we cannot stand back and take a good look at them. A little distance allows us to see the dynamics among the many elements that make up the life of the soul. By becoming interested in these phenomena, we begin to see our own complexity."

(Care of the Soul, Thomas Moore,1992, p.14)

You have been using the art of introspection to understand consciously what has been unconsciously driving your behavior, thoughts and feelings. You are aware of your inner child and the historical reasons for your thoughts, feelings, and behavior. What you are doing with this information will change your life. Most of my clients have a general awareness of their problem and how to fix it after doing inner child work. They are aware of a course of treatment to break free from their internal or external indulging.

Inner child work will trigger external indulgence due to the desire to avoid emotions, medicate the emotions or move towards the habit of indulging. When doing inner child work, one becomes aware of the possibility of becoming happy and whole, yet the internal and external indulgence remains. Your external indulgence will trigger or become the gateway for you to walk right back to your old script or behavioral choices. I would be remiss if I did not give a plan for healing from external indulgences as part of this journey to the soul. Inner child work will create freedom from past slavery while indulgences create the same captivity.

You can free your inner child from his/her past slavery, yet still not move into the promise land of God's rest or freedom. You may have a strong desire to stay free of old dysfunctional, emotional, and behavioral patterns, but find that your external indulgence is still active. Your captivity is like that of the Israelites. The Israelites were in captivity under Pharaoh. The Israelites had exoduses slavery in Egypt to live in the Promise Land, "a land flowing with milk and honey" (Deuteronomy 26:9 NASB) or "God's rest" (Hebrews 3:18 NASB). You may be asking yourself, what is God's rest?

God's rest is a reliance on God and not us. This reliance on God "is not temporary relaxation, but God's own perfect and continuing rest. This is not the cessation from creative activities, but the removal of the anguish which accompanies the labor of a person who has only his own meager resources to draw from" (The Broardman Bible Commentary, Vol,12, Editor Clifton Allen, 1972, p. 35). The Promise Land is a place of rest from your resources and a reliance on God's resources. The Israelites were led by Moses and freed by God. So, what happened? Once freed from slavery, they got stuck on a mountain in the desert for forty years (Deuteronomy 1:2).

"In Deuteronomy 1:2, Moses pointed out to the is Israelites that it was only an eleven-day journey to the border of Canaan (the Promised Land), yet it had taken them forty years to get there" (Battlefield of the Mind, Joyce Meyer, 1995,p.27). Then in Deuteronomy 1:6 it says "The LORD our God spoke to us at Horeb, saying, 'You have stayed long enough at this mountain" (NASB). The Israelites wandered in the wilderness or around this mountain for forty years, yet they could have entered the Promise Land in eleven days. The question is: Have you stayed long enough on your mountain? If your answer is yes, then it is possible to leave it. You can free your inner child from depression, anxiety, or an abusive relationship and still be captive to a host of indulgences.

What kept the Israelites in the wilderness or on a desolate mountain in the desert for forty years? They had a captive mentality based on a blind clarity. They knew the God of their forefathers freed them from slavery but had little faith in Him to sustain them in the desert. Their faith was colored by their learned script of their captivity. They were blinded by their past learning which stopped their progress to be totally free.

Most of my clients thought they would move into the Promise Land once they had freed their inner child and themselves from past emotional and mental slavery. They did not expect to travel through the desert to reach their goals. They, like the Israelites, wanted to not suffer through change. They still got tempted to return to their old behaviors and familiar defense mechanisms. Dealing with authentic emotions is still difficult because "repression appears less painful than discipline" (The Symbolic Quest, Edward, C Whitmont 1978, p.167). Becoming more conscious and not allowing their historic unconscious truths to color the present was one thing but using their conscious knowledge not to continue old habits was another thing altogether.

In the second month of freedom the Israelites wished they could return to slavery and even wish they died in Egypt. (Exodus 16:1-3). They wanted to go back to their learned captivity. Your learned captivity may have been growing up in an alcoholic or abusive household, marrying an abuser or experiencing years of emotional abuse. You may not want to return to your Egypt but are afraid to leave your mountain or external indulgence which continues to hold you captive. Later in this chapter, you will be given the tools to leave your mountain while addressing five mountains that are notorious for keeping people captive in the church and society.

Many of you have recognized the cost of living in captivity to your past script. You have re-written some of your storyline and need to take steps to be authentic. Now, you could make conscious decisions that are less affected by unconscious influences. You can take your heart's desires seriously while giving the child within you what he/she wants and needs to be whole. Becoming authentic does not guarantee you will break through old strongholds, internal, or external indulgences in your life. My clients got off their mountains and broke their indulgences by creating attainable goals and taking intentional steps. Intentional steps toward the promise land stopped their wandering around on their mountain.

## Failure to Plan is Planning to Fail

Most of this book deals with understanding, finding, and reclaiming your inner child. This chapter deals with rational thoughts and how to create a plan of healing to achieve your goals of stopping problematic behaviors in your life. You have identified and spoke with your inner child, yet you may have developed unhealthy behaviors over the years. You will have a chance to identify the problem and develop ways to deal with them. You will learn to create a plan of healing. If you choose not to create and follow a plan for healing, you will likely fail.

Does anyone plan to fail? My client failed because of their failure to plan. Planning is difficult for a problem you do not see. If you have been doing the exercise in the preceding chapters, you are aware of your inner child and have identified problematic thinking and behaviors. Over years of adapting, you may be stuck on a mountain that developed over the years due to poor boundaries, coping skills and avoidance of your authentic emotions. You have been reconceptualizing your early learning which creates healing for internal indulgences, but what about your external ones.

Now it is time to look at your adult's use of external indulgences. These external indulgences may have begun due to genetic predisposition, early learning, or avoidance of your authentic feelings. You can stay problem oriented or become solution focused. You can become solution focused (move towards the promised land) by identifying your problems and creating a plan for healing. A plan is necessary for healing. You can create a plan for healing by writing down what you are struggling with today. You are the one with the problem or mountain in your life and the one with the knowledge to solve it.

## Exercise: What Mountains Are in Your Life?

*This is not a regression exercise. There are no special instructions included. Answer simply and directly in your journal.*

Write them down here.

1)
2)
3)

Then, ask yourself: What would be two or three things I would change daily to deal with this problem or leave this mountain?

1)
2)
3)

These three answers will be referred to as your goals. Once you identify your goals then list two or three ways to accomplish or achieve each of your goals.

Here is an example.

Problems

1) Overweight
2) Negative thoughts
3) Watching so much TV and reading books

Here are three ways to accomplish your goal with the two solutions.

Example:

1) Overeating
    a) Drink an 8-16 oz. of water before I eat a meal

b) Walk at a pace faster than I normally walk for 30 minutes daily

2) Stop saying negative things about or to myself
   a) I will say "Stop" each time I say or think a negative thought about myself
   b) I will call a friend at the end of the day and tell them the words I said about myself
3) Stop sitting in front of the TV or reading my books
   a) Not more than 2 hours of TV or reading daily
   b) To journal 30 minutes a day

List two solutions to each of your problems.

Problem 1

List two solutions.

a)

b)

Problem 2

a)

b)

Problem 3

a)

b)

Now you have a plan with goals and solutions.

This treatment plan will use seven virtues taken from Erik Erickson's eight stages of psychological development. You will use the virtues of the second through eight stage of development: will, purpose, competence, fidelity, love, care, and wisdom. These seven virtues will lead to or create an installation of hope which is the first virtue of Erikson's eight stages of psychosocial development.

With a plan, you can enact your "Will." "Will has more to do with personal intention and how we decide to use our energies" (Gerald G. May, M.D, Will & Spirit, 1982, p. 3). You will need to be intentional and use your energies to follow your plan. Your will, intentions, and energies can help with the next virtue of Purpose. If you create purpose, no matter what the purpose is, you will have a greater chance to have mastery, success, and empowerment. You can look at purpose as meaning making.

Usually if you Will yourself to move toward or with your purpose it will lead to competence. Competence, mastery and success, will come as you take steps towards your Goal. In Philippians 4:13 it states, "I can do all things through Him who strengthens me" (Philippians 4:13 NASB). This Competence through Christ's strength only comes with practice and failure, failure and practice, then practice and success, which leads to competence.

In Matthew 7:7 it speaks of seeking with earnestness, diligence, and perseverance when it says, "Ask, and it will be given to you; seek, and you will find; knock, and it will be opened to you" (Matthew 7:7 NASB). This is a process which builds competence. Competence will build fidelity as fidelity builds competence.

Fidelity or faithfulness is usually linked with the sexual arena. Fidelity to your plan and goals will lead you to success. The number one reason that my clients failed to achieve their goal was because they quit and were not faithful to themselves or goals. Fidelity is like creating a budget and then allowing the budget to have control over your spending and savings. That is one way to look at faithfulness. This faithfulness stems from the next virtue of love.

Love is such a dynamic virtue. You may believe these virtues are not to be spent on simple things like losing weight or overcoming other external indulgences. That belief is a distortion and part of another type of deception. God loves all the small things about you. God would say your "small things" matter if He knows the "very hairs of your head are all numbered" (Matthew 10:30 NASB)

The next characteristic of having a healthy self is Care. Care is a form of love that is kind, tender and soft. Imagine if you had a friend with the same struggles as you and was working to achieve these goals. Would you give kind and supportive words, call to walk with him or her, let him or her know you are praying for him or her or bring him or her something health to eat? These are all kind things that you need to do for yourself. In the use of these characteristics of health development, you will attain your goals. You will also gain wisdom.

Wisdom comes from tribulations, crisis, and acquired knowledge of living life. You can use your wisdom gained after each of your attained goals or unsuccessful attempts. Wisdom will help you assess your next step forward. Wisdom comes from learning from your successes and failures. If you are not able to do your daily goals, then you will need to move closer to your target. If you do not move closer to your target to meet your goals, then you will stop pursuing them. Being wise is knowing how to change your steps or behavior to meet your overall goals.

A good example of wisdom combined with God's rest is the Serenity Prayer.

## The Serenity Prayer

God grant me the serenity to accept the things I cannot change; Courage to change the things I can; And the wisdom to know the difference. Living one day at a time; Enjoying one moment at a time; Accepting hardship as the pathway to peace; Taking, as He did, this sinful world As it is, not as I would have it; Trusting that He will make all things right If I surrender to His Will; That I may be reasonably happy in this life And supremely happy with Him Forever in the next. Amen. Reinhold Niebuhr

Many of my clients struggled with the "courage to change the things they can," due to the belief that they could not change. The belief that you cannot change is a core belief when you are in captivity of an indulgence and is a distortion that is not true. To confront this distortion, you will need to follow a plan for change or healing. Your plan for healing needs to have the strength, healing, or comfort of the Spirit of God (refer to "Soul Food" if needed).

When you bring God into your healing process you will be able to use your faith to confront the core beliefs that keep you stuck in your indulgence. An example of using your faith might be having a belief based on this scripture, "I can do all things through Him who strengthens me" (Philippians 4:13 NASB) and your "God will supply all your needs according to His riches in glory in Christ Jesus" (Philippians 4:19 NASB). Your faith in God ensures you will never be alone, and you will have the great comforter. In 2 Corinthians 1: 3, 4 it states that, "Blessed be the God and Father of our Lord Jesus Christ, the Father of mercies and God of all comfort, who comforts us in all our affliction so that we will be able to comfort those who are in any affliction with the comfort with which we ourselves are comforted by God"

(2 Corinthians 1:3, 4 NASB).

Back to one of my premises: you cannot give God or others what you do not have yourself. If you comfort yourself in your afflictions, then you can comfort others. God says he will comfort you so you can comfort others. You are helping others by helping yourself through your afflictions. Now you might ask, "What are afflictions?"

Afflictions in Greek can be translated as tribulation, oppression, or distress. The literal meaning of the Greek word for afflictions is *thlipsis. "Thlispsis"* is from thlibo, to press together" (Word Pictures in the New Testament, Archibald Robertson, 1931, p.209). The pain, hurt or anxiety is "pressed" into you. It is not a part of you and can be separated. The reason you might think you cannot change your beliefs are because you believe you are the problem rather than you have a problem. Your plan for healing will address the problem by being solution focused. You will find out you are okay. The Serenity Prayer will help you to have "the wisdom to know the difference."

This affliction was pressed into your life mentally, emotionally, physically, and spiritually. It is not a part of your being or soul. The reason indulgence was used instead of "addiction" was because our society relates addiction with permanence. Addictions cannot be separated from you. Our society is aware that an "Indulgence" is self-gratification with a lack of moderation. Indulgence is an action not a state of being. Addictions are said to be a state of being that are permanent. Both are associated with excess, lack of restraint, or being a habit. The state of being "dependent" is only associated with addiction which decays empowerment, freewill and independent choice.

Your affliction, tribulation, oppression, or distress may range from external causes like trauma, abuse, and broken relationships, to death of a loved one. Your internal indulgences may be from affliction or your historic learning. Yes, both are covered by defense mechanisms and will rob your soul of joy. God made you with the ability to make conscious choices: choices based on your will. Your will is the prime mover of your rational mind and gives you the ability or potential to transform. Transformation is a free choice that is not determined by "dependency," how you grew up or your status in life. You will have the ability to use your plan for healing to protect your authentic self, but it will take an act of your Will.

Before you go back to your plan, remember that God's "comfort" comes to you. This comfort can separate between your mind and body, bone and marrow and spirit or soul. This comfort fills your mind, body, and Soul. This comfort extends to life and death. The Apostle Paul was speaking about all God's mercy and comfort that transcends the natural and brings in the supernatural. This comfort will extend to you while moving toward your goals on this journey to the Soul.

Going back to your plan, remember to assess it monthly. Once you accomplish a goal for 2 weeks then increase your goal to get your desired outcome. You may achieve your goal for two weeks and be afraid of raising the bar. This fear is usually fear of failure. It is okay to fail if you learn from it and use your virtue of fidelity or faithfulness to stick with your plan. There is a Japanese proverb that says, "Fall down seven times get up eight." Getting up and continuing towards your goal will lead to success.

If you set a goal and are not able to attain it after a week of following your plan, then lower your goal. Do not allow your esteem or plan to be conditional on your success, especially during the first month. Remember, you are turning away from the old and putting on the new. You need to give yourself grace to keep from critiquing yourself. You can hold yourself accountable without being critical. Grace, God's favor, will be an important part of healing or your time to get off this mountain.

Healing is solution focused and not problem oriented. The focus of any healing is not how you got the wound but on the care of it. Your wound can have several names; the names are only important if they can inform the treatment of the wound. There will be five mountains or external indulgences addressed in this chapter. These five mountains are a problem in our churches and society today. Many of my clients spent years on these mountains. These five indulgences have kept many out of the "promise land" of being emotionally, relationally, and spiritually healthy.

# Gluttony

Gluttony can be the over-indulgences in anything. Gluttony can be the over-consumption of food, alcohol, wealth, sexuality, or pain. Most people in our society, associate gluttony with food. Each of the struggles will address the issues of over-indulgence. We will first deal with the gluttony of food, or its byproduct which is obesity.

Obesity is a severe problem in the United States. The last time I looked at the statistics concerning adult obesity, they were sobering. The latest statistics on adult obesity from the center of Disease and Control (CDC) are "More than one-third (34.9% or 78.6 million) of U.S. adults are obese."

Obesity affects some groups more than others:

- Non-Hispanic blacks have the highest age-adjusted rates of obesity (47.8%) followed by Hispanics (42.5%), non-Hispanic whites (32.6%), and non-Hispanic Asians (10.8%)
- Obesity is higher among middle age adults, 40-59 years old (39.5%) than among younger adults, age 20-39 (30.3%) or adults over 60 or above (35.4%)" (http://www.cdc.gov/obesity/data/adult.html) While "Childhood obesity in 2011& 12 was "approximately 17% (or 12.7 million) of children and adolescents aged 2—19 years are obese" (.http://www.cdc.gov/obesity/data/childhood.html).

You are considered obese if your body mass index (BMI) is over 30 and overweight if your BMI is between 25-29.9. These numbers are sobering, yet the sad thing is that adult obesity will increase the risk for childhood obesity in the United States. Currently, there are 25 million obese children. The causes of obesity, for many of the readers, are overeating and not having enough exercise.

It is crazy how our culture has accepted obesity. Obesity is a major health risk and takes away joy, esteem, and self-worth. Obesity is a difficult "addiction," "struggle," "sin," or mountain" to leave. It is difficult to get free from obesity since you must eat to live. It is important for over-eaters to know they can have "sobriety." In 12 step group sobrieties is associated with abstinence. Sobriety, the quality, or state of being sober, does not mean abstinence; it is a form of moderation that shows one not to be intoxicated. Sobriety is not over-indulging. I do believe a true alcoholic or drug "addict" could never be "clean and sober" if he or she needed to use 3 times a day like an overeater needs too.

You will need to know that I struggled with this beast for years and still flee the temptation to overeat. I know how difficult it is to eat small portions, to exercise, to struggle with getting clothes on, to be embarrassed when putting on a swimming suit or go to a formal function that makes it difficult to hide my weight. My heart goes out to anyone that has their soul imprisoned by food.

Being overweight is difficult due to self-criticism and the belief that other people are "laughing" and "judging" you. You know the experience of not being able to join into activities that require physical activity. You know how it feels to look in the mirror and hate the image that is looking back at you. Self-loathing or shame are mental and emotional bars that imprison your soul. Self-loathing will stop your success and your relationship with yourself, others, and God. Remember self-loathing is an internal indulgence that feeds your external indulgence. As your external indulgences increase your internal indulgence will also increase. This self-perpetuating cycle is not of God but of the flesh.

To free yourself from this prison is difficult and you may believe it to be impossible. The first step is admitting that you have a problem. This step, like many other "addictions," is the most important. The First Step is acknowledging your powerlessness when it comes to food. In Overeaters Anonymous, OA, they call this the "First Step" in recovery.

The First Step is admitting you are powerless over food and that your life is unmanageable. Acknowledging your life is "unmanageable" sounds easy but your defense mechanisms are strong. You can easily deny, rationalize, or minimize that you are overweight. The use of defense mechanisms keeps you in this indulgence, yet dealing with the emotions of hurt, shame or fear of being overweight is toxic to your soul. If you suppress or push down these emotions, then you will eat more to fill this void. It is a self-perpetuating cycle.

To break the cycle of gluttony, you will need to acknowledge that you are powerless and accept that your life is unmanageable concerning food. You are powerless now due to your present thoughts, feelings and behaviors concerning food. Empowerment comes by creating a plan of recovery and using these virtues or characteristics of healthy development. Hope is an intrinsic part of any plan. The plan for weight loss is "easy" due to all the literature on this topic. You can go to the internet and find diets and exercise plans in minutes. I hope that you will create a plan that considers your calorie intake and food choices without getting on a "diet."

Your "diet" is your natural food intake and the amount that you eat. Your diet which is creating weight gain is not working – it is unmanageable, currently. Do not get on a fad diet. You are not able to sustain a fad diet for life. You will lose your weight if your daily calorie intake is fewer than the calories that you burn daily. That is simple. The hard thing is to go by the plan daily. You will need to create the plan then gather your support system. You will need their accountability, support, and love on this journey.

I have seen hundreds of my clients go on "diets" and have a rebound effect once they stopped their diet. They did not maintain their "diet" due to not having a lifestyle diet that fits them. They went on a diet and lost 10 to 15 pounds then stop the fad diet. Once they stopped the diet, they gained back the 15 pounds and added another 10 to 15 pounds. This decreased their hopes and increased their guilt and shame. They were looking for a quick fix while not dealing with their emotions or their wounds that moved them to medicate with food in the first place.

For several years I did Bariatric assessments for clients that wanted Bariatric Surgery. Bariatric surgery removed part of their stomach and small intestines. It is an extreme way to lose weight. My clients saw Bariatric Surgery as a "silver bullet." The "silver bullet" did not work because they continued to eat to fill their emotional void or medicate their wounds. They were encouraged to get a support system and create a plan that included exercise and journaling. Rarely did they do so and many of them gained back their weight after losing over a hundred pounds. Many of the ones that stayed on their treatment plan lost the weight and kept the weight off.

The real issue was not their weight but their suppression of their emotions and going by scripted beliefs from childhood. The sad thing was that many of the bariatric clients had been sexually abused in childhood or suffered from severe emotional abuse, yet they kept being strong, not paying attention to their wound. Remember, a wound heals from the inside out.

I was stung by a black scorpion when I was 16 years old. I got extremely sick. My right arm was swollen, and my fever was 104 degrees. I went to a German doctor in town that everyone referred to as the "quack." He had broken English and usually odd treatment techniques.

I walked into his office and physically felt like I was going to die. He called me back to his examining room and asked me what happened, while he was pressing and squeezing my arm. The pain was extraordinary. The doctor turned and spoke German under his breath. He began to shake his head as to say no. He grabbed a clear glass quart jar and a knife. The knife had a one-inch curved blade.

The doctor walked over and grabbed my arm and stuck the knife in my arm. He got a Mason jar and put it under the knife. Once he pulled the knife out of my arm, he was able to fill the quart jar three quarters full of pus. Without a word, he took off his left glove and cut the tip of the gloves fingers so that he could close using the palm of the glove. Once he cut the finger, he rubbed the glove in a circle motion in his hands then pushed and tucked the glove into the cut in my arm. Once the glove was totally absorbed in my arm and out of sight, the doctor put a bandage on the incision.

I was in shock as I sat there on the table. The doctor asked me to come back the next morning and left the room. I was still feeling dizzy and lightheaded as I got up to leave his office. I got home and went directly to the couch where I fell asleep. The next morning, I was awake in time to go to my doctor's appointment. Once I got to the doctor's office, I was physically sick and extremely weak.

The doctor asked me to come back to the examining room and said "I don't think you be here today. I thought you might die." He said this with a straight face. I quickly responded, "Why?" He replied, "You had a red line from your arm over your shoulder going to your heart... Likely die." I ask him "Why didn't you tell me I was so sick." He replied, "If I told you. You would have run round and want to live and push the line to heart. You die." He went on to say, "You probably went home and sleep in bed because of poison in the system."

As I sat on a cold iron table, I noticed the doctor getting long tongs. He took the bandage off my arm. Then he opened the wound with his left hand and reached in the opening of the cut with the tongs. He pulled out, with force, the cut-up glove. The glove was a mass of clotted red and black blood clots with yellow or lite green lines running over it. It was three times bigger than the original glove that was placed in my arm. It looked like a placenta that comes from afterbirth. He threw it into a bucket on the floor which made a loud noise. I could not believe that he did not give me pain pills or a shot for pain. He grasped my arm with both hands then squeezed out the rest of the blood and other liquid. He asked me to "open wound every day."

I went home and after a couple of days and felt better. The wound closed and I felt little pain. I began doing normal things and felt great. About two weeks later, my arm began to swell, and my fever began to rise. The pain was back in my arm and I was sweating throughout the day. I called the doctor and got an appointment the next day. My arm was swelling and getting hotter with each hour that passed.

By the time I got to the doctor my arm was swollen, red with fever. I had a fever and was nauseous. Once I got back to the exam room the doctor looked at the wound, which had completely healed. The doctor reached over and got the curved knife, I became sick at my stomach. He shook his head and said, " You didn't open wound every day." Then he proceeded to open the wound with the knife. This time there was a lot less staph in the wound. He poured some medication which looked like methylate on and in the wound.

When I was leaving, he said "Open that wound every day. A WOUND ONLY HEALS FROM THE INSIDE OUT." You can be sure that I opened the wound every day and got any staph out of the wound. I was healed in a couple weeks. This is the same technique that you will need to do with any emotional wound. This would be one of the "silver bullets" that will help heal your past emotional or mental wounds.

The Seven Deadly Sins, mental illness, or automatic negative thoughts are the best way to open your wound, in addition to journaling. Make sure to include journaling as a part of your plan for healing. Journaling is the way to open your emotional wounds while dealing with the "staph" that poisons the soul.

Journaling takes work. The more time you take to write your thoughts and feelings, the more you will hear yourself. If you cannot hear yourself, how can you hear God? Journaling is a physical way to get the emotional toxins out of your body. You will be releasing the physical experience of your abuse as you are journaling. As you write down your words on paper or type them on the computer you are figuratively extracting the poison from your body. Then you will be able to lay this yoke of slavery down while God sustains you (Psalms 55;22). This book will be a primer for you to know what to extract and will lead you to a transparent guide, the Holy Spirit, which will give you peace, comfort and understanding.

There have been thousands of books to deal with weight loss and the underlying problems that fuel weight gain. Marianne Williamson in *A Course in Weight Loss* states, "Fat is not just inert cellular tissue. It is a repository of twisted, distorted thoughts and feelings that did not have anywhere else to go. If you remove the fat tissue but do not remove its psychic cause, then the fat might go but the causal imprint remains. And the imprint, in time will attract more substance with which to materially express itself" (2012, p.171). This is the reason you need to clean your wound by journaling and enlist support because the "imprint" will attract other indulgences.

If you struggle with gluttony, then create a plan (use the one mentioned earlier as a guide). Make sure you call your support system and get a journal. Stop spending money on magazines, fad diets and weight loss supplements until you do the work. Anything worth having is worth working for. You are your greatest asset. If you need assistance, get a counselor to work through your abuse issues, clean your emotional lens or change your script. Bring your Heavenly Father into the struggle to comfort, empower and guide you through this difficult time.

Here are some helpful hints to help you with your weight loss goals. Drink water, half of your body weight in ounces, every day. Write down your caloric intake every day to not exceed the recommended 2000 calories a day. Journal any negative thought or emotion every day. Lastly, you may want to shock your system by beginning your weight loss plan with a three day fast.

A fast can be with anything, but in this case, I am speaking of food. This means you will need to not eat any food for three days and drink your water. The first day you will crave food because you are breaking a physical and emotional cycle. The second day you will feel a little lethargic due to your body eating away at the plaque in your intestines and organs. Your body is cleansing itself. The third day you will be more aware of your thoughts and feelings. This brief fast will clean your body while breaking the habit.

This time of fasting is safe unless your health is poor, or you are on several medications. Check with your doctor before you take these steps. I have had hundreds of clients in poor health, overweight to obese that did great while fasting. Fasting is a good first step to stop gluttony.

## Compulsive sexual behavior

Compulsive sexual behavior is a prevalent problem in and out of the church. Martin Saunders is Deputy CEO of Youthscape and Contributing Editor for Christian Today writes that" Over 41% of men in church are addicted to porn. A new survey conducted by writer Marin Saunders reveals that a shocking 41 % of men in church are addicted to pornography. His survey uncovered that 30% of church leaders access porn on the internet regularly. He added that 75% of Christian men view pornography on a monthly or less regular basis and 10% of Christian men said that they have paid for sex. (http://www.theway.co.uk/news-9821-over-41-of-men-in-church-are-addicted-to-porn) The use of pornography is a silent cancer which keeps men and woman in captivity. Compulsive sexual behavior usually begins with Pornography or porn for short. Pornography is another distraction that will keep you from listening to your authentic emotions.

Patrick Carnes, one of the foremost experts of sexual addiction, has "a four-step self-perpetuated cycle that intensifies with each repetition:

1. Preoccupation – the trance or mood where in the addicts' minds are completely engrossed with thoughts of sex. This mental state creates

an obsessive search for sexual stimulation.

2. Ritualization – the addicts' own special routines that lead up to the sexual behavior. The ritual intensifies the preoccupation, adding arousal and excitement.
3. Compulsive sexual behavior – the actual sexual act, which is the end goal of the preoccupation and ritualization. Sexual addicts are unable to control or stop this behavior
4. Despair - the feeling of utter hopelessness addicts have about their behavior and their powerlessness" (Patrick Carnes, PH. D, Out of The shadows, 3rd Ed, 2001, pp.19 and 20).

Pornography is the gateway behavior to sexual indulgences that pervert the soul. It is like cannabis, marijuana or pot is the gateway for use of cocaine and methamphetamine. This cycle of indulgence begins with avoidance of your authentic emotions. This avoidance is medicated by conscious internal stimulation that can be called obsessing. This mental stimulation concerning sexual behavior moves to the ritual phase. This preoccupation and the behavior steps to enact the fantasy becomes the sexual act which I refer to as "acting out." Once you "act out" with a compulsive sexual action you will have increased unwanted emotions which perpetuates the cycle.

This self-perpetuated cycle gets intense due to two opposing reasons. First, you avoid your emotions and begin the cycle. Second, you are increasing more unwanted feelings due to the "acting out." This is not considering chemical stimulation in your brain. The "acting out" is a pleasurable activity which increases a neurotransmitter called dopamine.

"When you anticipate an experience that is pleasurable, the brain immediately makes a chemical neurotransmitter called dopamine, which turns the brain and body on in anticipation of that experience and causes you to begin to feel excited"(Joe Dispenza, D.C.,Evolve your Brain,2007, p.43). Dopamine creates a "good" feeling which creates an indulgent response. The desire to feel "good" by increasing the production of dopamine using Pornography or compulsive sexual behavior intensifies your desire to indulge. The self-perpetuating cycle becomes repetitive due to the emotional and physical stimulation of dopamine.

This indulgence cycle begins with the avoidance of images of historic abuse or past emotional trauma. The avoidance of emotions was done by obsessing over something other than your historic or present emotions. Obsessing will move you to mentally pleasurable thoughts or physical activities which moves you into a ritual phase. The ritual phase will have increase behavioral steps to get closer to the pleasurable thoughts or activity. When you are in the ritual phase, you are totally unaware of your past abuse, disassociated experience, or past emotional state that you are "escaping." This leads directly to Acting Out.

The acting out phase is where you are looking at pornography, finding a prostitute or acting out more deviant sexual acts. Acting out sexually or with any indulgence increases the neurotransmitter called dopamine in your brain. Once the pleasurable activity is over, your dopamine levels decrease, leaving you with your unwanted emotions and present experience of reality. Yet, "the pain the addicts feel at the end of the cycle can be numbed or obscured by sexual preoccupation that reengages the addiction cycle" (Patrick Carnes, PH. D, Out of The shadows, 3rd Ed, 2001, p.20).

Once the neurotransmitter dopamine is gone, then physiologically your neurotransmitters return "to normal" leaving your brain craving dopamine, and your emotional turmoil returns. The emotions that follow acting out are usually guilt and shame. Patrick Carnes now uses the word "despair" for this final stage of the cycle. I believe "unwanted emotions" might be a better description of the phase. Then the cycle will move back to obsessing to increase dopamine and away from your unwanted emotions. You will want to increase the "high" by acting out. This is called a self-perpetuating cycle.

This repetitive cycle will become more pathological and stimulus seeking, while the "acting out" will become more severe in form or function. Compulsive sexual behavior can begin with soft porn (magazines of nudity) - to hard porn (raw sexual or erotic acts) to lewd acts (voyeurism, exhibitionism, or rape). Sexual indulgence will become more intense each time you use it, just like any other indulgence.

The sad thing is that sexually explicit material can be found on the computer, smart phone, and TV now. Pornography can be seen at work, home, or church. It is at the tip of your finger all the time. Many will say "everyone does it" "I'm not hurting anyone," or "I'm just bored." This rationalizing, minimizing or denial of the problem or cost will keep you stuck in your indulgence or sin.

The greatest cost of compulsive sexual behavior is that it separates you from God. You will become a slave to it. In the book of John "Jesus answered them, "Truly, truly, I say to you, everyone who commits sin is the slave of sin" (John 8:34 NASB). Being a slave could look like dependency. Remember, your behavior separates you from God, but God is never separated from you because of your behavior or sin. The compulsive sexual behavior will have control like any other sin. You will be in idolatry with immorality and impurity as your idols. This influences your Soul.

I have seen my clients' progression from using pornography in magazines to voyeurism. Voyeurism is the watching of others to seek sexual arousal. This behavior can lead to rape and incarceration. I have had Christian men and women find stimulation with nudity on the internet. Their sexual indulgences progressed to infidelity or lewd sexual acts. Many have said to me "I don't know how this happened." They were unaware of their gradual loss of their moral or ethical standard. Their minds became perverted without them knowing.

In our culture this perversion of what is natural is attributed mostly to males. A 2015 study shows "a growing number of women are engaging in the use of pornography.

- 13% of women admit to accessing porn at work
- 70% of women keep their cyber activities secret
- 17% of all women struggle with porn addiction" http://www.sagu.edu/thoughthub/pornography-statistics-who-uses-pornography) About a third of my clients that struggled with sexual indulgences were women. Yes, females struggle with pornography or sexual indulgence too. Their sexual appetite increases for the forbidden and becomes more perverted with time. They followed Patrick Carnes addiction cycle like their male counterparts.

This indulgence creates relational issues. The primary issue for those active in the addictive cycle is less stimulation by their partners while craving the high of the forbidden use of pornography or illicit relationships. Though in my clinical experience, women were more aware of the problem of their "addiction" than my male clients. Women were less likely to deny or minimize their behavior. Yet the sad thing was women, like men, got pulled away from intimacy with their spouse and got caught in this indulgent cycle. I had a female client that was caught in this web of lust.

## My Story: Sandra

Sandra was 49-year-old white female with three kids. Sandra had been married for 11 years to her second husband. Sandra began "looking at porn 3 years ago" because "I was home, and all my kids are gone. I had too much time on my hands." Sandra found porn on the "Internet." Sandra moved from pornographic pictures and videos to interactive pornography. Interactive pornography was where Sandra would talk to a male while they would undress and acted out being sexual with her. "I love him talking to me and wanting to be with me." Interactive Pornography was expensive. It costs more than pornographic pictures or video due to the per minute price. It is like a 1-800 call that can last from 20 minutes to an hour. Sandra, via her webcam, did it when "no one was home."

Sandra got caught by her husband because she had "23,800 dollars on my credit card." Sandra's husband took the credit cards and paid the bills to protect his wife. Sandra followed the new norm of finding men to have sex within a moment's notice via the Internet. Sandra was on four social media sites where she could instantly "hook up with someone." She "loved the passion when I wanted it." Sandra's relationship deteriorated with her husband and ended in a divorce. When she left therapy, she was with a man that she was having an affair with when she got divorced.

Sandra never admitted to having a problem with pornography. She began with soft porn and advanced to having sexual experiences with both males and females. She had no knowledge of who the men were personally. She only had pictures of what they look like and a brief description of what they wanted sexually from a web site. Sandra was driven by lust and greed; she had little remorse. Sandra left therapy because she neither hit bottom nor did she want to change. A bottom is where the addict admits to themself that their life is unmanageable, and they admit they are powerless at that moment over their indulgence.

I have seen many women, like Sandra, that were caught up in over-indulging sexually. My clients that acknowledge their problems, had a support system, and followed their treatment plan had better prognoses. Most of my clients had hit a bottom with their sexual compulsive behavior before recovering from this indulgence. They wanted to stop their sexual indulgence due to increased "shame" and "guilt." Their bottoms ranged from broken marriage and sexually transmitted diseases (STD's), to being incarcerated for lewd acts. They became aware of their avoidance of past traumas or sexual abuse issues. Many reclaimed their inner child and found their authentic self.

Breaking indulgences of a sexual nature is difficult like any other indulgence. The clients that successfully broke the cycle of sexual "addiction" did work to stop it. They struggled with creating a treatment plan and following it. They had increased isolation and decreased support due to their fear of judgment or rejection by others. My clients with a good support system had better prognoses. My clients that had faith in God usually had increased shame at the beginning and increased forgiveness and hope at the "end" of recovery. Recovery is a constant battle with any indulgence, due to the craving for the stimulation and wanting to escape from reality. My clients that broke the cycle had increased life without pursuing their sexual craving. They were aware of their "powerlessness" over their sexual indulgence and planned accordingly to be empowered. They used their self-awareness to FACE God and flee temptation. They grew emotionally and spiritually while finding their authentic selves. They began living free of their indulgence and created dopamine through doing meaningful things in their lives. They dealt with their unwanted emotions and historic memories. Recovery began with acceptance of their problem.

If you are struggling with lust, you will need to take the First Step of recovery. The First step is "admitting your powerlessness" over the activity or substance and that your life is "unmanageable." This will help you flee the temptation to use. You could make a good argument that God knew you were "powerless" over temptations and indulgences.

It is crazy, as a Christian, that you can "rebuke Satan" (Jude 1;9) but not temptation. You are to flee temptation (2 Timothy 2:22-24). A good example of fleeing temptation was Joseph (Genesis 39; ff). Joseph was a servant in Potiphar's house. Joseph was "handsome in form and appearance" which Potiphar's wife wanted to "lie with" him. "Now it happened one day that he went into the house to do his work, and none of the men of the household was there inside" (Genesis 39:11 NASB). Joseph declined her verbal seduction and stood up for his God and Potiphar (vs 9). Once Potiphar's wife was alone in the house with Joseph, she increased her seduction.

In Genesis 29: 12-13 Joseph had great temptation by Potiphar's wife: "She caught him by his garment, saying, 'Lie with me!' And he left his garment in her hand and fled and went outside. When she saw that he had left his garment in her hand and had fled outside" (Genesis 39:12, 13 NASB). Joseph fled, he didn't rebuke her or speak of his belief in God due to the power of temptation. He fled. When you are tempted with seduction you need to flee.

Now fleeing temptation with a history of sexual indulgences is difficult. It is difficult because your brain carries the images or fantasies in your mind. Many overeaters will argue that they cannot have sobriety from food due to the need to feed their bodies to live. Not being able to abstain from food makes breaking that indulgence difficult. Now just think: with sexual compulsivity you can abstain and still have the images playing in your mind. What is worse is that you have a "response set" that goes with the mental images. The response that is "triggered" from your mental image is called a response set. It is a set of responses that follow an action or response.

The response set (mental images or memories) or trigger will stimulate your amygdala or feeling center. This stimulation will create increased molecules of emotion (MOEs) in the form of peptides, along with a present desired response or emotions. This response set is difficult to break because it recreates old "good" feelings." For example, when you have a sexual fantasy, your brain immediately releases peptides that turn on hormones/ secretions that make you ready for intercourse. Hormones also act as ligands to bind to other tissues to further stimulate systemic activity "(Evolve Your Brain, Joe Dispenza, 2007, p. 289). This physiological process ties the mind and body together. You have triggers of old experiences, increased stimulation of the amygdala (intense feelings), with increased peptides that stimulate hormones and secretion in the body. This process takes less than two seconds. This makes it hard for you to be rational.

When you want to be "strong" by not fleeing the temptation, your mind and body are already responding to the past action and priming itself for the next response. What makes a response set or mental relapse more difficult is that this chemical and physiological response will continue after the initial trigger for approximately 30 minutes and longer. If you are actively sexualizing your mental images or pictures, then you are having a mental relapse, and this will increase the use of your sexual indulgence.

You will need to flee all temptation and clean your mind at the same time. The cleaning of your mind is an active process which moves you away from your mountain. The cleaning is a process that begins with acknowledging you are "powerless" and that your inappropriate sexual behavior is unmanageable. In AA they say, "one drink is too many and 50 is not enough." Once you acknowledge you are out of control then you will need to create a treatment plan. It is hard to ask others for support due to the fear of judgment and rejection. I hope you will face these fears and build a support system. Patrick Carnes says "All forms of addictions or conscious because they further the inability to trust others. Yet without help from others, the addict cannot regain control because the addiction feeds itself "(Out of the Shadows p. 31).

Getting a support system is difficult due to your shame, guilt, and fear. You may not know how powerful the fear of others' judgment or rejection can be. Many of my clients will not get a healthy support system due to these fears. Support for sexual indulgence is necessary from a recovery and spiritual perspective. The support and accountability are so important with this indulgence. You will need accountability in different ways while dealing with this deadly sin of lust.

You will need accountability in the form of having an Internet nanny. You can get good computer programs to monitor your computer use. This computer "nanny" will send your accountability partner a notification when you view any website with elicit material. This accountability allows you to process your struggle or reasons for your relapse with your support system. “Net Nanny” is a good program to monitor your use of the computer or phone. Your support system will be able to confront your defense mechanism when you get triggered and help you process new choices.

Remember, your brain has created neural pathways with millions of neurons to create a neuron network that "craves" the stimulation from sexually explicit material or activities. Your brain has created a physiological response to your behavior which brings a "high." This mind-altering experience is the reason that many professionals call indulgences addictions, though they do not mention that neuron cells that do not fire together do not stay together. You are changing your brain by changing your behavior.

## Exercise: Sexual Indulgences

*This is not a regression exercise. There are no special instructions included. Answer simply and directly in your journal.*

Once you have acknowledged that you have a problem with compulsive sexual behavior then you are ready to create a plan of recovery. Write down three problems that stem from your sexual indulgences:

Write down three goals:

-
-
-

This is an Example of a plan that deals with problems.

Example:

Plan

1) To stop looking at Pornography
   a) To get Internet nanny like triple X or Covenant Eyes
   b) To stop mental relapses by calling your support system when it happens
   c) Monitor TV shows by pre- taping with DVR
2) To do the 12 steps of recovery
   a) Go to 12 step group bi-weekly
   B) To get a sponsor
   c) Work on 12 step material or the steps daily
3) To stop daily thoughts or mental images of lusting
   a) To read Sex, Man and God or Everyman's Battle
   b) To pray for the person you are lusting or objectifying

c) To journal about emotions when you are triggered to lust
d) To read scripture on God's promises and on lust

Your goals can be:

- to increase time with my spouse
- to have daily quiet times
- to eat and watch tv together
- to go on a date once a week
- to start doing my old hobbies

My clients that followed their plan had success. They had mental and physical relapses along the road to recovery. Their success came by getting back on their plan immediately. The cycle ends and begins with emotion. Unwanted emotions are avoided at the beginning of the cycle and returned after the acting out. The key to recovery is dealing with your unwanted emotions and not moving into the obsessing or preoccupation stage with your thoughts of sexually indulging. Once you begin to think or obsess about looking at porn, calling a prostitute, or lewd sexual acts, you are having a mental relapse. Immediately call your support system, attend a meeting, or follow the acronym F.A.C.E.

***FACE stands for:***

F - Fleeing temptation
A - acknowledging God
C - confessing if you indulged or taking captive the thoughts to indulge with truth or your knowledge of God
E - enlisting the Holy Spirit

As you FACE away from your indulgence you are breaking Carne's cycle of addiction and freeing yourself from an old response set while building another one. It is important to know that breaking any habit will slingshot you back to racket feelings or authentic ones that were avoided. By dealing with your authentic emotions, you will break your captivity and truly be able to rest in God.

The goal is stopping the "addictive" cycle and then living life being "sober." Sobriety, according to the 12-step model, is time without using or abstinence from consumption of any mood-altering thought or activity. It is difficult to be "sober" when you can consume, use, or act out your compulsive sexual behavior in the privacy of your mind. You will weaken the bars of your bondage of lust each time you abstain from acting out on lust. The greater your sobriety the more you can "become clean" by dealing with your historic thoughts, emotions, or dissociative trauma. You will decrease your shame and guilt in sobriety which were triggers. When you stop your avoidant behavior and attend to your inner child, the desire to act out on lust will greatly decrease. This temptation of lust is normal. Your sobriety will help you deal with reality; being clean will lead you to your authentic self and the ability to rest in God.

## Adultery

The next struggle of the church comes from three of the Seven Deadly Sins. These three are of envy, greed, and lust. This sin is pursued, found on accident, or comes by a desire to be loved. It wipes away the virtue of fidelity. Faithfulness is shattered by the lust of the heart. The lust of the heart begins by desiring the "good" in another person which is usually lacking in your relationship and the desire to have more "love" than you already have in your relationship. Envy, greed, and lust feed your flesh to avoid the true image of the soul.

Adultery is a sin of great consequence – emotional, relational, and spiritual. It was taken so seriously in the Old Testament that it was called for death. "If there is a man who commits adultery with another man's wife, one who commits adultery with his friend's wife, the adulterer and the adulteress shall surely be put to death" (Leviticus 20:10 NASB). Today, you would be safe saying that 50 % to 60 % of married men and women will be unfaithful to their spouses before they die. In Proverbs, adultery was tied to destruction of oneself, stating, "But whoever commits adultery with a woman lacks heart and understanding (moral principle and prudence); he who does it is destroying his own life" (Proverbs 6:32 AMP). Your life is affected due to your "unstable" soul." Peter 2:14 speaks of this unstable soul that is full of greed by saying, "having eyes full of adultery that never cease from sin, enticing unstable souls, having a heart trained in greed, accursed children" (2 Peter 2:14 NASB). Adultery is the seventh of The Ten Commandments. Deuteronomy 5:18 says "You shall not commit Adultery." Adultery is a commandment for you to know God's thoughts on the matter. What about the relational aspects of this sin?

The one good thing about adultery is that you know if you are having an affair or not. The question is, will you admit to it? Yes, most people minimize, rationalize, or intellectualize the reasons they are having an affair but deny having one. Most people are not aware of the cost emotionally, relationally, or spiritually of adultery. They are moved by the emotions of the moment and are not counting the cost. The high is caught in a dream catcher that leaves only broken dreams and hearts.

The reasons for an affair can be by those that move with greed of the flesh to the envy of it. They are more like perpetrators of hearts that want to fill their fleshly desires. The carnal desire of envy has the belief that the affair has the aspect of true love. The experience is colored more by the emotions of the affair than the sexual component. Then those that move from lust of the flesh are more focused on the erotica of the physical or sexual experience. All these "reasons" to have an affair ends in pain, destruction and sometimes death.

The adulterer that moves with lust or erotic love will mirror that of a sexual compulsive indulgence. Sexual compulsive behavior and adultery has the same cousins of infidelity and lust. Infidelity and lust are common denominators of the two. Another common denominator is "sexual anorexia." In Sex, Men and God by Douglas Weiss there is a "Sexual Anorexia Self- test" that could be helpful for you if you struggle with a sexual "addiction" or infidelity. This test is: "Answer yes or no to the following questions relating to the course of your relationship.

1. Would your spouse feel you keep yourself so busy that you have little time for her (not family time, but just time for her alone)?
   Y____ N_____

2. Would your spouse feel that if problems arise in the relationship, you are more likely to focus on them as the problem before owning your side of the problem?
   Y____ N____
3. Would your spouse feel that you withheld love from her (not sex)?
   Y____N____

4. Would your spouse feel that you withheld praise from her?
   Y___N____
5. Would your spouse feel that you withheld yourself spiritually and emotionally during sex with her?
   Y___N____

6. Would your spouse feel that you are unwilling or unable to discuss your feelings with her?
   Y___N____

7. Would your spouse feel you have ungrounded or ongoing criticism of her?
   Y___N____

8. Would your spouse feel that you use silence or anger as a means of control in the relationship?
   Y___N___

9. Would your spouse feel that you control or shame her in financial issues?
   Y___N____

"(2003, P.43). Weiss' says if you answer "yes" to five or more of these questions, you might have sexual anorexia in your relationship with your spouse.

Healing from adultery is not like healing from other struggles due to the nature of joining with someone emotionally, physically, sexually, and spiritually. Adultery is more than just getting "laid." It is a fleshly desire to fill the voids in your life and soul. Adultery breaks the marital covenant with God and your spouse, not counting the harm done to another person and his/ her family. I am not saying that other sins are not damaging. I am saying an affair affects the soul of the participants and their families. You have also broken a covenant with God. Other addiction, struggles, or sins mentioned are not breaking a marital covenant that God had sealed.

Many believe that sin, and this one particularly, will cause you to lose your salvation. Yes, adultery is breaking a marital covenant with God but not a blood covenant sealed with Christ's blood. Your salvation, saving your Soul from sin and death, was sealed by Christ's blood. In Hebrews 9:14 "how much more will the blood of Christ, who through the eternal Spirit offered Himself without blemish to God, cleanse your conscience from dead works to serve the living God?" (Hebrews 9:14 NASB). This blood covenant will not be broken due to God's sovereign love for you. Your covenant with your spouse was broken by the lust, greed, or envy of the flesh in an adulterous act. You will need to create a new covenant with your spouse if adultery was committed. Unlike God, neither you or your spouse are sovereign, nor do you all have unconditional love.

Part of your covenant with your spouse and God was broken due to your envy, greed, and lust. Your marital agreement or covenant was to be faithful to yourself, spouse, and God. This covenant was sealed with your marriage vows. The need for healing then is for yourself and your spouse. Like any spiritual covenant there must be a death or sacrifice. Your covenant with God was sealed with Christ's blood. Your sacrifice is to die to your way of life and put on a new way of life. First, you must remember your old covenant with your spouse. Remembering this covenant will help you recover what you have lost.

Your adultery created emotional, physical, relational, and spiritual losses to you and your spouse. You will need to look at these losses for many reasons: First, awareness of the losses can create true empathy, which can lead to true healing of your spouse's heart. Empathy can be the fuel that stops the deception of yourself. Secondly, your awareness of the losses will allow you to break the power of envy, greed, and lust. If you continue with infidelity, you will lose sight of the heartbeat of your soul.

## Exercise: Dealing with Adultery

*This is not a regression exercise. There are no special instructions included. Answer simply and directly in your journal.*

Make a list of problems:

-
-
-

Then make a list of Goals:

-
-
-

Then create your plan to stop being unfaithful:

1) To stop all contact with the seductress
   a) To erase their number and block their calls
   b) To stop all rituals that were tied to the other man/ woman (places you meet, ate, and went)

2) To build relationship with your spouse
   a) To do Love Dare book daily
   b) To create a list of ways to love your spouse and do them daily

3) To be happy with myself
   a) To increase time at the gym and with your friends
   b) To spend time journaling
   c) To have daily quiet time with God

## Workaholism

The three deadly Sin of greed, envy, and pride are highly active in the next behavioral indulgence called Workaholism. Workaholism is affecting your soul's health and relationships. Workaholism, compulsive behavior of working, has its own 12 step recovery group. You could call workaholism a compulsive disorder and not an indulgence. I do not believe workaholism is a compulsive disorder, but it does have a compulsive component. Most "addiction" has a compulsive component like Internet, gambling, and shopping addiction. Workaholics are compelled to work.

The major difference between workaholism and other behavioral indulgences is our cultural perspectives concerning work. Workaholics are praised, get raises, and promotions. This is not a bad "addiction" to have, is it? The workaholic gets toys that are envied by neighbors and friends. The church loves and praises a good workaholic because of what they give the church financially. Their family will praise and esteem them. This is not a bad indulgence to have, is it?

Well, I guess you need to ask their nuclear family. Like any indulgence, the dysfunctions show up behind the front door where the emotional, physical, sexual, and spiritual costs are counted. The family gets ignored, must be perfect and misses the time, energy, and attention of the workaholic. The mistress of workaholics is work. The pursuit of money, power and prestige is her seduction. The workaholic does not have control; the seductress has the control. No longer is the goal to work to live but live to work in this progressive cycle.

The workaholic's esteem is performance based like a Codependent is "others" based esteem. There is no concrete sign of workaholics, but the following provides a good indication there is a problem occurring:

-If you are the first one to work and one of the last to leave
- If you think about work and cannot sleep at night
- If your spouse complains that you work too much
- If you do not have time to exercise
- If you stop doing meaningful things,
- If you are thinking of the next project before the last one is finished
- If you stopped attending your kids' after school functions
- If you get sick when you go on vacations
- Sets extremely high standards
- Have an increased desire to control others or situations
- Have difficulty with delegating work to others

These signs can arise when moderation is present. Once this external indulgence reaches moderation then what appears are the internal indulgences of self-doubt and shame. The struggle while working with self-doubt and shame is how to build self-esteem that is not performance-based esteem. So, the question is "How do I have value and worth without performing?"

Most workaholics come from authoritarian parents that have strokes on performance which is the foundation for this indulgence. Some workaholics learned to over perform or compensate for permissive parents with indulgence and uninvolved parents with decreased order or success to be ok.

A workaholic has high standards and a need for control in personal relationships. The workaholic loses peace and joy outside of work. When a workaholic is without his or her mistress, they experience chronic fatigue, irritability, anhedonia (a lack of pleasure in things that were once pleasurable), increased isolation and depression due to the lack of balance in their life. These signs may be what some call "burnout."

If you are a workaholic and want to break the cycle of this indulgence, then create a plan.

## Exercise: Workaholism

*This is not a regression exercise. There are no special instructions included. Answer simply and directly in your journal.*

List the problems:

-
-
-

Then list your goals:

-
-
-

Then create your plan

1) To increase time with the family
   a) To schedule time with each family member daily
   b) To attend one scheduled activity a week
   c) To schedule a date night with your spouse once a week

2) To increase time with friends
   a) To join a team sport
   b) To call a friend daily
   c) To get involved in weekly bible studies

3) To decrease time at work
   a) To not work over 50 hours a week
   b) To delegate 3 things a day
   c) To not do any work or accept calls when you are not at work

Workaholism is difficult to break due to being conditioned or seduced by money, power, and prestige. You may need to cut back or get rid of some toys. Workaholics will want to deny their problem of workaholism and will constantly defend the fact that it is not mentioned as a sin in the bible. It is amazing how difficult it is for them to work less and create moderation. They usually run into their authentic fear and anxiety on the road to moderation or recovery. It is difficult for the workaholic to establish moderation unless they have health issues, a life crisis, or present problems. When the workaholic decreases external indulgences, they will run into their authentic fears.

## Sloth

What is a sloth? The times we live in affords one to be slothful. You are slothful if you are spiritually, emotionally, and behaviorally inactive or apathetic. This is not depression but mimic it. It is not laziness, but many people would label sloth that way. Laziness, aimlessness, or carelessness is a part of being slothful. You could be active, but you do not want to do it. Slothful people have the "Take Care of Me Blues" as their background music. The sloth struggles with the internal indulgence of shame, self-pity, or self-loathing yet they wear the mask of grandiosity, entitlement, or self-preoccupation. They are passive narcissists.

There is an entitlement or arrogance that surrounds their mountain. The other six deadly sins are active while this one is passive. Yes, there is a sense of pride surrounding this mountain. Now, I am not being tongue in cheek, but I know a slothful person will not care to do this work. They are content in their "misery". An example is when a slothful person is hungry, he/she will come over to your house to eat. You know you will cook, and he/she will want you to bring them the food to eat. They are inactive and work hard to stay that way.

The sloth I have seen in therapy had permissive or uninvolved parents. The permissive parents were affectionate and nurturing yet were indulgence, inconsistent with boundaries and used little of their control. The uninvolved parents were rejecting, self-absorbed with little to no boundaries. The sloth would use the permissive parents' love and nurturing against the parents to get their needs met or critique their parents' indulgent behavior, inconsistency, and lack of boundaries to be a victim to get their needs met. The sloth with uninvolved parents would get his/ her needs met by being a victim or martyr when criticizing their parents' poor boundaries, neglect, and rejection of them growing up.

Sloths mask their self-loathing, pity, or shame by wearing the mask of entitlement. By wearing the mask of entitlement, they get their needs met by demands and criticism of their parents and others while remaining inactive. They learned being under responsible would get others to take care of them.

I worked for a nonprofit for years. I saw people on a sliding fee scale. I would not see people for free because I wanted them to be invested in themselves and value my time. I saw a lot of slothful people. They usually came to therapy to get others to help them or get them to be quiet. They wanted to be slothful in peace.

## My Story: Tim

I had a client, Tim, that was slothful. You would not have known that he was slothful. He was well groomed and dressed nice for a 39-year-old male. He complained that he did not have a job, his mom made him come, and his truck needed tires. He spoke of how tired he was of hearing his mother "whine" about working so hard. He complained that his sister got a new car, his friends did not ask him to go fishing and his dad was on his case.

When I asked, "Tim, what do you want out of therapy?" Tim did not answer the question but told me what he did not like about others. I asked, "Tim, do you have a problem you want to work through while you are here?" Tim spoke of the problems of others and not his own. I asked, "Tim, do others think or call you lazy or think you need to care for what they care about?" Tim said, "I had a lot of people judging me." Tim had many characteristics of a slothful person, but it was hard to diagnose slothfulness.

Tim voiced that he wanted to come back for another session because it "might get everyone off his back." I told Tim that his payment was based on a sliding fee scale and how much could he pay. He told me, "Mom is going to pay the full fee." I told Tim that this was his therapy and not his mom's therapy. Tim was confused and told me he did not have any money. He asked for a free session. I told him I did not work for free. I asked Tim, "You can pay with what money you have of your own." I let him know that I had faith in him, and he would earn money to pay his bill. Tim went to his truck and brought in a handful of pennies, nickels, and dimes. I took the coins and filled out his slip and wrote the amount of his payment. He got mad at me for taking his "last dime." He was "embarrassed" to pay this amount. He went on and told me he was not coming back to a place that "likes to embarrass people so much."

Tim was slothful and struggled with sloth. Tim did not have a problem because everyone else had the problems. Tim was apathetic and did not care about much because he was taken care of by his parents. He wanted others to take care of him and got mad when they did not do so. He was envious of his sister getting a new car that she paid for herself. The greatest treatment plan for sloths are for others to stop enabling them.

A slothful person would not make it this far in the book due to their apathy and inactivity, but an enabler of a sloth would read this for the slothful person. An enabler is still wanting to know how to help their slothful daughter, son, or spouse. The enabler or codependent has the problem. The codependent works to make the sloth in his/her life feel better to lower their own anxiety. These enablers need to stop enabling their slothful loved one. Enabling has not helped the slothful person yet, has it? You can enable them to take steps to further their life or stay stuck being a victim. If you are enabling your sloth, stop today. The enabler must leave the mountain before the sloth will entertain the idea. It is never too late for you or the sloth to leave that mountain. The Israelites took 40 years for an 11-day trip to enter the promised land.

It is difficult for codependents and enablers to know how to get off their Mountain because the codependent does not know where their mountain begins and the sloth's ends. Codependency is " any suffering and/or dysfunction that is associated with or results from focusing on the needs and behavior of others" (Healing the Child Within, Charles Whitfield,1987, p.28) codependency "leads to a process of ' nonliving' which is progressive." It is hard for a codependent to leave the sloth because they are projecting what they would want and need if they were struggling and their fear of conflict if they do not please them.

Yet the sloths can speak from their masked self-pity, self-loathing, or shame. These projections of their wounds are laid on the codependent or enabler. The codependent personalizes or believes the critic and judgments of the sloth and enables out of guilt.

You will need to recognize that you are powerless over this family member. Most enablers do not know they have a problem because they are over focused on helping the slothful person with his/her problem. Here are some goals:

- To not give money if it is not earned
- To not give rides if they are not paid for
- To not help if the sloth is able to do it themselves
- To give sloth responsibility matched with accountability
- To not get into power struggles with the sloth i.e. Do not argue or explain your reasons with the slothful person.

These are goals for the codependent that address the problems with slothful people. Remember to "ask yourself, 'What will I Will myself do today, to move towards my daily goal or PURPOSE which will increase my Competency? How will I be Faithful to my daily goal while loving and Caring for myself? What Wisdom did I gather from yesterday that I can apply today?" A codependent will need to ask and answer these questions daily to move into recovery.

Sloth mountains stem from years of being mentally and emotionally in captivity. Sloths find ways to avoid being authentic in our culture. Due to social acceptance of their victimization and the church's desire to help the less fortunate allows them to stay stuck. these mountains can exist without help or hopes of freedom. Many would blame the church for neither dealing with these seven deadly sins nor helping those struggling with these external indulgences. Yet, note in Mark6:5 "And He [Jesus] was not able to do even one work of power there, except that He laid His hands on a few sickly people [and] cured them" (AMPC). This verse states that God's son, Jesus "was not able to do even one work of power there."

Jesus, God incarnate, was unable to minister to those in the crowd. Christ, like our churches, can only help those who acknowledge their problems and His power. My church clients rarely admit their internal or external indulgences to the church, and many believe God would not use His power due to their sin. They were not aware that God loved them enough to honor their free choices and/or their poor choices. Sloths will be victims to get his or her needs met or move from entitlement and demand others to meet their needs. The codependents or enablers can increase accountability by confronting the sloth's poor choices and enabling the sloth to be accountable.

This apathetic arrogance called acceptance only Instills more shame and hopelessness for its victims. The victims' bars of captivity are now invisible without accountability. These invisible bars must first be acknowledged by the holder of the keys or captives themselves. Leaving these mountains and breaking historic self-perpetuating cycles which lead to "nonliving" must be addressed to move to the promised land. Once the sloth acknowledges the invisible bars then he or she is one step away from leaving your mountain.

The next or first step may be the hardest one of the entire journey. This step is acknowledging you are powerless to move your mountain alone. This step leads to calling out to something greater than yourself. By enlisting the creator of all things through faith you get clarity and directions to the promised land. You will find freedom and rest. You will be able to listen to your authentic self.

## Remember:

If you have any of these or other indulgences in your life, then you need to leave them to be authentic. They are based on unconscious fears and conscious shame of past captivity. You will not be able to free your inner child from their captors if you are still living by invisible bars of the past perpetrators of hearts. You cannot teach your inner child what you do not know yourself. You will be able to provide more safety and security to your inner child by leaving this mountain. It is hard to get to the promised land if you are still wandering around in the desert. Now is the time to get off this mountain.

# CHAPTER THIRTEEN

## WHEN THE THUNDER ROARS AND THE CLOCK STOPS

"Brethren, I count not myself yet to have laid hold: but one thing I do, forgetting the things which are behind, and stretching forward to the things which are before, I press on toward the goal unto the prize of the high calling of God in Christ Jesus. Let us therefore, as many as are perfect, be thus minded: and if in anything ye are otherwise minded, this also shall God reveal unto you."

**KEY POINTS:**

1- You will likely be triggered before and after recovery of your inner child.
2- Returning to your past captivity and dysfunction is optional.
3- Life crises offer opportunities to regress into old patterns or strengthen your new storyline.

**Reflections:**

1- Have you stopped and looked for opportunities to grow in your life crisis?
2- Have you been loving, nurturing, and mentoring the child within you?
3- Have you taken steps to be a Wounded Healer to others?

# Welcome.

"The soul would have no rainbow if the eyes didn't have tears."

Ancient proverb

You have already sat in your Holy of Holies and experienced the part of you that was hurt, bruised, or abandoned along the way. As many of my clients have reported experiencing the following findings from their journey:

- One with self and God
- Understand the inner child
- Became your authentic self and not hiding behind the mask
- Found peace and joy
- Feel valued

Words cannot explain this Renaissance. You are now a Soul warrior, survivor, or fellow struggler. You have received the priceless gift that never stops giving and one cannot buy. You have discovered the relic of God within you.

Life now gives you more meaning, and one can see this as you smile, which radiates love and life, not one painted by the mask. Peace and joy are truly experiencing and not a destination. You know the peace that passes all understanding. The question becomes how can you keep it while not allowing your old dysfunctional behavior to bring back your old lifestyle?

Your childlike mind still wants to confirm his/her old dysfunctional beliefs and craves the old familiar emotions or lifestyle. You still live in a world that has missed the mark. Yes, you have had a renewal and celebration that words cannot describe, and poems are written. You too understand what Virginia Satire meant when she said " -- I want to Love you without clutching. Appreciate you without judging. Join you without invading. Invite you without guilting, criticize without insulting. If I can have the same thing from you then we can truly meet and enrich each other. " You have given this love to the child within you, yet it may be difficult to give others.

This love has not faded, but it is hard to live around and experience life with others that hide behind the mask you once wore. The world still cannot see the lies they are living which, brings you a different type of loneliness. You want to love while being loved but learn imposters cannot experience this type of intimacy. You crave for others to have and know this unadulterated peace and joy, but you find that they cannot understand innocent intimacy without a mask. They are still moved by their old beliefs, dance with their indulgences, and use defense mechanisms. They do not understand the experience behind your words and eyes. They still do not have eyes to see or ears to hear. You are doing the same dance that they are but hear a different tune.

The good news is that you have changed your life by changing your words, thinking, and behaviors. These changes came by changing your inner child's responses. You have learned to change your responses by changing your early beliefs about yourself. The part of you that was hidden by shame and guilt now dances with peace and joy yet craves fellowship. It is like you are living with zombies. The people you love and want to love to have no idea of the cost of their mask. It is like you are at a party and you are the only one that is not drinking the Kool-aide.

Have you ever been around others that were drinking or drunk? They think they are behaving normally. They are slurring their words and moving at half the speed, while laughing at things that are not funny. You are sober while conversing, but they cannot hear you. They are seriously dancing to another tune. This would be tolerable if you could leave the party, but this is life. You know you are high; and it is not because of drinking. Your heart hurts because you see the people you love living a lie without knowing it.

You have the choice to step into their dance and give up your priceless gift. You yearn to have like-minded conversation and are not willing to join into their counterfeit lives. The belief that you can teach them about true joy and peace is an illusion. You still crave others to have what you have experienced and crave fellowship with like-minded people. You are like the boy that put the world together by first putting the man together.

I heard a story about a father and a son. The father had been playing with his son all morning. He wanted to relax, but his son wanted to continue to play with him. The father saw a picture of the world in the paper. He began to tear it into several small pieces. He called his son over to him and told him "When you put the world back together, I will play with you."

The father sat back to enjoy his paper. Several minutes later his son came back into the room with all the pieces of the world taped together. The boy's father was in disbelief. He asked his son " How did you put the world back together so quickly?" The son replied:" I put the man's face together on the other side and the world came together."

This is a powerful story about psychology, sociology, and theology. The truth is, you have put the "man" or yourself together and the world will change. Every system you are in will change as you take off your mask. Instead of working to change the world or others, you have changed yourself, yet you are surrounded by others still trying to put you and the world together. They do not see the picture of the man on the other side. Others who are putting the world together will attempt to change you.

It is important to be mindful of the changes you have made to keep them. The seduction of the world does not stop. I had a client, Sara that had lost 73 pounds and reclaimed her inner child. She had stopped the roar of the thunder and the lightning strikes were faint memories. She was amazed at how chaotic her world became. She found that as she lost weight that "everyone wants to feed me. My husband is now judging me for being skinny. He thinks I need to stop losing weight. My friends believe that I think I am better than them. I'm just amazed at how everyone is acting."

Sara wanted and believed that others would be happy and celebrate with her. She did not know that her sickness found and fostered sick friends. She thought since she was better, her family would be better, not knowing that they had played a part in her obesity. Sara had brought order into chaos which created more chaos. She was no longer a part of this lie or the people who supported the lie. She had peace and joy to comfort her. She would not give herself up again to make others happy.

Sara, like many of my clients that got healthy, found sanity in an insane world. She had to actively seek out others that had taken off their mask. Sara had become whole. She was not willing to be around those that were blind by past shadows of their yesterdays. Sara sat down and made a list of her new beliefs and sought out other soul warriors. You may need to make a list of changes that you have made to continue moving toward them.

## Exercise: Examining Your Changed Beliefs

*This is not a regression exercise. There are no special instructions included. Answer simply and directly in your journal.*

What beliefs about yourself have changed to this point in your work?

-
-
-
-

What do you need to do to continue your growth?

-
-
-

As you put the picture of yourself together, every relationship and system you are in will change. Stop and think of how others are responding to changes you have made to this point. List changes in other responses:

-
-
-

As you continue to grow, you need to know you can count on changes happening. Hopefully, you are picking the direction you want to go. The choices of those around you will change, but you cannot control their changes or choices. If you are giving yourself a voice and protecting the child within you, then the people around you will have a different response to you.

Let us say you have not had a voice due to the belief that you were not worthy. When you begin having a voice, you may find those that love you will honor your thoughts and feelings. Also, you may discover that your loved one is getting angry when you are voicing your thoughts and feelings. They will most likely try to get you to stop. When I have clients changing their codependent traits by taking themselves seriously, I can count on their spouses changing. The controlling spouses, which once encouraged them to come to counseling many times, tried to make them stop coming back. While others will pull closer and celebrate their growth.

## Time Races on as the Clock Stands Still

You are getting healthier by listening to the child within you. You are using your adult rational mind and not your child's emotional logic. You are changing your early script while exploring your new self. You are growing spiritually and experiencing the Fruit of the Spirit. You need to continue growing in your new self, even when life crises arise. You can count on life crises to come your way.

It is easier to pick your direction for change when you are conscious. It is difficult to pick the direction of your change when crisis or tribulation comes into your life. The urgency of the moment no longer has power over you. You are aware that time is important, but you are more important than time. If you are not intentional about the direction you are going, a life crisis can throw you back in time. Most people regress to old childhood survival skills when in crisis. The question is, will you?

Crisis offers you the opportunity to regress to that familiar place and have regressive coping skills. You know the cost of regressing without your present insight covering the inner child. By reclaiming your inner child, you are less likely to use regressive coping skills. Those of you that are more integrated with your inner child due to increased communication, safety and intimacy will be less likely to go back to the old. You need to know that you can go back to the old thinking and coping skills. Yes, a crisis can take you back to your old regressive thoughts and feelings. This is not as alarming as it sounds. You have developed a strong sense of self. You have strengthened your adult coping skills and can quickly begin your emotional clock and not give the crisis the power to use your past against you.

At times of crisis, it is important to reach out to your support system and not lean on your own strength. If you move into any historic memories, thoughts or feelings that occurred at the time of the abuse, you need to reach out immediately to a therapist, pastoral counselor, coach, or friend that understands regressive coping during crisis. It is not an emergency if the child within you goes back to its old historic learning. It is an emergency if he/ she moves back to the time of abuse. I believe that you never need to go back to that time. You will recreate lighting strikes on your soul. You can hear the thunder roar and get the child part of yourself to your safe place. The child within you will rest in you.

Most people do not do soul work because they fear spontaneous regression. The sad thing is they are more likely to live in or create more abuse for themselves by listening to their fear. If your adult can hear and see your Inner child, you can calm the storm. The storm can have value for your life.

When you are conscious, your "life crises" are a chance for growth. In the urgency of the moment, the crisis of the day will likely deepen your "core" beliefs. You will recognize patterns of reactions from your early learning. When you "react," something on the outside has control. The Chinese word for crisis is made of two symbols: They are wei, which means "danger" and ji which means "opportunity." You have the chance to pick the direction you want to go. The English word crisis is derived from the medical model which meant a turning point in a disease. You can tip it one way for healing or decay. Another word for crisis can be tribulation.

Tribulation can be any persecution, affliction, or distress in your life. Present or past distress and affliction can take away all your joy, peace, and happiness if you allow it. It is difficult to recognize the opportunity when you experience death of a loved one, loss of a job or a severe health issue. Where is the opportunity in a date rape, a wreck or being verbally abused by your spouse? When you are depressed or having a panic attack, how do you not see "danger?" How do you see the opportunity? Write down any present "life crises" and list a couple of ways they are opportunities:

-

-

You may not see the opportunity in your crisis yet. It took me a while to recognize the great opportunities after being terminated from my job of 20 years. I did not see the opportunity to write this book, do Skype sessions with clients all over the world, or the time to rest and play. I acknowledge that my relationship with God made seeing opportunities much easier.

If you do not have a relationship with God, it is difficult to see the opportunities. Tribulation was created to break up the Earth's soil with sharp metal objects. This tool had sharp objects which pressed through the soil. This tribulation of the ground allows the seeds to get deeper into the earth. The deeper the tribulation, the more nutrients, water and safety the seed has from the weather. The ripped apart ground will soon be covered by vegetation while protecting it from rain, wind, and sun. The vegetation will later give back nutrients to the soil and give the ground the ability to breathe and take in more water.

In crisis, you are normal, if you are not looking at the opportunities and do not understand "Why me?" "Why God?" It does not matter if you or others caused the crisis. You will still have a choice to make it an opportunity or a danger.

I would like to tell you that all you should do is to stand on your faith and trust in God. You could stand on verses like Philippians 4:6,7 that says " Be anxious for nothing, but in everything by prayer and supplication with thanksgiving let your requests be made known to God. And the peace of God, which surpasses all comprehension, will guard your hearts and your minds in Christ Jesus" (Philippians 4:6, 7 NASB). You will hear scripture verses and words from well-meaning people.

It is difficult to stand on your faith because of the crisis, which triggers your early learning. You will find and use your old coping skills of your childhood. This form of regressive coping bypasses your adult coping skills, while using those of your childhood. Joan Borysenko spoke to those who constantly use regressive coping. In her book Mending the Body Healing the Mind she says, "regressive copers back away from stress and dwell instead on their own repetitive emotional reactions. They stay in a rut, are alienated from life, feel powerless to change things, and are therefore threatened by anything that rocks the boat"(98.) Regression copers have little adult oversight. This is like regressive coping.

It is amazing how easy it is to regress back to early learning. I had over 20 years of clinical experience as a Pastoral Counselor and a Licensed Marriage and Family Therapist. I was an ordained minister and the director of a Pastoral Counseling Center for over 20 years. This is important for you to know because I had difficulty accepting Philippians 4:6 or any other scripture with my last life crisis. As a reader, you need to know about regressive coping and the cost of a crisis on a wounded healer.

I started this book three days before I got terminated from being the director of a non-profit counseling center for 20 years. I received the notice of being terminated on Sunday evening. The locks had been changed on the center doors, all my furniture, books and charts were still at the center. I would like to tell you that I could see the opportunity in my tribulation, but the truth is, I saw danger. In the danger, I experienced mental, physical, and spiritual illness. The sad thing was, I had knowledge of what was happening and how to "fix it." As you could believe, this knowledge made my illness worse.

The 10 % of the iceberg that I was standing on got overtaken by the 90% under the water line. The ability to know and have awareness of what was happening became a weapon against me. The loss of my 20-year pastoral counseling ministry was only one loss. Being a workaholic made this loss even greater. I made work, as all addicts, my life. Not only did I lose my job and friends, but I lost my identity as a minister.

I went into shock. I was numb and detached myself from reality for a couple of days. The shock created a physiological storm that led to physical illness. My brain was producing tons of the neurotransmitter norepinephrine due to my crisis. Norepinephrine created increased anxiety which triggered my natural fight or flight response. The fight or flight response increased the "stress hormone" cortisol. Cortisol was being produced by my adrenal glands to deal with the crisis.

Cortisol can be good in small doses to increase memory, energy and restore homeostasis or sanity, but I was overdosing on it. The amount of prolonged stress elevated my cortisol, which increased memory deficits and difficulty regulating my affective control. I was losing consciousness fast. The physiological affect continued taking me out of reality. My emotional center of my primitive brain was triggered, which created a fight or flight mold. This fight or flight response to the crisis triggered old unconscious memories and regressive coping skills. The present crisis, the changes in the chemical reactions in my brain, and going back to my primitive learning started mental illness.

The increased stimulation of the amygdala and the present danger created panic attacks. The old relics of depression, low self-esteem, and hopelessness from childhood was triggered, which increased the depression and intensified the present danger. The norepinephrine was creating waves of anxiety. I was primed for a fight even though nothing was there except fear and the unknown.

My locus cerulean continued to be simulated and created more norepinephrine, which triggered old intrusive images and flashbacks of my childhood trauma. Regressing back to my early traumatic memories of growing up with an alcoholic father, these physiological factors increased my sign of posttraumatic stress disorder (PTSD) and depression. My mental state got ill with the increased signs of PTSD, depression, and grief. The loss of my job, friends, and lifestyle were compounded by further threats. My anxiety made all probabilities possibilities, which colored my reality.

The threat of losing other things had increased over the weeks. The need to get a job loomed heavy on my mind. I was terminated due to accusations of ethical violations of my LMFT license. This threatened my marriage, professional, and ministerial career. The worst was to come; I was already suffering from physical and emotional illness. The emotional and physical illness had affected my spiritual foundation.

Spiritually, I had a strong faith in God. I used my knowledge and faith in God in high school and built on it in college. I went to seminary to get my Master of Divinity to further my spiritual growth. I practiced daily bible study, prayers, and ministry for over 25 years. The loss of my job and the threat of losing my ministry as a Pastoral Counselor, increased the deterioration of not only my mental and physical, but also my spiritual health.

My spiritual lens began to be colored by my past beliefs and experiences of childhood. My first God image was a critical, demanding, and abusive alcoholic father. Without knowing, I looked through these dark colored lenses of my soul. It was difficult in crisis to know if I was looking out of the window of my soul or its mirror. I began moving away from God based on my old childhood belief that God was critical and judgmental. My life began to become unmanageable.

I turned to working out, which had sustained me before in stressful times. Exercise usually balanced my mental and physical state. Now, exercise was difficult due to my depression. I had decreased energy, concentration and sexual drive with increased anxiety and anhedonia (lack of pleasure). This unhealthy stress was now affecting me more and more each day. I had to will myself to get out of bed and had little energy to workout.

I had constant anxiety, which increased my cortisol levels and adrenal glands while decreasing my serotonin level. My serotonin was being depleted due to increased obsessing and no healthy outlets to increase it. As my serotonin decreased my depression increased. The depression seemed to get bigger and heavier daily. The grief was getting more intense due to the daily reminders of no job and no friends, so I thought, and no ministry.

This was a perfect storm. I sat in my chair and asked myself, "What would I tell my clients going through a perfect storm?" An internal storm that was taking their mental, physical, and spiritual health. An external crisis, which took their job, friends, ministry, and a large part of their identity. A storm that raised their unconscious memories and coping skills of their youth, while decreasing conscious awareness and choices. I sat quietly for a couple of hours and then created a plan. The goal of this plan was not to confront old thinking; it was to preserve my adult's mental health.

## The Plan

Physically, the plan was to see a doctor and get testing of my blood and hormone levels, then follow the doctor's advice. This was a hard step to take. Like many men, I hated to go to any doctor; my regressive coping was to be strong and not to be weak. My "be strong" driver did not want to rely on medication. The plan gave me a week to call the doctor and schedule an appointment. I planned to workout 4-5 times a week. Even if I just showed up to work out and then left, which I did, counted. I had a long list of vitamins and herbs to combat deteriorating more mentally and physically.

My mental plan was to begin doing daily journaling and build a support system. I needed support. I decided to reach out to three people to check out my thinking, to voice my feelings, and to sustain me during this difficult time. This was more difficult than my physical plan because of my early learning in an alcoholic home. I learned to keep the secret, be strong and not to feel my emotions. These beliefs make mental health hard and being vulnerable with others even harder. I knew that these steps were going to be difficult because I truly had no energy, and my mood would range from sad one moment to severe panic the next moment.

My spiritual plan was to have daily prayers and a devotional. I was to create a 20-minute daily devotion time to dwell in my temple. I knew that this quiet time would give me the ability to hear God's word or the Holy Spirit within me. I was to have spiritual music to go with my spiritual meditation. I was to be vulnerable and ask for prayer daily from others. This all seemed difficult because I was looking through my regressive lens, the mirror of my past, and seeing my first beliefs about God.

My early learning suppressed emotions, and dysfunctional beliefs stormed in my mind as past emotions of hurt and fear flooded my Soul. My alcoholic father once again stood in my God Spot. The God I knew was all loving, knowing, present and powerful was vanishing by the hour. I was to begin immediately with my plans and check my progress each week.

My anxiety and depression made following my plan difficult, especially during the first month. I willed myself to follow the plan. My wound was opened daily by my clients, referral sources and friends wanting to know: "What happened?" "Why were you fired?" "How are you doing?" These questions were asked out of concern and love. The love of others made the ability to be strong and functional almost non-existent. I hated grieving and mourning with others. This grieving, in hindsight, was the very thing I needed to clean my wounded heart.

The second month was a little better, I found out through the medical test that I had five times the normal cortisol levels of a normal male, low testosterone levels, and a deficiency in vitamin D. I began taking a cortisol blocker, testosterone, and vitamin D supplement. These supplements work slowly to help my alertness, memory, and mental and physical strength. The medical diagnosis helped me know my physical signs of weight gain, low energy, and muscle loss were not all mental. The awareness of cortisol "poisoning" helped me know there was help for my memory, concentration, and anxiety.

The second month also brought increased clarity emotionally and mentally due to the daily journaling and meditation. My journaling gave me a release for my emotions, while beginning to inform me of my present needs and help me not step into old forgotten memories: memories of my dysfunctional beliefs and coping mechanisms of my 12-year-old self. My time with God through prayer calmed me. I began to be aware of my truth and God's truth concerning my present situation. By the end of the second month, I had increased awareness that God was actively loving, sustaining and providing for me. I was still weak and faced with daily warfare.

I am using the word "warfare" because this was not a battle of flesh and blood. I knew these afflictions could be from God. It was a spiritual battle with powers and principalities to stop my ministry and destroy me. I knew God had called me to write this book, which I ignored and ran from for over ten years. I was like Christ in the garden praying for this cup to pass over me. I did not want to start a Skype ministry for counseling. I worked hard to stay away from these internal convictions of the Holy Spirit. This knowledge furthers my burdens and like prophets of old I wanted to hide and run. The mantle of writing a book on healing while I was bleeding and beaten down made even less sense to me.

I wanted to sit back and heal, wait to take steps, and not start anything new. I feared what could happen next. God continued to prompt me to start a Skype ministry and to continue writing my book. Neither of these did I have the desire nor energy to do, yet the "pressure" or moving of the Holy Spirit continued daily. People called and wanted Skype and FaceTime sessions. I had several people ask me out of the blue about my book. These inquiries confirmed God's calling yet increased my anxiety. The book began to take form as the pain and suffering of the tribulation gave it life. My anxiety began moving me toward my goals rather than away from them.

I knew I had to follow the plan for my recovery. I grew stronger each day. The plan eventually gave me direction: it sustained me. My circumstances received less attention as I took steps towards meaningful things. My regressive coping gave way to my knowledge and wisdom. My adult mind became more active as the seeds of the plan took root. These roots got daily attention and the fruit of opportunity grew over time. The fruit of this tribulation sustains me today.

My tribulations were like anyone else's. I had faith in God most of the time and knew He would never forsake me. These tribulations can create life or death. The important question was, "How will I make this present tribulation an opportunity to grow?" The seed of opportunity took root by me following my plan. Instead of focusing on my circumstances, I rested on Gods promises.

What does it take to see the trials or tribulations as opportunities? It begins with you taking yourself seriously, acknowledging the problems and creating a plan to honor you emotionally, mentally, physically, and spiritually. You need others' support and accountability. You need accountability to honor you and to hold yourself accountable. Accountability is needed in the difficult times or tribulations. You need a support system to sustain you during your difficult times, to check out your reality and to hold you, encouraging you to take the appropriate steps. Remember that a chain is only as strong as its weakest link. Being aware and maintaining your emotional, mental, physical, and spiritual link is easier said than done. Tribulation will break up your emotional soil. In your garden of your Soul you will need long suffering as the soil is broken up, knowledge of the right seeds to plant, help planting the seeds, and patience as the seeds grow. The garden of the Soul is usually torn apart by the weeds of old and not the present tribulation. You will need to protect yourself against the seeds of old weeds beliefs and behaviors because these will not help your present condition. Planting seeds that are a solution and God focused will grow into hope, this hope will not be problem or crisis oriented when it comes to your Garden of your Soul.

Creating a plan is an adult coping skill combating your repressive coping skills. You have worked hard to reclaim your inner child and built your sense of self. These strengths will stand strong in life's weather. Storms of life can invite you to regress your early learning, poor choices, and dysfunctional coping "skills." This storm is not a danger, but an opportunity to grow. Life's tribulations handled appropriately will bring more fruit into your life.

I now stand on the other side of my tribulation. I now count my losses as a blessing. I prayed for years to be off Fridays. My goal was to start this when I was 50 years old. Those who knew me would laugh because I was a workaholic. God has given me what I could not give myself. Being terminated from my job gave me time to finish the book God placed on my heart. I can now have face to face sessions via the internet. I would not have been able to do this if I still had my license as a Marriage and Family Therapist. I experienced an extraordinary God whose radiance helped me see in my darkest hour. Romans 5:3,4 which says, "And not only this but we also exalt in our tribulations, knowing that tribulation brings about perseverance; and perseverance, proven character; and proven character, hope" (NASB). I am thankful.

This book ends with a plan to take care of your adult self. Your inner child can only reach your level of growth. You can now reach beyond ordinary limits by creating a plan and not planning to fail. Planning to succeed allows you to be successful in your pursuits. God wants you to have the desires of your hearts, while my hope is you will take your desires seriously by creating a plan. While living East of Eden, you will need to protect your adult mind from life crises, bad habits or old beliefs by making yourself a priority. Your mind will continue to be a battlefield. You can fight life's battles with a Plan, temptation with the FACE intervention and another regressive pattern of belief by loving and mentoring the child within you. You can eat soul food and move closer to your target. By loving yourself, you will be able to disregard your mask and be a companion to others. You are becoming a self-portrait of your God.

I learned a lot through my healing journey to the Soul. I learned by reaching out to others and having them reach out to me: fellowship brought more of God's presence and healing into my personal situation. I now understand and practice what Henri J.M. Nouewen, author of The Wounded Healer, says, " for a deep understanding of our own pain makes it possible for us to convert our weakness into strengths and to offer our own experience as a source of healing to those who are often lost in the darkness of their own misunderstood sufferings"(The Wounded Healer, henri J. M. Nouwen, p.93).

## Remember

Accountability is needed in the difficult times or tribulations. You need a support system to sustain you during your difficult times, to check out your reality and to hold you, encouraging you to take the appropriate steps.

I pray this book and your ministry "can indeed be a witness to the living truth that the wound, which caused us to suffer now, will be revealed to us later as a place for God in the intimated [making known] a new creation" (p.102).

Now your journey begins. God bless you.

# ABOUT THE AUTHOR

Walter W. Swinhoe has been in ministry for over 30 years as an Ordained minister. He was the director of a nonprofit counseling ministry for 20 years before starting The Family Christian Wellness Center. He practiced psychotherapy as a Licensed Marriage & Family Therapist and Pastoral Counseling for more than 25 years. His pastoral ministry included individual, marriage, family & group counseling. His pastoral identity models unconditional positive regard, presence, grace, and hope. He graduated from the Southern Baptist Theological Seminary earning his Masters of Divinity Degree in 1990.

Walter ministers today as a Wounded Healer, leading others through a psycho/spiritual healing experience. He lives in a small rural town in Texas raising cattle with his wife, Courtney. His passions are hunting, fishing and floating the Guadalupe River.

# ABOUT THE EDITOR

Anne Morrison Smith has bachelor's degrees in Biology and English Literature from the University of Missouri and a Juris Doctorate from the University of Missouri-Kansas City. As she develops her skills as a wounded healer, Annie will forever be grateful to Walter Swinhoe, her counselor, advisor, mentor, and friend. In her spare time, she enjoys reading meandering novels, weekends on the lake, and the general mayhem of life with two young sons and a large extended family.

# ABOUT THE LINE EDITOR

Hannah Daniel is on track to graduate with a Bachelor in Spanish and Bachelor of Arts in Psychology from Midwestern State University. Influenced by Walter's remarkable impact on her life, she has decided to pursue a Master's in Psychology and counsel children through equine therapy. In her free time, she enjoys adventures with her dogs and horses and volunteering at her church's horse ministry, where she and other members use horses to share God's love with the youth.

Made in the USA
Columbia, SC
17 May 2021

38131002R00205